The
FREEDOM
of the
CHRISTIAN MAN

The

FREEDOM

of the

CHRISTIAN MAN

A CHRISTIAN CONFRONTATION WITH THE SECULAR GODS

BY

HELMUT THIELICKE

TRANSLATED BY JOHN W. DOBERSTEIN

HARPER & ROW, PUBLISHERS
NEW YORK AND EVANSTON

CONTENTS

TRANSLATOR'S NOTE

IN A NATIONWIDE RADIO AND TELEVISION BROADCAST, DELIVERED IN Germany on June 6, 1962, Helmut Thielicke spoke the following words, which so aptly express the theme of this book that the translator deems them worth including here:

"Freedom is never bestowed without our having to struggle and pay for it. . . . In the East the man who sets his freedom against the system risks his life. Among us the man who stands up for his freedom pays for it at most with his comfort, sacrificing the paltry ease which is sought by all who do not want to be bothered, all who act in accord with the law of least resistance and play the conformist game. Even if we had a welfare state in which we received for nothing spectacles, toothpaste, and whatever else you can think of, we shall most certainly never get freedom for nothing. Freedom will always cost something; it always requires risk, venture, and willingness to sacrifice. . . .

"We are in danger of becoming a generation of constant demanders. Our dogma is the cry: 'We are entitled to it!' . . . But the real question and challenge that is thrust upon our conscience is how we shall use the chance that freedom gives us, whether it becomes an invested talent or whether we squander it in shabby selfishness."

These chapters, all dealing with the theme of Christian freedom in the modern world, were supplied to the translator by the author in manuscript and pamphlet form. They represent lectures, addresses, articles, and study papers. This explains the difference in tone and style which the reader may become aware of as he proceeds from chapter to chapter. The translator, however, has not found it desirable to eliminate evidences of spoken address which appear in some of the chapters.

Chapter I is the address delivered by Dr. Thielicke on the occasion of his assuming the rectorate of the University of Hamburg, November 9, 1960. Chapter II, reflecting a primary concern of the author for the younger generation, addresses itself particularly to young people. Chapter III is an address delivered to the Overseas Club of Hamburg on November 22, 1960. Chapter IV represents some of the author's studies in Marxism. Chapters V to IX are addresses and articles written for various occasions. And Chapter X is the address delivered by Dr. Thielicke to a mass audience of Christians from both East and West Germany at the *Kirchentag* in Berlin, July, 1961.

The title and the chapter arrangement have been provided by the author. The index has been supplied by the translator.

Mount Airy, Philadelphia   JOHN W. DOBERSTEIN
August, 1962

I

WHAT IS FREEDOM?

ONE OF THE MOST VENERABLE ELEMENTS IN THE GERMAN UNIVERSITY tradition is that it is oriented around the idea of freedom. It is a normative principle that underlies—explicitly or implicitly—every discussion that revolves about the questions of research and teaching, of the functions of scholarship and education, of self-government and supervision by the state. In December when we shall celebrate —vicariously for our brethren behind the Iron Curtain—the one hundred and fiftieth anniversary of the founding of the University of Berlin, Hans Wenke's sesquicentennial address will show us the creative impulses which men like Humboldt,[1] Schleiermacher,[2] and Steffens[3] caused to flow from an idea of freedom that we, the children of a later century which is sicklied over with pragmatism, are in danger of losing.[4]

---

[1] Cf. Humboldt's prospectus of 1810, "On the Internal and External Organization of the Higher Institutions of Learning at Berlin," in *Die Idee der deutschen Universitat*, Darmstadt, 1956, pp. 375 ff.

[2] "Occasional Thoughts Concerning Universities in the German Sense. . . ," *ibid.*, p. 725.

[3] "On the Idea of Universities," in *Philosophische Bibliothek*, vol. 120, p. 205. More problematical—in any case more dialectical and indirect—Fichte; cf. with this "A Deduced Plan for a Higher School to be Established at Berlin," in *Die Idee der deutschen Universität*, especially pp. 30-33, 165 ff.; also pp. 176 ff.

[4] I am referring to statements such as those in Humboldt's prospectus of 1810, to the effect that true knowledge is never to be gained from purely professional education, but rather "must be informed with the spirit of the whole," and that

The term "freedom" has acquired such a variety of different meanings in our generation that we may well ask ourselves whether the concept of freedom is not in danger of losing its meaning altogether. The territory it covers ranges all the way from the Hegelian-Marxian definition, which defines freedom as insight into necessity, to Sartre's precisely opposite idea of a "total" freedom which is not qualified by any necessity whatsoever.

For Sartre's opinion, man is not hampered either by the necessity of an unfolding entelechy or by the necessity of a God-given *assentia.* He is left to himself to create himself in freedom. Man, thus freed from any form of *nomos,* is therefore obliged to usurp the freedom of God. He exists in imitation of the Creator of the world and His *actus purus.* It is a desperate freedom that manifests itself in anxiety rather than in the joy of liberation. It is a freedom that is weary, not because it has grown weary through exercise, but even before it begins to operate.

Our ordinary Western ideas of freedom are to be found somewhere on this scale between the extreme positions of Marx and Sartre. And again these ideals are so varied that it is difficult, if not impossible, to compress them into a rallying cry that would give wings to the spirit and equip us with the kind of authority that is capable of defying the pressure of the channelized freedom of the Eastern bloc.

But we cannot wish to be free unless we know what freedom is. Only that which provides meaning can acquire the status of a real motivation in our life.

Paul de Lagarde once said: "He is not free who can do what he wills, but rather he who can become what he should."[5] Our understanding of freedom is threatened with disintegration *because* we do not know what "we should become," and therefore because we have lost our sense of what we were intended to be. The confusion in what we mean by freedom is only a reflection of our uncertainty concerning what man is. For the freedom to produce and apply technical means appears to increase in direct proportion to our

scientific knowledge is engendered only by "spontaneity," that is to say, through freedom. For only the scientific knowledge that springs from within and can be implanted in the inner man is capable of transforming character. (*Ibid.,* p. XV.)

[5] *Deutsche Schriften,* 2nd ed., 1934, Vol. I, p. 79.

lack of freedom to incorporate these means in a meaningful *telos*. As Einstein once said, "We live in an age of perfect means and confused ends."

There are many symptoms that clearly show that in the minds of the broad mass of people the term "freedom" has in fact degenerated into the notion that one can "do what one wills," and that even then this means only that one is allowed to make claims upon life and assert one's individual rights over against the community. I content myself with mentioning only one of these symptoms.

In deceptive analogy to mechanical and therefore impersonal processes, freedom is interpreted as that area in which we have "free play" in what we do or do not do, without any necessity to give an account of oneself, explain one's actions, or to consider what "should" be played in this area of "free play." Not until this mechanical simile is humanized, that it, not until it is made clear that our human existence constitutes the area in which we enter into play and that this game has only a fixed time to run and that this time has its *telos* can we see that freedom is a task that is set for us. But then we shall also see that it is not only a gift, but also a burden, that it is not only an opportunity, but also a temptation.

No wonder then that freedom has long since ceased to be praised as an ideal (except in festival speeches, which are usually rather liberal in pouring out the pathos). Countless thousands of people today, instead of crying out "give me liberty, or give me death," would rather, and certainly more honestly, say, "Just let me be a functionary who carries out orders." In any case, they would agree with Sartre when he says that we are "condemned" to freedom and it is our lot to bear the burden of freedom. Sartre may perhaps be a noxious insect in many respects, but if this be true, then at least this insect provides a kind of inoculation that will immunize us against some of the sentimental talk we hear from the freedom-shouters. For we are studiously at work shaking off the burden of freedom from our shoulders. Our officials are familiar with the office-holder's constant desire to be furnished with "regulations"—even for the interpretation of recent history—in order that he may be "covered" and not be obliged to take the risk of making a decision on his own. The courts charged with the task of adjudicating the crimes of Germany's recent past and faced with legally definable, or legally undefinable, murderers are constantly receiving this stereotyped answer: "I was only acting under orders."

True, these men had an ethos: it was obedience to the free will of the stronger, the freedom of the man in command who gives the orders. But it was not by exercising one's *own* freedom that this obedience was brought into such disrepute. The degeneration of this ethos consisted rather in the fact that it had deteriorated from a personal responsibility for making decisions to a purely instrumental responsibility for carrying out orders. Wherever the burden of freedom is shrugged off—and this is exactly what happened here—then fidelity is nothing more than fidelity to regulations; the only law that is left is the law of following the line of least resistance, and the functionary—or better, in order not to offend any profession (which is far from my purpose), the "functioner"—is nothing more than a "will-less" molecule in the collective, because the cadre is now made up only of the cadavers of what were once individuals. People whom, in more solidly based times, we called "personalities" have now been relegated to the retired list as far as their individuality is concerned.

Hence it is no wonder that this reduced sense of freedom should be so exceedingly insecure and vulnerable to all kinds of external incursions and infiltrations. Formerly it was the omnipotence of the state that was regarded as the main threat to individual freedom. But this threat was at the same time a kind of creative provocation that drove men to assert their right to freedom. The reason for this, in my opinion, was that the omnipotence of the state represented a clearly defined vis-a-vis to which one might react. Today this freedom, which has already become atrophied by long disuse, is also being further weakened by methods of influencing the subconscious which have been developed with the aid of psychoanalytical tests. By means of these tricks, employing certain methods of subliminal motivation, the personal center of decision is, as it were, circumvented and subjected unwittingly to remote control.

The consumer is rendered incapable even of freely choosing a paltry box of soap. The presentation of the product ("The most gleaming white I have ever seen") is enacted on the television screen in such a mystic ecstasy that the consumers suddenly feel they have discovered a new ideal of life, that they have discovered the Platonic idea of "whiteness" or even whiteness itself. By the time this almost mythical imbuement of inspiration has done its work, the theme "soap power" has long since faded into unsubstantial shadow. The appeals to be "a man of the world" by smoking a certain brand of cigarettes or to become the envy of one's neighbors by driving a particular make of car have created something akin to a consumer ideology, which by analogy with all other forms of ideology, blocks the actual exercise of one's freedom. However, any method which is capable of rendering people powerless when confronted with everyday trivialities like soap powders and cigarettes will be equally effective as a depotentiating force when it comes to making really important decisions.

How are we to be able to understand the nature of freedom if there are so many interpretations and so much confusion with regard to its application, and when the concept itself is threatened from all sides?

Allow me to take as my starting point a definition formulated by Henrik Steffens in his lectures on the idea of the university—again a reminiscence of the founding of the University of Berlin: "We call free that which is itself in inner harmony with its nature."[6] In the interpretation of this definition we need not dwell at length upon the question of what is meant here by the term "nature." It may be sufficient to point out that it is meant to state a negative and a positive element.

The negative element of the term "nature" implies that freedom is possible only when the self acts spontaneously and of its own free will, and not as the result of any direction by another will, i.e., when it is not the object of a *heteros nomos*. The imperatives "Do this!" and "Do that!" would thus become the result of direction from an outside source, a dictate, an *octroi*, which would make the self functionally dependent, hence depriving it of the freedom of self-determination. We are already aware of the importance of this negative element in Kant's theory of autonomy.

The positive element in Steffens' definition of nature implies that man's capacity for freedom becomes active only when it is used for

---

[6] *Philosophische Bibliothek*, Vol. 120, p. 263. Cf. also: "Self-determination is the inner root of our being, and whenever it disappears we cease to be inward," *Ibid.*, p. 236.

the purpose of self-fulfillment. We may leave open the question whether in this definition the *telos* which is implied in the concept of the self is synonomous with entelechy in Goethe's sense, in which the self is the "minted form" stamped upon us by Nature and which "develops as it lives,"[7] or whether it is synonymous with the idea of "humanity" in the thinking of idealism or romanticism; or whether it is synonymous with the Christian idea that we are the "children of God."

In any case, the formal analogy in *all* these forms of free self-fulfillment is that freedom can be realized only within the confines of certain limitations, and hence that the mystery of this co-ordination of freedom and limitation must be the first consideration in any doctrine of freedom.

Let us now check the opposite theory. An unrestricted freedom which would allow us to do anything we pleased would obviously only disguise a worse form of tyranny. For if we were permitted to do exactly as we pleased, we would be subjected to the law of least resistance, and therefore to a *law* which again would deprive us of our freedom. That is to say, we would be driven by whatever urges were strongest within us, for example, by the desire for power or the sex instinct, and would thus be subjected to an anonymous form of bondage. The road into the far country described in Jesus' parable of the prodigal son is in this sense the road from the restraints and obligations of the father's house into the license of unlimited self-determination. But it ends, characteristically enough, in a pigsty, in an extremity of bondage in which one is driven like a slave. It ends therefore in the opposite of freedom. In fact, it *is* the antithesis of freedom.

Real freedom, on the other hand—the freedom "to become what one should"—must be defined as a definite form of bondage or obligation, in a word, as what one *should* do. Real freedom is a bondage and nothing else. The chains of unfreedom are broken, not primarily by liberation from bonds, but rather by entering into a genuine commitment to, and acceptance of, obligations that sustain one's very existence. Therefore the difference between un-

---

[7] The reference is to the last line of the first of Goethe's *Urworte, Orphisch:* "*Geprägte Form, die lebend sich entwickelt.*" (Trans.)

freedom and freedom is not the difference between being bound and unbound, but rather between false and true bondage.

It was none other than Kant who made this clear when he said that our consciousness of freedom is explained by the fact that we are aware of the unconditional "thou shalt" of the practical reason. Because the ideal goal of human existence imposes upon us an unconditional and categorical claim, we know that we have an obligation to strive for this ideal goal, and therefore we also know that we possess the freedom to achieve it. Kant expressed this in his axiom, "You can, because you ought."

We can also put it this way: the obligation to strive for self-realization "empowers" us to achieve freedom. Underlying the ability to be free is therefore an act of empowerment. What it is that thus empowers me to be free varies considerably, depending upon what philosophy of life I hold. For Kant, it was the practical reason, which deprives me of the excuse that, since I am a creature bound by causality, I cannot follow it, and thus—paradoxical though this may sound—compels me to achieve freedom. For Christians, freedom, as distinguished from enslavement under the Law, arises as a result of my being empowered to be a responsible child of God and to learn to will what God wills. Freedom here becomes the unimpeded spontaneity of love.

In any case, however, freedom is always based upon this sort of impowerment or enablement which I receive from the aim of my life and actions, or, to express it in terms of a very precise concept, from my predestination, from that which I was intended and destined to be.

It is this very quality of being bound to his *telos*—and only secondarily, his freedom to achieve his *telos*—that marks the difference between the human being and the animal. "In the case of animals and plants," says Schiller, as does also Herder, "nature not only appoints the destiny but it alone carries it out."[8] In other words, it implants in its creatures an automatism in which there is no freedom whatsoever. "In the case of man, however, nature provides only the destiny and leaves it to him to carry it out." In

---

[8] Cf. H. Thielicke, *Theologische Ethik*, 2nd. ed., Vol. I, § 796 f.

other words, in man nature links his destiny with his own decision to relate himself to the fixed and ordained *telos*.

We may therefore say that human freedom is always a freedom that is bound. In this sense it has both an ethical and an aesthetic variant. For, after all, the poet realizes the utmost freedom only by expressing meaning in language which is "bound" by rhythm and meter. The sculptor does so by binding himself to a given material that puts limitations upon his own arbitrary will, and the painter reduces the range of choice he has for fashioning a picture by resorting to limiting colors, forms, and compositions. Else the very limitlessness of the materials for making a statement would void the freedom of his skill. And therefore such epigrams as "Brevity is the soul of wit" and "Restraint reveals the master's hand" are epigrammatic statements of the relation of freedom to the power of restraint that makes it possible.

Hence anyone who wishes to develop a philosophy of art *or* to make any statement whatsoever about the nature of freedom—whether it be thought of as ethical, aesthetic or religious—will be able to do so only if he takes into account the importance of this power of constraint which corresponds to freedom, and without which freedom is impossible.

It is apparent that this power of constraint is exceedingly ambivalent in structure. And in my opinion much depends upon our understanding its inner dialectic, for it is this inner dialectic that permits it to be moved by two opposite poles. The two extreme possibilities which it combines led Kant to dissolve the unity of this power of constraint and make of it an antagonism of two powers: On one side stands the causality of nature that seeks to bind man. Ethically speaking, its effect is that it threatens to abandon man to a eudaemonistic drive for happiness and thus subject him to the automatism of sensual desire. On the other side stands the call of the practical reason that ordains him to freedom over against the causality of nature.

That which we have termed the power of constraint here divides itself into two heterogeneous, opposing forces: duty and inclination, so that the binding force no longer presents itself as a unified identity. Thus sometimes it confronts us as an enslaving power; at others as an empowering force, at one time binding, at another liberating, sometimes calling human nature into question, sometimes confirming and corroborating humanity.

Schiller sought to resolve this antagonism by means of his ideal of the "beautiful soul" and thus restore the unified identity of the power of constraint and make of it an antagonism of two powers. necessity of spontaneity and also by poking fun at Kant's dualism in a series of pointed epigrams.[9]

Although Kant's dualism has always been regarded as a secular version of the Christian ethos, I am of the opinion that the form of the problem of freedom which is most exciting theologically (if I may be permitted to use this somewhat emotional expression) emerges where this power of constraint embraces both freedom and necessity at the same time and presents them as two different aspects of one and the same thing.

I mention three examples of this interpretation of the power of constraint: first, the entelechic; second, the tragic; and third, the Marxist form of a unity of freedom and necessity.

1. The *entelechic* combination of freedom and necessity was, if I may so express it, Goethe's specialty. The "minted form" which "develops as it lives" cries out for freedom inasmuch as it is in accordance with natural laws, but is at the same time demanded by the imperative, "Become what you are." In Goethe's view, therefore, necessity (*ananke*) is not, as in Kant's view, pitted against freedom, but rather merges with it in order to allow man to want to be what he is, and thus to fuse man's will and natural law into a unity similar to that which obtains in Hegel's doctrine of the "cunning of reason" or in Fichte's theory of genius. It is described in astrological symbols in the *Orphic Sayings:* "Then it is as the stars decreed: limit and law, and all will is only a willing, simply because we should." Translated into the language of Mephistophelian irony, this means that the freedom implied in the words "become what you are" is interwoven with the necessity (*ananke*) implied in the words "you will still remain what you are." (These are the words used in the Study scene in *Faust*.)

Now it is precisely this interweavement of freedom and necessity

---

[9] "Gladly do I serve my friends; but, unfortunately, I do so by desire. Thus I am irked because I am not virtuous." This is dealt with in greater detail in H. Thielicke, *Theologische Ethik*, 2nd ed., Vol. I, § 228 ff.

that is the main premise of the anthropology that underlies Luther's doctrine of justification. For that which he calls the *servum arbitrium* (the enslaved will) is by no means a determinism that operates from transcendence, but is rather the expression of man's bondage to himself. His conduct, his good works, and even his Faustian efforts to overcome himself do not make it possible really to change the basis of existence, but are simply enacted upon this same basis. They are like the passage of waves over an unchanging ocean bed. As Luther says in *De servo arbitrio: "Hinc fit, quod . . . velit, cupiat, faciat taliter, qualis ipse est."*[10] "So it is that man wills, desires, and acts in accord with what he himself is." Even if he were to achieve ethical perfection in his conduct, this could not change him; it would only be an expression of himself.

In other words, in our conduct we can objectify, but never transcend, ourselves. Between man's being and his conduct there reigns a necessity which cannot be eliminated by any intervention of man's will. Wherever such an intervention is set in motion the result is not self-transcendence, but Titanism; the given nature is merely intensified and concentrated to the highest possible degree. For—and here I Luther quote again—"it is not good works that make a good man, but rather a good man performs good works."

Without such an anthropological presupposition one cannot possibly understand why the Reformation doctrine of justification advocates the thesis "by grace alone." This thesis draws its very life from the premise that man's being possesses primacy over his will and not vice versa. To this extent man is helpless at the point of the real and ultimate theme of his life, since his will must always run back in a circle to his given existential situation and therefore must always end in religious, philosophical, and ethical forms of self-confirmation.

Liberation from this vicious circle becomes possible only if he is given a new *being*, which in turn provides a new *will*. But, in the terminology which I have been using, this is simply to say that the *power of constraint* that encompasses all freedom is changed. In the place of inevitable self-realization, i.e., in the place of enslavement by the old Adamite self, comes the new necessity which is

---

[10] WA 18,709.

characteristic of sonship to God and the spontaneity of the love of God. For the one who loves is free precisely to the degree that he surrenders to the necessity of love. This new bondage of our exist-ence, this new creation (*kaine ktisis*) which is freed in order to love, permits the human heart to will what the heart of God wills. Ex-pressed in theological terms, this means that then the power of constraint is no longer "law"—for the law rivets man to himself and only intensifies his being what he is—but rather the "gospel" of free sonship to God. For sonship bestows the free and inevitable spontaneity of love.

2. The second type of interweavement of freedom and necessity is represented by *tragedy*. When Oedipus slays his father and commits incest with his mother, this has nothing to do with guilt in the sense of a wrong moral decision, but rather occurs through operation of an inescapable fate (*moira*), which brings guilt and fate into congru-ence, so that it is impossible to tell where one ends and the other begins. Similarly, in the Oresteia it is "the old Avenger, stern of mood for Atreus and his feast of blood," who compels Clytemnestra to commit the act of bloodshed, and yet at the same time the chorus declares that she cannot clear herself of guilt by pleading that the fault lies with beguiling fate. The chorus accentuates, not the fateful, but the guilty, aspect of her crime, in the sense of the individual's unique, inescapable responsibility (Heidegger's *Jemeinigkeit*):

> Thou guiltless of this murder, thou!
> Who dares such thought avow?
> Yet it may be, wroth for the parent's deed,
> The fiend hath holpen thee to slay the son.[11]

This interweavement of freedom and necessity in tragedy cannot be understood without an appreciation of its mythological back-ground as this is expressed in certain cosmological conceptions. The world—at any rate in the unusually crass conception found in Teu-tonic mythology—is formed of tainted, curse-laden matter. Pre-existent gods and Titans have incorporated accursed matter into the very structure of the world, burdened it with a primeval mortgage, that is now working itself out in history and becoming more and more virulent. (This is the case, for example, in the concept that the

---

[11] Translations from *Agamemnon* by E. D. A. Morshead. (Trans.)

world was formed from the corpse of the slain giant, Ymir.) Whatever man does in his freedom is therefore encompassed by the same necessity by which the cosmogonic material develops, enters into, and co-operates in all human actions.

The tragic self therefore always has about it that hidden ambivalence which is apparent in Clytemnestra's dialogue with the chorus: it is at once the causative subject of guilt and the victim of compulsion. It must point the finger of accusation at itself and at the same time it can also point away from itself. *Amor fati,* that ultimate resort of tragic catharsis, therefore finds the solution of the insoluble problem in the acceptance and affirmation of causative destiny and of the congruence of guilt and fate, freedom and necessity, which reconciles the hero to the challenge of the cosmos. In this way Oedipus becomes the saint in Colonnus.

The Christian antithesis to tragedy—for it is nothing less than this —breaks through this congruence of guilt and fate by adding to the *anthropological* premise of the doctrine of justification (which asserts the precedence of being over action) a *cosmogonic* premise.

This cosmogonic premise consists in the doctrine of *creatio ex nihilo,* the creation of the universe from nothing. The point of this doctrine lies in the affirmation that God the Creator did not make use of already existing, curse-encumbered matter which he then formed into a cosmos. In this respect there can be no analogy between the creative work of God and the work of a human artificer. The Hebrew term *barah* is therefore purely a *terminus technicus* that is to be reserved only for the creative action of God. But if creation is thus understood to mean *creatio ex nihilo,* then man caught in the toils of guilt can no longer claim that he is the victim of a flaw in the material of which the creation is made. He is deprived of the pathos that attaches to the tragic victim. Since apart from himself he knows nothing about his origin except that he came from nothingness, his attempt to "derive" himself is frustrated from the outset. He cannot interpret himself as being the effect resulting from a cause outside himself. Any attempt to do so presupposes the intention to transform guilt into fate and thus resolve the burden of responsible freedom into the exonerating necessity of a process.

Thus *creatio ex nihilo* says in mythical cipher-language that man must say "I" to himself as a whole and undivided being and that he is fixed to himself.

The cosmogonic premise of the doctrine of justification may therefore be formulated as follows: I have received my self from the hands of God, and, what is more, received it exclusively from God, without any co-operation of the elements of the world; therefore I must give my self back to him in the same state in which I received it. The discovery that I cannot do this, that I am incapable of "reporting back" in the original state in which I received my self, fixes and binds me down to the same state of being which we found to be the starting point of the doctrine of justification, namely, that I have lost the freedom to be my self; there is a *rift* in the original relationship between man and God, a loss of "peace" which I do not have the freedom to restore. The liberation to a new "ability to be" must come from outside my self, from the other side. What is needed is the freedom of grace and thus the peace which the world cannot give.

3. The third problem to which we must address ourselves is the one presented by the Marxist synthesis of freedom and necessity. Here our generation is confronted with issues of fateful moment. I shall restrict myself merely to a clear definition of the theme which not only confronts us with a task of hard thinking but is also instinct with the obligation to make some elementary decisions, both political and existential.

Wolfgang Leonhard, in his now famous book *Child of the Revolution*,[12] gives an account of the strange impression which the freedom proclamations of the Western press made upon the young functionaries in the Communist party colleges.

For us freedom meant insight into historical necessity. We were free because we were the only ones who possessed this insight on the basis of scientific theory; whereas people in the West, who lacked this scientific theory and simply confronted historical evolution with an unreasoning, desperate opposition, to the point of being simply the playthings of that evolution—these were the ones who were unfree.

In other words, the West thinks freedom means the ability "to do

---

[12] Trans. by C. M. Woodhouse, Regnery, N. Y., 1958, p. 488. (Trans.)

what one wills," but is quite unaware of the hidden forces that are interwoven in its alleged freedom and make it illusory. One cannot ignore the seriousness of the question this poses. If we were to answer it merely with the profession that we in the West stand for a free way of life, then this would be nothing but empty pathos. It makes me shudder every time I hear the sound of these clanging cymbals among us. They are the sounds of a smug security that is not only unseemly but actually perilous on the edge of the abyss. This is the point where we must do some hard thinking.

What is the meaning of this statement that freedom is insight into necessity?

Dialectical materialism advocates the thesis that in nature as well as society there is no such thing as chance, but that necessity reigns supreme. Hence everything in the realm of history and thus also in the sphere of human action is controlled by objective laws. They are as stringent as natural laws. Since Communism views itself as a liberation movement and consequently wishes not only to interpret but to change the world, it simply cannot escape the problem of freedom. For the will to change the world logically presupposes the freedom to be *able* to change it.

The answer to the question of the relation between freedom and necessity within the limits thus set can only be that of the famous definition of Friedrich Engels: "Freedom does not consist in the dream of independence of natural laws, but in the knowledge of these laws and in the possibility this gives of systematically allowing them to work toward definite ends."

Accordingly, freedom is not active intervention in the laws—how could this be possible!—but rather consists in collaboration with these laws, in systematically *allowing* them to work.

Naturally this collaboration presupposes a knowledge of these laws. And this knowledge is understood as being the rules that govern the material and economic substructure of history.

Superimposed upon this *historical* structure of freedom, as being merely the discernment of necessity, is the *eschatological* freedom that will come with the consummation of history. This second, eschatological form of freedom will bring about what Marxism-Leninism calls the "leap into the realm of freedom." For when society seizes the means of production, the rule of the product over the producers will cease. And this will mean that the necessity of the previous course of history, which has had the significance of an *octroi* for men, will also cease. The "objective alien forces that ruled history hitherto will come under the control of men" and make man the subject, rather than the object of these forces. And this eschatological stage of history will bring the final emancipation of man from the animal world, allow him to exist wholly in and with himself, and open up the chance to be a complete human being.

Anybody who is familiar with Hegel will have no difficulty in seeing that this is a materialization of Hegel's doctrine of spirit: As man develops into a subjective spirit he becomes free and discerns in all reality the manifestation of that spirit which comes to self-consciousness in him as a finite spirit. In recognizing that he is identical with everything that permeates objective reality he becomes absolutely free. For to be free and not to be determined by anything outside oneself are one and the same thing. "I am free when my existence depends upon myself"; in other words, I am free when I will what the world-spirit wills and when that which is willed is no longer an *octroi* for me. Because history is progress in the consciousness of this identity, "the history of the world is none other than the progress of consciousness of freedom."[13]

The eschatological realm of freedom is therefore also a realm of perfected humanity in the sense that man will then be a "self-contained existence," existing "in and with" himself.

Thus the Marxist, following Hegel's footsteps, views the ascent to freedom as assured because he knows by name the anonymous forces, which the bourgeoisie faces blindly, and conforms his program of action with his knowledge of the laws by which they operate. In this way he no longer wears himself out in struggling with the inevitable forces of history, as the Kantian dualism of freedom and necessity requires, i.e., in struggling with economic trends, the laws of mass psychology, and many other factors in the realm of history beyond the individual, but rather exploits their gradient, directs all their currents into his mills, and thus potentiates his history-changing dynamic with the forces of history itself. In other words, he treats

[13] Hegel, *Philosophie der Geschichte, Philos. Bibl.*, pp. 32, 40 (*Philosophy of History*, trans. by J. Sibree, in *Great Books of the Western World*, Vol. 46, pp. 160, 161).

history homeopathically (if I may be allowed the expression—with a bow to the medical faculty) in the sense of treating like with like, rather than opposing it allopathically.

It should be noted that here—*unlike* the philosophy of Hegel!—an economic argument is introduced; namely, that it is a waste of energy to resist the trend of history, and conversely, a saving of energy to multiply by many times the power of one's own will by bringing it into line with the dynamic trend of history. The economic factor is not only the *subject* of Marxist thinking; it also determines its method of mastering this subject intellectually and then actively influencing it.

We are aware of the great fascination that this view and this program of action must engender. If I am not mistaken, the attractiveness of this concept resides less in its materialistic background—for here the polemical "ifs" and "ands" immediately come into play —than in the realization that here freedom is not merely being proclaimed as a goal to be wished for, but that it is being subjected to the pressure of reflection. This reflection brings to light certain controlling factors in history which really make it possible to achieve freedom and without which freedom is blind and degenerates into an empty phrase. Anyone who speaks of freedom without being aware of that necessity with which he has to come to terms in one way or another is really saying nothing at all.

Therefore the so-called free West cannot declare and define its freedom merely by saying that it "wills" something different from its Eastern counterpart; it must rather declare that it "thinks" differently. The freedom to exercise our will—in opposition, say, to terror and ideological tyranny—can therefore mean only that we want to *think* about freedom in a different way. Freedom must be based on something, it must be *grounded* upon thought, otherwise it has no foundation. I purposely use these terms in order to emphasize the double meaning of the word "ground," in both the sense of a logical category and the sense of a real foundation for life.

To that extent Marxism-Leninism addresses to us a very fundamental question that cannot be answered merely with declamation but only with argumentation.

The problem of how this question is to be answered seems to me to be *the* great task of thought and decision that now faces the mature minds of the West. If the University of Berlin were being founded today, the idea of freedom which was set forth by Humboldt, Schleiermacher, and Steffens at that time would undoubtedly appear in this form.

If I were to formulate this task of thought set for us by the Marxist synthesis of freedom and necessity, I would seek to do so in two ways:

First, we need to examine whether the Marxist definition, which states that necessity is inherent in the autonomous processes of the material substructure of history, is correct or not, and whether the interaction of spirit and matter is not far more dialectical than has appeared to be surmised and claimed, at least since the publication of Stalin's "letters on linguistics." As long as the Central Committee decides what is "necessary," it is obvious that freedom cannot be defined as insight into necessity, but is actually nullified by submission to those who *allege* that they have insight into necessity. In the place of the logic of history, which in principle should be capable of elucidation—at least according to the Marxist conception—there comes the positivistic assertion of the will of a privileged caste which exercises rule.

The popular and somewhat naïve observation commonly heard in our circles that terror and tyranny hold sway on the other side of the Iron Curtain is therefore correct enough in the last analysis. Nevertheless the mature minds among us must not simply repeat this without having thought it through, in order that they may then make this diagnosis more intelligently and meaningfully.

This thinking will start from the question of why it was that Marxism-Leninism is forced to commit this inconsistency in its doctrine of freedom, why it was forced into precisely the position where it was *not* able to make the necessity of history the object of insight and thus to render freedom possible, instead of substituting for it a positivistic assertion of will that must be obeyed. The answer to this question leads directly to a critique of the Marxist definition of necessity and hence to the determining function of the economic substructure.

Second, the Marxist synthesis of freedom and necessity contains —in spite of its materialistic error—the following quite respectable thesis: Consciousness and actual existence of freedom are possible only where the consciousness of freedom says No in the face of the powers that would restrict it, in other words, where it stands firm against the fact of necessity. Even though we deny the Marxist definition of the relationship between freedom and necessity and thus deny the concept of freedom implicit in it, the very fact that Marxism even starts out with this definition constitutes an unmistakable challenge to self-examination.

The question is whether the Western idea of freedom is not in danger of losing its specific gravity and becoming an empty, weightless phrase, either because we no longer have any common consciousness of the forces that limit and restrict freedom, and are therefore not really entitled to speak about freedom at all, or because our common consciousness so overestimates the forces that limit freedom, especially the almost blind overemphasis upon milieu and infatuation with environmental theories, that the very words "freedom" and "responsibility" are choked off before they reach the threshold of consciousness.

Today we can no longer honestly utter the word "freedom" unless we have previously come to grips with the theories that lie behind the idea of the forces of necessity, such as autonomy in economics and politics or the determinative importance of environment. Anybody who takes the words "freedom" and "human dignity" on his lips or sings the songs of liberty in the songbooks must do so in the face of these forces and in defiance of them. Otherwise it all becomes mere bleating. Moreover, we are no longer permitted, even in Kant's sense, to think merely in terms of the entelechy of the intelligible ego when we speak of personhood and conscience. In fact, we can speak of personhood and freedom only as we have explored—not least with the aid of sociology—their relation to the limiting forces which we have discovered to be "necessity" in the historical dimension.

These forces are certainly of a kind different from those which Marxism thought it had discovered. Nevertheless they are there. It is not only Christian ethics—though it, above all others, must do so—that is obliged to define its doctrine of freedom in the light of these factors.

To be sure, these forces that limit freedom do not have only this character of necessity, this quality of a trend that operates as a law. Freedom "to do what I will" is also limited by *normative* factors.

These may be represented by the interests of the community or reasons of state or even by my immediate neighbor who represents a barrier to my personal freedom. The paradoxical fact is that the rights of citizenship and the freedom they guarantee can remain in force only if I do not lay claim to all my freedom, only if I abstain from some of my privileges and do not exercise the full latitude of my constitutional rights.

This ethical limitation upon freedom, which is very difficult, and sometimes impossible, to define in terms of law, becomes an acute problem, for example, in the ticklish question of the freedom of the press, the freedom to publish fairly extreme pornography, the freedom to break to some extent the taboo of personal privacy. An indication that here we recognize the task of exerting some self-limitation upon our freedom is the establishment of corporate self-controls, such as those for films and press. They are institutional symbols of the possibility that freedom may erupt in self-destruction and at the same time of the conviction that the law must not hesitate to accept some of the hazards of freedom in order that it may not become the total regimentation of tyranny.

This rounds the circle of our thinking, which throughout has been revolving about the question of what kind of dialectic is inherent in the relationship between freedom and necessity.

This problem has many different aspects, and we have endeavored to address ourselves to several which are of particular significance. The essential conclusion has been that freedom is possible only within certain limitations and a framework of obligations, if it is not to become a playground of neutral values and thus a force that produces mere chaos. In our thinking together we have seen that at some times the binding factor can take the form of a power of constraint and that it is present in this mode in the numerous variants of necessity. But we also have seen that it can appear as a factor that empowers freedom. Behind all the ciphers in which this empowering factor appears, stands the ultimate author of empowerment, none other than God, who has called us into existence and provided our existence with a *telos*.

In the state of free, mature sonship to God, into which we have been called and for which the Christ-event is representative, we enter into the bondage that makes us free of all the bondages and false empowerments we meet in the created world. For the Father has authorized and empowered everything that may legitimately limit, rule or empower us. The free, mature son, however, has immediate access to his Father, he possesses the standard and the criteria by which to judge these authorized courts (the state, for example), and therefore stands apart from them by virtue of his immediate relationship to the Father. This is what Luther meant when he said that the Christian man is the lord of all things and subject to none. He who is close to the *norma normans* can no longer be subject to the *normae normatae*.

I know of no place where this question is so graphically stated and dealt with as it is in Jesus' parable of the prodigal son. This son, who strove to get away from his father into the far country, was fundamentally seeking only himself and his own free development. In other words, he is afraid that if he remains within the confining tradition and value-structure of the parental home, he will not be able to find himself in freedom, but will just go on doing what others do, or, to use a modern phrase, that he will remain an unfree function of his milieu. So he separates himself from his father in the hope that he will find himself on the free paths of the far country and be able to develop himself in freedom. He hopes, as it were, to become autonomous. But, instead of finding freedom, he falls under the dictatorship of his homesickness, his ambition, his urges. The freedom to do what he wills subjects him to the tyranny of the law of least resistance. The very lack of binding restraints that he willed leads him to the pigsty—a highly symbolical term—and makes it utterly clear that he has not exchanged his bondage to the father for freedom (which is what he really wanted), but rather for bondage to inferior powers.

This is his catastrophe. It is *our* catastrophe. When the son found the father *anew* by the roundabout way of wandering in the far country he realized that he had also found himself in this bond, and therefore had arrived at real freedom. We have only to choose between bondage to the Father, which makes us free, and bondage to the powers of this world, which enslaves us. Only he who finds God finds himself. In Hegelian terms, he is "in and with himself." This insight should be the key signature that precedes everything we have been thinking about in this chapter.

Therefore, mindful of our responsibility for the brethren beyond the Curtain, I cannot close without raising the question of self-examination: What is the concept of freedom on which the West is really acting? Is it, for many of us, anything more than the freedom to achieve a certain standard of living? Is freedom just another item among the consumer's goods that contribute to our common comfort, which we use and use up—in a word, consume? We have become consumers of freedom.

Are we still really producing freedom in our own lives? Do we still have a source of supply? Freedom which has forgotten the empowering factor—or better and emphatically, the One who empowers—very quickly degenerates into irresponsible libertarianism. For a brief interim it leads the half-life of an idea, the source of which is not remembered and which is therefore no longer nourished by this source. The well-known saying that mankind is on an incline leading from divinity to humanity to bestiality is a beacon. He who wants the freedom of man must seek for that which is more than man.

I close therefore with what is a basic question. This is not the time for eloquent, emotional perorations; rather what is needed is sharp Socratic interrogation, for only he who is called in question can become a mature adult. Therefore it is the glory and worth of a university to ask questions and then to teach men how to stand firm and face questions.

II

IDEALS IN A FREE SOCIETY

THE TRUTH OF THE ATOMIC AGE, A TRIUMPH OF RATIONALITY CARRIED to its uttermost limits, has proved itself to be superior to many previous truths. Not a few of them have been shown to be mere prejudices. And yet, now that this kind of truth has reached a climax, it is becoming clear that, though it does discern and bring to extreme technological development the functions of man, it nevertheless has not understood the *bearer* of these functions, man himself; that to it man's person has become a mystery and above all a critical dangerpoint in a calculation in which it has "reckoned without its host." This is the point where the question arises: What is man? Or, to put it in terms of our theme, What do the ideals of man say concerning his nature?

A. THE MAN BEHIND THE IDEALS

I should like to show first that man conceals himself behind his ideals and some of the ways in which he does so. Back of the ideal image of what he ought to be, man hides his real being. And this in itself is revealing. For in the way we conceal ourselves and above all in what we hide, we reveal our secret. But in order to develop this point further we shall first have to get a clear understanding of the terms involved and thus proceed in a workmanlike way. Since for reasons of space we cannot deal at length with the literature in which these terms are sometimes used with a different shade of meaning, we are here concerned more with clarifying our terminology, particularly the terms "idea," "ideal," "utopia," and "ideology."

I start with this thesis: to have ideals means to be convinced that we ourselves and the real world around us are no longer congruent with what we were intended to be. The ideal therefore has within it an accusation; one might even say that it contains a judgment upon us. So, before we dare to sit in theological judgment and criticize the fact that ideals are self-chosen or that they are often high-flown and visionary or illusory, we must first give due regard to the ciphered message of repentance which our ideals proclaim to us. Frequently enough, of course, this message of repentance is not ciphered at all, but quite candidly takes the offensive. Thus the ideals of the Youth Movement were coupled with very aggressive criticism of respectable society and of adults in general. Both of these, the ideal goal and the critical offensive, belong together. How closely the two can be linked together may be seen in the ethics of critical idealism. For example, we shall fail to understand Kant's ethics if we do not see that his ideal of humanity contains a tremendous protest against man as he actually is. Kant's concept of duty launches an offensive against things as they are. It is therefore a message of repentance. Nobody ever expressed this protest character in such fine philosophical laughter as did Wilhelm Busch when he said, "The good—this rule is hard and fast—is always the evil from which we abstain." But I can only "abstain from" something which has already been given, something that has being (or at least potential being, and thus is a "possibility"). The criterion by which we establish the discrepancy between what is and what should be we call the idea. For example, when we compare ourselves with the idea of "humanity," as defined by Kant or Schleiermacher or David Friedrich Strauss or Feuerbach, we see that as actual persons we do not measure up to this idea, that at most we have only a potential relationship to it. The actual man–woman relationship falls short of Goethe's idea of the "eternal feminine," and the idea of the state, of "statehood," is always above and beyond all empirical states, no matter how superlatively they may be realized, say, in a consistent democracy.

When we understand the idea to be a kind of critical principle, which subjects our actual existence to judgment, and when we then accept it as a goal to be attained, so that it becomes an image of what we should be, then the idea becomes an *ideal*. This is our second definition.

Let me illustrate this distinction between an idea and an ideal in this way. Friedrich Rückert said:

> In every man there lives an image
> Of what he ought to be.
> As long as he is not that image
> He ne'er at rest will be.

This image of myself is the idea that slumbers within me, and is therefore what Goethe called the "minted form," the "entelechy" within me. When I measure myself by this image, I note that I am not identical, not congruent with the design which I should realize. Thus my own idea of myself becomes a judgment upon me, which, because of the discrepancy between the ideal and what I actually am, may cast me into dissatisfaction and dissension with myself, perhaps even into melancholy dejection, the acedia of the medieval monks. At the same time, however, this ideal is something imposed and laid upon me; it assumes the role of the normative ideal toward which I must strive. And not until I achieve it will I be "at rest."

We need still further definitions, however. The ideal which has thus come into being may take several forms. Either it may exist in my consciousness as an abstract normative concept, such as the idea of the state or the eternal feminine. Or it may shake off this abstractness and become a virile, imaginative concept of a very concrete state of the world, a blueprint of a world (think of Kant and Albrecht Ritschl) in which humanity is organized "in accord with moral laws" or on the "principle of love." Or it may produce a picture of a world in which there is no more poverty, no hunger, and no disease. When the ideal is thus given concrete form and when on top of this the hopeful thesis is maintained that our world is actually capable of reaching this state, that this perfection can be wrung from it and that we are therefore committed to ensure its realization, we speak of this as *utopia*.

A utopia is therefore an ideal envisioned in concrete terms, applicable to a state beyond the personal sphere, and held to be capable of realization. This is our third definition. And here again we give an example, not one of the classical utopias, but one which is impressive just because it is so naïve and casual. It comes from the French physicist Perrin, who not long ago made the following statement: "Will not all our desires, even the most daring, gradually become realizable through technology? Does not technology lead to an ever-growing wealth for mankind and a progressive reduction of the oppressive burden of labor? As machines do our work, men will gain time to devote themselves to enjoyment and the cultivation of the nobler goods of civilization. And as ever more rapidly increasing wealth not only eliminates poverty and social injustice but at the same time removes the causes of strife and eruptions of war, mankind's ancient dream of equality and freedom will be fulfilled in the harmony of equal rights for all on a planet where disease has vanished and age and death have been conquered." The transition from the idea to the ideal to the utopia takes place as it were on a plateau on which the relative rank and level of these three thought-images is essentially retained. But this transition can turn into a steep descent if its course heads toward a fourth thought-image. That is to say, it can happen—and perhaps it must of necessity happen—that the ideal and the utopia may not be revered at all because of their intrinsic value and the binding truth they contain, but that men may see that they are psychologically attractive and effective for mobilizing people and then proceed to utilize them for their political potential. In this case the result is an *ideology*. Hence we shall understand this term "ideology" to mean an ideal that has become *pragmatic*. This is our fourth definition.

At the same time these definitions provide us with an architectonic structure for our thinking. We shall deal first with this trend toward ideology, discussing it as the ideal jeopardizing itself. In a second section we shall deal with the ideal as it is jeopardized by us.

B. THE IDEAL JEOPARDIZED BY ITSELF

The first of these two themes (we may divulge this right at the start) has in it an undertone of irony. For it will become apparent that, strictly speaking, there is no such thing as self-jeopardization of the ideal, but rather that it is always we ourselves who ruin the ideal.

We trace first, then, the course that leads from the utopia to the ideology, because this is the course that goes through the process in which the ideal jeopardizes itself. To do this we must characterize more clearly what is meant by utopia.

1. UTOPIANISM

If I see aright, there are three completely different classes of utopias: first, the utopia as a faith that the world has a predetermined design; second, the visionary utopia; and third, the history-transcending utopia.

a) The utopia as a faith that the world has a predetermined design may be illustrated by the utopia of Thomas More and by contrast with Machiavelli. As is well known, Machiavelli describes history as an ethically neutral play of forces without meaning or goal; and he taught his prince how to play along with these forces and come out on top. History is a kind of drama or spectacle of nature, a tempestuous storm of natural forces, the course of which one explores, so to speak, meteorologically, in order that one may not only ride it out, but also take advantage of it by channeling the elemental torrents as much as possible and making them run one's own mill.

Thomas More, on the other hand, viewed man as a being who has a purpose and destiny and who therefore must realize this destiny, with which he was created, in every area of his existence, and above all in the area of the *state*. In the order and peace and welfare of the state this destiny of man's being must also find perfect expression. The utopian state, so understood, objectifies and institutionalizes the *being* of man.

As is immediately apparent, we have here two fundamentally different points of departure in thinking. But, if I see aright, this difference does not consist in the fact that Machiavelli held a pessimistic, realistic view of man, while Thomas More was a visionary, idealistic, and optimistic dreamer. Realism and utopianism cannot be differentiated quite that crudely. That this will not do is apparent from the fact that Thomas More, the utopian, is fully aware of the dubiousness of man, of the passions and above all the greed and egoism, by which he is driven. His ideal state is a thoroughly studied and well-thought-out structure that actually provides *dams* against the torrents of human passion and furnishes outlets for its pressures. Moreover, there is a strain of skepticism that runs through the whole of it: man cannot ultimately be changed from what he is. Only to a degree can he be kept in check by institutional means and then only by partially subduing his avarice through provision of comforts and social equality. This is the most that can be done.

Here the question may arise: how is it that a person who was so realistic and sober-minded should come to write, of all things, a utopia, and then into the bargain become famous for it? My opinion would be that the reason lies in the fact that Thomas More saw that there are two sides to man. He saw man first as he is *de facto* (and here man shows himself to be avaricious, egoistic, sensual), but he also saw man as he was meant to be, in the light of his destiny, his real, intended being. And from this point of view man is a being in whom the spirit triumphs over desire, justice over egoism, and the peace of God over violence. Once we see this we shall not be inclined simply to dismiss utopias in the style of Thomas More as unrealistic figments of dreams. On the contrary, this kind of a utopian is envisioning a state of the world or a social structure in which we have an objectification of the essential image of man's being rather than of the empirical image of him as actually he is.

Consequently, one can discover from the utopias man constructs what he thinks of as being his real, innermost nature—this nature which, though it is present in the real life he now lives, is nevertheless hidden beneath distortions. Hence the utopias contain very definite assertions about the nature of man, assertions which may be thoroughly realistic and aware of the sin and the degeneration of human existence. The important thing for the understanding of such utopias, however, would seem to me to be that in them man is not conceived of—as in Machiavelli—as a mere force of nature, which can simply be posited as such and taken into one's calculations, but rather that they see in man a being who transcends himself and is designed for a purpose.

If one wished to say, in the context of such a utopia, what man is, quite the wrong way to go about it would be to describe him in his *de facto* condition and say, for example, that man is a murderer, a thief, an adulterer, egoistic and greedy for power. Thomas More certainly would not have denied that this description of his *de facto* condition is largely accurate. (There are clear indications in his book that he would have agreed.) But what he would have objected to just as strongly is the notion that man's essential *being* can be defined by such descriptions of his present condition. In the same way, the Christian, however realistically he interprets the world by the standard of the laws of God, would demur if anyone were to say that "man after the Fall" is the real and essential man. No, the real and essential man is rather the one who came from the Creator's hand as the image of God and gazes upon us undistorted from the face of Jesus Christ.

The decisive difference from Machiavelli's anthropology therefore is that Machiavelli identifies the being of man with his *de facto* condition, that he sees him as one who is driven by his passions. Thomas More, on the contrary, still sees the being of man apart from his *de facto* condition. He regards him as one-who-ought-to-be in conflict with what-he-is. He sees him as a man in contradiction to himself. Correspondingly, he also does not construct his ideal state by proceeding to describe the empirical conditions of the state, making a distillate of their best characteristics, and then setting forth the highest degree of functional efficiency in a state. He rather constructs a visionary image of the state that is adapted to the real destiny of man and then subjects the empirical states to the judgment of this essential image. Reduced to a simple formula, it might be said that Machiavelli sets forth what man and his state are, while More presents what they should be.

We Christians especially will have to concede, indeed, even declare, that this conviction that man must be described not merely in terms of his condition but also in terms of his essential being is one of the main theses of our faith. The publicans and harlots of the New Testament are not defined by the fact that they are publicans and harlots; rather their essential being (and therefore that which is in the last analysis to be defined here) consists precisely in that which transcends their actual condition: they are the children of their Father in heaven who is grieving for them. The love that causes Jesus to seek them out and that determines his relationship to them is nothing else but the charism of penetrating beyond the condition of lostness and addressing oneself to this essential being.

Only if we take into account this point of the utopian statement, which is directed to the essential being, will we understand one of the very important phenomena of history, namely, that utopias have a tremendous mobilizing power and that they are capable of generating revolutionary movements, and have, in fact, done so repeatedly. The yearning of man to find his way through to himself and his essential being, which is appealed to in utopias, is a political force of the first rank. It is by no means the case (as Machiavelli thought) that these elemental forces are only the cruder urges of man, his hunger for happiness and well-being and power, for bread and circuses. His longing, often very dim and hardly understood, to find his way through to his destination is a force that creates history. That this is so can readily be seen in the political importance of utopias (we need only to think, for example, of the utopian dreams of Marxism). The idea of a peaceable kingdom, of a state of justice or of social equality has actually unleashed fanatical movements and thus has been a high-powered motor of historical progress.

It would therefore be quite wrong to interpret the utopias, in any case those in the style of Thomas More, as mere fairy tales. Fairy tales always take place outside oneself, in a detached, nonresponsible zone. This is why they generally have their effect only upon children, who still cannot distinguish between what is inside and what is outside, between reality and fantasy. But adults are capable of making this distinction! So for them fairy tales are merely a kind of dreaming that leads to a higher or lower form of entertaining idleness or perhaps to dreaming oneself back into the land of childhood, thus seducing one into sentimentalism. In any case this would not help us to understand the political potential of utopianism. Rather this political potential can be explained only by the fact that the utopian images of ideals and ultimate goals have a correlation with the essential being of man, with his "potential being," and that man recognizes himself in them, recognizes in them his essential being as it should be. The utopias are therefore filled with the pathos of what man could be and was intended to be. They are, to use a term employed by Nietzsche, a "monumentalistic history" projected into the future. The peaceable kingdom or the classless society is never merely the antithesis to present conditions; these utopian kingdoms rather depict as mature, fruit-bearing trees what is already present in embryo in man as he now is.

b) The second form of utopia we call the visionary utopia. The negative characteristics of this form of utopia are that its ideals are not accommodated to the real possibilities of history (though they may be to its ultimate possibilities) and that it has lost sight of the abiding conflict between man's essential being and his actual condition. Instead of this it sets up *absolute* goals. When this is done in Christian terms, the result is that the laws of the kingdom of God, which transcends history, are simply carried over into this aeon. Thus, as in the case of the sixteenth-century fanatics, or, in a different way, Tolstoi, the commandments of the Sermon on the Mount are made into a constitution for this world and a kingdom is proclaimed in which there will be no more force, no military, and no police.

There are two reasons why this utopian dream is always frustrated. First, because here the kingdom of God is no longer the object of expectation and faith, but is forcibly wrenched into this aeon, skipping over history between the Fall and the Last Judgment. Then faith leaps, as it were, from the state of waiting, hoping, and trusting into that of "seeing," which is forbidden, and thus eliminates the boundary between the "now" and the "not yet." It loses its ability to say, "Nevertheless," and insists upon "having" the object of faith immediately.

This indicates the second reason why this kind of utopianism breaks down. The violence with which the interim of this aeon is brushed aside shows that here the kingdom of God ceases to be an eschatological *act* of God and becomes instead a goal of human action, a *work* of man. In this way faith is compromised in two ways: first, in the sense that it insists upon "seeing" (by forcibly dragging the kingdom of God into the actual conditions of the "now"); and also in the fact that faith is made a work (by making the kingdom of God something that can be forced into being by man). Therefore this form of utopia is based upon an illusion, which is usually followed, at latest in the second generation, by disillusionment.

c) There is the third form of utopia, which I call the history-transcending *"utopia,"* though not without a certain hesitation and some strong conceptual reservations. For I am quite aware that this form of utopia is not in the same category as the others; indeed, that it is really a *"judgment"* upon the others. But the very fact that for a moment we include this history-transcending ideal among the utopias, well safe-guarded with quotation marks and italics— in the same way that we may sometimes call the gospel a religion —makes it clear at once how far removed it is from all other utopias.

What I mean by this third form of utopia is what the Bible means by the *eschaton:* the paradise, the kingdom of God, and all the absolutes that are behind the demands of the Sermon on the Mount. Here again it is man's essential being, man as he should be, that is addressed. One needs only to think of the radicalizations of the Mosaic law in the Sermon on the Mount (radicalizations in which not only the realm of man's ethical conduct but also his thoughts and the depths of his heart are claimed for God), in order to see that here man is being addressed at the point of his ultimate being and destination, at the point that transcends what he is now. For here man is addressed as if he had just come unspoiled from the hands of God, or as if he were already existing in the fulfill-ment of the kingdom of God. He is addressed as a created being *and* an eschatological being.

In the pertinent passages of the Bible (that is, wherever it deals with paradise, the kingdom of God or with the *eschaton* of the Sermon on the Mount), the purpose is not to take this man as he is, this man who it is hoped will become what he was intended to be, and set him up as the definitive figure in this aeon and to visualize him as realizing an actual condition of perfection. No, this man is at one and the same time the man who has passed away and the man he will become after his resurrection. He is the man who does not yet know "what he shall be" (I John 3:2) when God will have made him congruent with his original design in his king-dom. The Sermon on the Mount makes its demands upon us as if we were still in our original state and as if the kingdom of God had already come. And this makes it a judgment upon our condition in this interim state.

Of course, it would be quite wrong to conclude from this that the ideals of the Sermon on the Mount must simply remain outside ourselves, that they belong somewhere beyond the horizon of our real world and actually have nothing to do with us (as if they are something like Platonic ideals). It is true that Bismarck once said that the world could not be governed by the Sermon on the Mount, because it is domiciled in another dimension and because things do not get done in the political sphere of our world without opportunism and without getting one's hands dirty. But a historical comparison between Bismarck and Hitler will show that the Sermon on the Mount does penetrate into this world nevertheless. Bismarck knew the Sermon on the Mount. And therefore he was also conscious of the dubiousness of the business of politics. He suffered in conscience over the fact that in this aeon might must repeatedly be allowed to supersede right and that often one must "let well enough alone." But it was precisely this dubiety that kept him sane and sound. For him, if I assess him rightly, it was like a bit of surgical gauze in the wound of this world that prevents it from healing and guards it from succumbing to the illusion that it is healthy, unwounded, and "in order."[1]

I believe that, seen purely from the point of view of practical politics, here lie the roots of Bismarck's sober moderation—a moderation which, given this multidimensional, activistic, vitally energetic personality, could otherwise hardly be explained. Hitler had no understanding of the Sermon on the Mount. He had no sense at all of the dubiety of political calculation. The condition of this world, as he diagnosed it, contained within itself the imperative for his own action: he believed that the condition of this world is determined by the fact that man's nature is that of a wolf; therefore his policy was, "Let us run with the wolf pack!" He believed— and in this he may even have been correct—that in our world might

---

[1] Cf. full treatment of this subject in the chapter on Bismarck in Thielicke, *Ethik des Politischen* (The Ethics of Politics), *Theologische Ethik*, Vol. II, 2, § 111 ff.

is usually right. So for him it was clear that he must be prepared to break any contract and twist any law if the interests of pure power so demanded. For him there was no *eschaton* that called this his world into question; for him there was no gauze in the world's wound. Therefore for him it was a sound body that could serve him as a model of natural action and reaction. The condition of the world prescribed for him the law of his life, since he did not recognize the dualism of condition and essential being. He roamed without restraint on a forest path and thus lapsed into the uninhibited state of the animal.

But let us go back to the problem of the utopia. The *eschaton* of the kingdom of God, which runs through the Sermon on the Mount as an ideal, therefore has only one thought in common with the utopia, namely, that what is expressed in it is man's authentic being, his being as it was intended to be, his eschatological being. But this *eschaton* differs from the utopia in that it is neither wrenched out of the context of transcendence and proclaimed as a visionary goal which man can achieve by his own autonomous effort (as in the case of the fanatics), nor understood as a historical possibility of a relative ideality, as in Thomas More.

Nevertheless, as we have seen, the kingdom of God does keep manifesting itself in secret signlike realizations and in a hidden presence as judgment and grace in this aeon. Therefore only the first two forms of utopias, namely, the utopia as a vision of man's predetermined design and the utopia as a visionary anticipation of the kingdom of God, can be considered utopias in the genuine sense of the word. They both break down: either because they demand too much of man's ability and imagine that man's essential being can overcome his actual condition, and thus for this very reason produce a picture of the land of utopia which, as the word itself says quite literally, is a "nowhere"; or because they forcibly translocate the kingdom of God into the present and put works and sight in the place of faith. This brings us to the point where we can draw our first conclusion.

We conclude, then, that the utopia may be the first step toward the self-jeopardization of the ideal. (As we have indicated, this is said ironically and we shall presently disclose the purpose of this irony.) In other words, the utopia, since it is a dream, albeit one that contains many elements of truth, including some protests against things as they are, which are to be taken very seriously, may actually refute the ideal. It can expose the ideal as being un-substantial, disobedient, unrealistic—and thus wreck it.

There are, it seems to me, two main forms in which man's utopian protest against things as they are, man's revolt against the transiency of his existence, can occur. One form of revolt is the unwarranted prolongation of the world. This is the idea that the world will continue to go on as it is, ending in icy death after millions of years, or continuing in an infinite progression. This makes the in-dividual a particle in an unending stream; he loses his immediacy to God and he eliminates from his existence the accent of uncondi-tionedness and once-for-allness which he has when he confronts the face of God. At this point Christians like Albrecht Bengel, for example, who believed that the Second Coming was imminent, were closer to the truth even though their dates may have been wrong.

The other form in which man protests against his transiency is the opposite of the prolongation of the world; it is a premature break with the world. The signal for this abrupt retreat from our aeon is given by those who make a utopia of the kingdom of God. The prematurity of this break with the world very frequently ex-presses itself in sectarian fanaticism, in impatient insistence upon having the goal immediately. This attitude is often found among doctrinaire pacifists, who want the lion and the lamb to lie down together and the tiger to eat grass here and now. This gives rise to the unwillingness to accept and endure the fallen state of our world and be content with that grace which comes as a light into our darkness. Therefore the attempt to transcend this fallen world by resorting to utopianism and to employ the message of the king-dom of God as the Magna Charta for utopianism is *hubris* and idolatry. One may find many things to question in Luther's doc-trine of the two kingdoms, but its fundamental intention is un-mistakable: it makes every effort to show the worldliness of this world and to prevent the kingdom of God from being turned into a utopia.

Allow me to make one further comment concerning the utopias.

It may look for a moment as if the utopia could be something in the nature of a Christian vision, since after all it does, at least in Thomas More, make the distinction between man's essential being and his present condition. But this flash of truth is swept away in the very next moment by the real trend of the utopian passion. This real trend is impelled by the postulate that the essential being of man can be realized by man, that his ideal form can be achieved by him, in himself and in his institutions. This visionary confidence of man in himself, which is the ultimate generative power in the utopias, betrays itself when man strays from his real nature and reveals himself to be a beast. In times of bestiality, times of Gestapo and GPU, torture and brainwashing, the praise of Christians can still rise unchanged to heaven. Their petition "Thy kingdom come" is not discouraged by darkest night or silent, unanswering heaven; it only becomes more fervent. For this kingdom is no utopia that stands or falls with man's self-reliance, but is secure in the hands of Him who knows our frame, and the more conscious we are of what we are, the more fervidly we may pray for his intervention and comfort. It was precisely when the utopian dream of a messianic kingdom collapsed in the dark night of Golgotha that the dying Christ was able to pray, "Father, into thy hands I commend my spirit." But the utopian, whose ideals are centered upon creative man, undergoes a shocking disillusionment when man's bestiality to man shatters his confidence in himself. Then his utopias suffer a gruesome sea-change and become apocalyptic horrors, spectacles of a world filled with synthetically fabricated test-tube babies (as in Aldous Huxley's *Brave New World*), or a world daunted and discouraged by the staring mask of the omnipresent dictator (as in George Orwell), or dominated by robots (as in Jack Williamson).

The ideal, here presenting itself in the form in which it jeopardizes itself, is therefore an ambivalent, ambiguous thing at its innermost core. It has its truthful side; it reckons with the fact that man is not congruent with his destiny, that he does not "possess" his essential being, but must seek it. But the ideal also has its demonic side, because it cherishes the confidence that man can either achieve this goal or at least move toward it and lay hold of its approximate values.

Not until we put it in this way can we state the conclusive reason why the kingdom of God cannot be interpreted as a utopia, namely, that God, and not man, is the Lord of the kingdom of God. The one who is Lord, however, is greater than his kingdom. One who makes a utopia of this kingdom sets it *above* the Lord. Then he cares more for the condition of peace, nonviolence, and a full stomach than he does for Him who bestows all these things and whose hand is greater than what it gives. Jesus said after feeding the five thousand, "You seek me, not because you saw signs, but because you ate your fill of the loaves" (John 6:26). What he was saying was: You are not seeking me; you are seeking your own satisfaction. You are not seeking the gift that reveals the Giver; you are seeking the gift as an end in itself. You are not seeking the Savior, but only salvation. You are not seeking my hand, but only the pennies in my hand—like one who flings a prayer to heaven when the bombs come screaming down and the next moment forgets it, because what he wanted was preservation and not the presence of the Preserver. The eyes that leer and lust for bread can never wait. Only he who looks at the hand that gives the bread can say, "The eyes of all look to thee, and thou givest them their food in due season" (Ps. 145:15), which means at a time which is "in his hand" (Ps. 31:15). He who sees the bread and not the hand loses the sense of the "due time". He wrenches everything out of its due season and wants it this moment.

The utopian wants the kingdom and not the Lord. Therefore he cannot wait, therefore he thinks he himself is the savior who can bring in the kingdom. For him, time is not in God's hands; it is only raw material he can parcel out in his date book as he pleases. But when he is disillusioned (and how could this fail to happen!), then his utopia becomes an apocalypse, the prophet becomes an existentialist, and the dreams of hope become visions of anxiety. This is the self-jeopardization of the ideal, this is the double-faced ideal, the dark face triumphing over its bright face.

2. IDEOLOGY

The breakdown of the utopias, however, is still not the last stage in the self-jeopardization of the ideal. It is the ideology that stands at the nether end of this destructive declivity. The term really requires extensive analysis, including historical analysis, but I must confine myself here to only one of its significations.[2]

The ideal and the utopia still retain, as we have seen, genuine and essential affirmations. They still express a "truth." The ideology, however, grows out of quite different soil. It springs from a pragmatic consideration, and everything in it that looks like truth and scientific substantiation is nothing but a subsequent intellectual alibi which it seeks to provide for itself.

The ideology arises from two considerations which are fostered above all in totalitarian governments, in other words, in ideological power states.

The first consideration goes something like this: We observe that ideals and utopias exercise a kind of fascination upon people; the one who has control over this fascination gains in power. The result is the myth of the "Third Reich" or the "classless society," cultivated because they are visionary ideals that possess attractive power and thus provide motivation for the passions and the will. Hence, the first consideration stems not from the question whether these visions are *true,* but rather from the question of what can be done to make people *believe* they are true, because then, having become convictions, they can be used to mobilize fanaticism by way of fantasy and thus perform the function of a productive self-delusion. These intellectual constructs, devised for a purpose, are called ideologies.

The second consideration runs as follows: The totalitarian state has at its command almost limitless physical and organizational means of power. It exercises, for example, the dictatorship of terror. Since there is no area, no association, no school, no union of employees or employers, and no vocation that escapes the control of the state, there is not even a desert into which the inhabitant of such a state could flee or be sent. (Perhaps this absence even of a desert best expresses the utter gloom that pervades the scene in a totalitarian world.)

Nevertheless, the totalitarian state is confronted with *one* limit to its power, which no terror can eliminate. The inhabitant of the totalitarian state can clench his fist in his pocket, he can "emigrate"

---

[2] More comprehensive studies on the origin, nature, and structure of ideologies may be found in the third volume of Thielicke, *Theologische Ethik,* II, 2, 154 ff. (*Ethik des Politischen*).

into himself. This opposition of the inner man, who flees into himself where he is ultimately uncontrollable, can only be destroyed by bacteria that penetrate a man's skin and infiltrate into his personal center. These bacteria are the ideologies. Their function is to overwhelm the recalcitrant reason. Hence they make use of argument and construct a pseudo-scientific façade. Even the conscience must be overcome, because it is especially dangerous politically. For anyone who acts ethically makes decisions, and anyone who makes decisions can decide to differ and go his own way. He can say: Here I stand, I cannot do otherwise. But if he does this he removes himself from the role of being a well-oiled functionary and may possibly become sand in the social machinery.

Consequently, it is not possible to win over the conscience by activating it and then winning it, in other words, by appealing to the conscience ethically. Even a conscience that has been won remains uncontrollable and is therefore an uncertain quantity, as long, that is, as it continues to be an alert, living conscience. Therefore it must be overcome and circumvented by launching the attack upon a point other than the conscience and the personal center. This other point is the nervous system. The means employed here is propaganda, which does not make appeals to conviction (since these would have to be addressed to the conscience), but rather operates with nerve stimulants, such as slogans, sound effects, eye-catchers, and monotonously repeated attacks upon concentrated goals. Consequently, the ideologies are always associated with propaganda, the preferred style of totalitarian exercise of power. The ideologies are therefore pragmatic to the extent that they are intellectually militant. One thinks of the Marxist expression "to forge the intellectual weapons of the proletariat." The ideologies, consequently, are not integuments of a truth which is a real authority for people, in any case not for the esoteric circle of the wielders of power. They are rather cynically utilized means for the exercise of power.

The ideologies therefore differ from the ideal in that they make an absolute of a by-product of the ideal. The by-product consists in the fact that ideals and utopias mobilize men's inner potential and possess a tremendous activating and suggestive power, which the ideological power-holder desires to put to his own uses. To him it is relatively immaterial whether the ideologies are true. What interests him is not the truth but the function. But if the function is to function, it cannot get along without the suggestive power of the truth. It therefore changes its clothes, doffing the robber's garb of pragmatism and putting on the robe and identity of serious science. So there comes into being the academic masquerade of ideology. Then we have the stupid fakir's trick of somehow being able to reconcile the alleged objectivity of science with obligation to the Party, which means the pragmatic submission of science to the interests of the Party.[3]

3. FROM THE IDEAL TO IDEOLOGY

The question arises at this point whether this degeneration of the ideal into ideology is a necessary process. Is this decline irresistible? Is nihilism, at least nihilism on the part of those who are in the esoteric circle, the inevitable end of the process?

It is easy to illustrate the course of this process with specific examples. When Emperor Wilhelm I said, "The people must be held to religion" (and in *his* mouth this certainly was not meant in an ideological sense), this could, and often still does, mean: I, who am expressing this opinion, do not have any regard for religion personally, but the masses need something like this, since, after all, religion makes good subjects, and we need it as a kind of inner curb and psychological means of constraint. This is, of course, an ideological abuse of religion. In this case, it has no authority for me. I disassociate myself from it and perhaps even laugh at it. But I use its pragmatic by-products, which consist in the incidental effect it has of making it possible to bind and control people. For me, personally, the Last Judgment is a joke, but the fear people have of this judgment is a tool I can use in my psychological strategy.

In the same way it is possible (I say, it is possible; it need not be so) for me to make an ideology of humanity, of the idea of man, as is done not infrequently under the watchword of "human relations." Here we have exactly the same process. I say to myself: My purpose in life is to earn money and gain social prestige. The people who help me to do this, my workers and employers, are of no concern to

---

[8] Look at the first pages of any textbook on "Political Economy."

me whatsoever. To be quite honest about it, I have no use for people. But I cannot let anybody see that this is the way I really feel, because this would affect the climate of the plant and the volume of production would fall. For, after all, there are irrational factors that have their effect on business, and this climate is one of them. I know that when men are happy in their work production increases and good treatment increases a person's joy in his work. ("Strength through joy"—of course that makes sense.) So I have to act sociably and humanely. Employees' welfare, company picnics, a friendly inquiry about the wife and kids, a smiling face as you go through the plant—all this is quite as important as the maintenance of the machines. As I have said, all this humanitarian nonsense makes me sick; for me, human beings don't exist, only market reports and figures. But naturally I too take advantage of the economic potential of a good technique in the handling of people.

It is not that "human relations" need be interpreted in this way. I am simply indicating how the idea of "human relations" can degenerate into an ideology. This degeneration exhibits the same form that it can take in religion: I utilize the by-products of humanitarianism and neighborly love, namely, their capacity to tap the human potential and make people happy, enthusiastic, and willing. But I personally disassociate myself from the thing itself. I despise people, but I use the potential that is released by having regard for people. So I play the part of the social-minded and humanitarian; like the wolf in *Little Red Ridinghood* I cover my paws and disguise my voice.

Have we ever really thought through the question whether many of the phenomena of secularism have not actually been evoked by the fact that men have seen through the intention of ideological religion and resented it? Has not ideological religion actually been used as opium for the people? Is not the adjective "Christian" in many cases nothing more than covering for the wolf's paws? Have we ever really faced the question whether the distrust that exists between partners in the social enterprise does not go back, in part at least, to the fact that people simply cannot believe in a society which is thought of in purely economic terms and that therefore the distrust has an ideological cause?

C. THE IDEAL JEOPARDIZED BY "ME"

Remembering that David Friedrich Strauss once said that the history of dogma is the judgment upon dogma, in other words, that it reduces itself to absurdity, one may well be inclined to believe, after all that we have said, that the history of the ideal is its judgment, since its history is nothing more than a descent which keeps dragging the ideal down to the level of ideology. But to come to such a conclusion would be to fall victim to a disastrous optical illusion. That is to say, the ideal itself cannot have a history at all; only our relation to the ideal has a history.

We men tend in a mythologizing way to attribute a history to things and forces, and particularly at points where we should see that it is really our own history that is in question. Thus, for example, Jacob Burckhardt says that power is evil and then describes its tendency to be insatiable, to accumulate and expand. We also speak of the demonic character of technology and talk about it as if technology had a being of its own, as if it were the subject of a history in which we human beings are carried along without any will of our own. So we also speak of the ideal as a seductive power and act as if the ideal were a kind of mythical person, a kind of siren or Lorelei who bewitches us with her song in order to lure our boat to destruction. Power, technology, and the ideal are especially popular objects of this kind of mythologizing by means of which we sheer away from our own history and divert attention from powerful, technological, and idealistic man in order to excuse ourselves and lay the blame somewhere else. The implication is that the chief culprit and actor is technology and the ideal, but that you and I are merely figurants and supernumeraries, tragically misled, and perhaps even victims.

A world seen in this way begins to take on an apocalyptic tone. All around us lurk fiends and furtive powers. Everything becomes a menacing danger, carrying a concealed dagger, literally everything: science (since it produces a knowledge that is suicidal power), language (since one can use it to tell lies), art (since it leads us to the principle of art for art's sake), the great cities (since they spawn the works of darkness), the church (since it contains the seeds of clericalism and theocracy). So the mythological projections, which in reality are nothing more than man's maneuvers to divert responsibility from himself, run riot.

If we undertake the demythologizing that is so urgently necessary here—and this would seem to me to be far more fruitful and also more relevant than demythologizing the New Testament—then surely we must state the situation in this way: it is not power as such that is dangerous or even evil; it is only the *way* in which power is used that can be saddled with this verdict. It is not the ideal that is a temptation; it is rather the way in which I deal with the ideal that proves me to be temptable. It is not the ideal that degenerates into ideology; it is I who turn it into an ideology.

The demythologizing of "things" and "powers" leads therefore to the obvious conclusion that it is I who am turning these seemingly autonomous processes into autobiography, and that I must rid myself completely of the tragi-sentimental illusion that I am merely the victim and object of powers which I have previously mythologized and personified, and learn to understand that it is only a pigheaded maneuver of my old Adam, who refuses to beat his own breast and is looking for lightning rods to deflect the judgment from himself.

But then we ask, which way of dealing with the ideal is at fault? Or, to put it more precisely, how do I go wrong in my relationship to the ideal? And to give the answer I could go through the whole first part of this presentation once more and from this point of view interpret the stages of decline autobiographically or existentially (or whatever adverb seems appropriate to us). The result would be to show, for example, that in my handling of the ideal, I am taking advantage of the by-product of its mobilizing power and "pragmatizing" it into an ideology; or that it is my urge to be autonomous which is creating a utopian alibi by wresting the kingdom of God from God's hands and taking it into my own hands, in other words, by changing faith into sight and into works.

D. THE RECOVERY OF OUR IDEALS

How can our ideals be cured; what is the therapy? The basic answer to this question would certainly be that, if the fault lies in our handling of our ideals, then the cure must begin here.

If I see correctly, all our wrong attitudes toward the ideal have one thing in common: they all dream of a material and nonpersonal perfection. Recall here the examples we have considered. The utopian dreams of a perfect world order and puts it in the place of the Lord of the world order. God then is important only because of his kingdom, just as Christ is important only because of the bread he provides for the five thousand. The "thing" and the "order" crowd out the person. Or we may recall the example of ideologically motivated "human relations"; the perfect economic apparatus crowds out the human person through impersonal relations. Indeed, we can add a further point: even when man makes himself the ideal in the form of a mythical *Führer* or hero, he depersonalizes himself. He then turns himself into an abstract, docetic bearer of attributes who seems unreal and bodiless, and then—an ironical vengeance—it becomes the most delicious fun to see him as his valet sees him, with his face covered with shaving soap.

It seems to me that an important clue to therapy lies in these depersonalizations or reifications ("thingifications") to which we are misled by our wrong attitude to the ideal. That is to say, we must try to find an attitude to the ideal that keeps intact the *personal* relationship and thus prevents the intrusion of a dividing wall between us and our neighbor in the form of an apparatus or a utopian stage set. The ideal can be legitimate (i.e., it can be saved from being rebellion against God) only so long as it keeps us related to our neighbor and does not consign our concern for him to some perfect system.

The criterion by which we judge whether we are still related to our neighbor, however, is whether we are capable of loving. It was Jean Paul, if I am not mistaken, who said, "Love is the power to idealize." This thought of combining love with the ideal may perhaps help us in our search for a solution—at any rate it could if we understood "idealize" to mean, not an act of trivial glorification, but rather an act in which we see the idea, and therefore the essential being, of the other person and address ourselves to that. If there is such a thing as a form of idealizing that does not spring from a pragmatic motive or from human *hubris*, but is born of love, it could indicate to us where we as Christians must look for the legitimate idea. And in fact I believe that the origin of the ideal does lie in love, in personal nearness. When a child says to its mother, "You are the most beautiful person in the world," this idealized mother is an image that springs from the event of love. I may illustrate this with another, much more sensitive, example. And I do so despite the fact that it may touch some sore spots and, as it were, invade some unresolved neuroses. (I think it is dangerous, now as before, to be influenced by the Nazis—even in the form of negative reactions—so that we allow certain values, such as that represented by the word "fatherland," to be considered shocking, merely because the Nazis did their dirty work with them and succeeded in infecting us with complexes that still continue to smolder.) The national anthem *"Deutschland, Deutschland, über alles"* may serve as a good illustration of the two basic forms of the ideal, the ideal that springs from love and the ideal that has been perverted into an ideology. In its original intent it was certainly a song that was an exact parallel to the child's declaration of love for is mother: "Thou art the most beautiful land of all, with thy castles, streams and woods; for me nothing in all the world surpasses thee." It is simply a declaration of love for one's country, which might be expressed by every inhabitant of every country. To read into this declaration an objective assertion that some people are better than others and that one's own people are paramount would be just as silly as to say that the child's declaration "You are the most beautiful" has the character of a diagnosis which is based upon exact test comparisons of his mother with other women. But this same ideal of one's country, which springs from love, can in the next moment become (and we have seen it happen) an ideological stimulant of nationalism and then be interpreted as a paraphrase of that other song that reads, "For today Germany belongs to us, tomorrow it will be the whole world."[4]

If we want to purge the ideal, if we wish to strip it of its idolatry and *hubris,* of its work character and its insistence upon sight instead of faith, then this can be done only by filling our idealizing with personal content, or better, by *discovering* its possible personal content. But this is possible only if we do not allow our idealizing to consist in mere goals and visions of perfection, but rather seek

---

[4] It is probable that the original text read: "For today Germany hears (*hört*) us" instead of "belongs to us" (*gehört uns*). Later the variants of the text prevailed.

in our idealizing the act by which we actually move toward people as they are.

In concrete terms this means that the "state," the "kingdom," "democracy," can never be ideals in the strict sense; for they are ordinances, apparatus, "things," which in the strict sense we cannot love. But though we cannot love them, we of course do so again and again, just as we worship idols in spite of the fact that this is basically impossible. The practice of such impossibilities immediately brings with it retribution in the form of the perversion into which we fall. Objects, which are not lovable but are loved nevertheless, drive people into illusionary idealism, into the "isms." But after the feast (*post festum*) the fetish is turned into a whipping boy. Nationalism is one of the most momentous examples of this kind of fetishism.

It is possible, however, for "my country," my "fatherland," to be my ideal because I can love it. For it is the land of my father and fathers, the "land where my fathers died," it is filled with the image of my neighbor. As my homeland it is the embodiment of that realm in which I am related, through homes and streets, valleys and mountains, memories of the past and the present, to persons whom God has put into my life and made a part of my own destiny.

If we face the terribly painful question of what the German soldiers in the last war really died for, we shall find ourselves plunged into an agonizing aporia if we look for the meaning of their death in any utopian idea. For which Germany did they die? What political idea did they die for? For the Third Reich? But perhaps we may say this: No matter how mistaken and misguided the ideals of many of them may have been, back of the false slogans was their willingness to sacrifice for wife and child, parents and friends, whom they believed to be threatened, even though this belief may have been put into their heads by wielders of power who were nationalistic but nevertheless devoid of real love for their fatherland. (To get some appreciation of this feeling, read the letters of students killed in the war.) For the ethos of the soldier of today and the days to come it will be of utmost importance that his willingness to fight be based, not upon nationalistic, or even utopian, humanitarian, grounds, but upon a sacrificial love for wife and child, friends and comrades, and therefore upon things that are filled with real human relationships.

So now one thing seems to me to be certain: False ideals, such as

those generated by nationalism, cannot be overcome by demythologizing the ideal and disillusioning people, but only by legitimate
ideals, that is, by ideals that spring from love. We cannot cope with
Bolshevism, for example, by refuting it rationally and unmasking its
ideal of a classless society as an ideology, thus merely demythologizing it. It would be useless to attempt to overcome the dynamic of
demonic ideological obsession by a mere intellectual argument exposing its faults—this would be a truly absurd undertaking. We can
only combat the false, ideologized ideal with the *legitimate* ideal.
And how could this be any other ideal except the ideal generated by
our love: wife and child, whom we do not wish to see enslaved, living communities which should not become collectives; a freedom
which should not become the submissiveness of the functionary. It is
not simply that we have ideals that are different from those of
Bolshevism; we have an essentially different kind of ideal.

With regard to this element of personal relationship in the true
ideal, it has always been significant to me that Jesus never says
anything at all about the structure of the kingdom of God and that
therefore it is never even suggested that it has anything to do with
a perfect material world, but rather that he brings the kingdom
by coming to meet his actual neighbor. It is present in the midst of
us, where he is present, acting and loving; that is to say, where the
lame walk, the blind receive their sight, and the poor have good
news preached to them. Albert Schweitzer does not proceed to draw
up an ideal order of society in which "reverence for life" is the supreme constitutional principle, although he certainly has the qualifications to do so. He simply goes to Lambarene and "lives out" his
reverence for life in such a way that as an ideal it issues directly
from a concrete act of love, remaining confined to this act, and thus
does not float about in the air like a loveless, utopian principle.
Schweitzer, who in this case is an infinitely instructive paradigm,
therefore does not merely proclaim the ideal of bringing some kind
of perfection to underdeveloped peoples, but goes on from day to
day, lancing the abscesses of individual suffering, afflicted persons.[5]

---

[5] Far more important with respect to the legitimate ideal than dreaming about
the ideal of a planetary society, as Eugen Rosenstock does, would be the establishment of a peace corps for the younger generation in the industralized
nations to help in the building up of the underdeveloped countries (though, to

E. THE IDEAL OF LOVE

Love for the ideal can be controlled and made whole only if the ideal grows out of love. Therefore the excesses of false idealism cannot be removed by rationalistic attack; they can be fought only with the power of idealizing which is bestowed by love. Consequently, we do not need to decide against the ideal. For the ideal contains within itself the decisive question whether we are going to deify and make an absolute of it or whether we expect that it will perform the heuristic function of an ideal.

This can be illustrated in the case of the teacher. The teacher cannot do more than evoke certain ideal images in the youthful mind that is receptive to images. As a youth leader or teacher he may perhaps himself endeavor to be such a model or example. If he is a Christian, it will be part of his witness—and this may well be one of the most impressive testimonies he can offer—to make it evident at some time or other that he too is in solidarity with even the poorest sinner in his class or youth group, that he too is a faulty, sinful man. The point I wish to make is that in this way the ideal has a part to play in history, that many phases of history could not exist at all without this background of interimistic idealism. For if a child, without having gone through an interim period of idealizing were to say, as it were, a priori, "Our teacher, our youth leader is not a bit better than the rest of us," there would of course be an element of truth in what he said, but we would take no pleasure from it.

Nor are we impressed when a teenager declares in a school essay that Goethe is the greatest of all poets. It is merely painful, even though what he says may be quite true. We don't care to hear this from a callow youth—just as we don't care to hear certain truths, as Nietzsche said, "from toothless mouths." "For every truth has its time, its age, its hour," in the words of Luther. Anybody who utters such truths prematurely may be precocious, but not wise. This is why many a student of theology—I am thinking especially of a certain self-confident type—who juggles with truths which the great in the kingdom of God have acquired only after a lifetime of disci-

---

be sure, Rosenstock has advocated this also). This would fill the ideal with personal content because it would issue from love toward concrete persons for whom other concrete persons accepted responsibility.

plined thought, is like a country boy whose mother has made his pants too long; he must first grow into them. So the ideal and the stage when the ideal becomes a relative thing have their age, their time, their hour. Quite apart from the existential untruth that is inherent in a premature resort to skepticism, without having gone through the experience that precedes it, there is, from the human point of view, hardly a less enjoyable sight than a precocious skeptic, who can neither enthuse over, nor "engage" with, anything and is therefore himself pushed into the blind alley of resignation, the snobbish, count-me-out attitude.

Pedagogy particularly, and especially Christian pedagogy, can confront us quite elementally with these questions if we take the time to think through its fundamental problems. For Christian pedagogy is different from humanistic pedagogy in that it does not educate toward the model of the ideal man, because it knows that a fully rounded development of man's inherited structure not only develops man's essential, created being, but also promotes the demonic side of his being, and that in the process the nocturnal adversary of God is always at work sowing his poisonous seed amongst the wheat (Matt. 13:24 ff). Hence, the dynamic of Christian education is based, not upon ideal images which man has ahead of him, but rather upon the events of creation and justification which are behind him. But just as the law goes along with the gospel, and the Word never consists only of "one" Word, but always of "two," of both judgment and grace, so this truth that lies behind man is not the only truth about him. I need these interimistic, lawlike ideals to strive toward as a goal, simply because my mind possesses an "image level," because I must think in images, if my God-given gift of imagination is not to atrophy.

At first these ideal images play the role of the "law" for me, because—as we showed in the case of critical idealism and the utopias —they put me under judgment, until in the stages of life's experience, and therefore in actual existential acts, I see that these ideal images are themselves subject to judgment. But the person who in this way arrives at his skepticism, and thus at a kind of "godly grief" (II Cor. 7:10), is quite different from one who in his precocious skepticism thinks he knows all this beforehand and still has not experienced and acquired it as his own at all. The person who reads *Faust* as one who is "engagé", and therefore reads it with enthusiasm and then begins to raise his questions and doubts is in a different stance (and also takes *Faust* seriously in a wholly different way) from the Christian know-it-all, the pharisaic snob, who thinks he knows from the start that there is nothing to be got here and that this is a detour that he can skip. In the end the prodigal son and his elder brother shared the same insight, namely, that the far country is by no means an ideal; but they possessed it in totally different ways. For the one had had a history, it had become a part of the living story of his life; but the other sat at home, missing the history of it. That's why heaven rejoiced over the son who came home. But not even the reader of the story can rejoice over the snobbish and premature knowledge of the elder brother.

I try to practice this insight in my pastoral care. When the poor neo-pagans tell me that they cannot "take" all these dogmas, but that for them Jesus is the ideal of love and religion, I do not start by trying to talk them out of it. Often enough I keep to myself my knowledge that the truth is altogether different from what they affirm and I say: Very well, start where you are; try to interpret Jesus ethically and psychologically; seek your ideal in him. But really *search* for him! And that means, don't fall in love with your own ideal conceptions of him, don't remain confined to your own ideas. Read the text of the Gospels, listen to the testimony of those who learned from experience in encounter with Jesus. Then the time will come when you will see that he does not fit into your idealistic concepts and your ethical and psychological patterns. And when that happens you will have arrived at the real essence of the matter.

So I ask again: Can this essence of the matter be gained by direct attack, by prematurely passing through skepticism and demythologizing? We always want everything too directly, we want it too cheaply; we want it, in other words, without the personal history that goes with it. The modern form of visionary fanaticism no longer consists, as it did in the Middle Ages, in an illegitimate anticipation of the *eschaton*. Now it consists in the premature and illegitimate conclusion that the ideal is done for, which, after all, is a conclusion that can be reached only by traversing the whole road. "The main thing is to keep step with God and not always be rushing a few steps ahead of him," said Dietrich Bonhoeffer. But we always want to be a step or two ahead. We want to be skeptical—we call it, with some affectation, soberness and clear-headedness!—and in doing so we spare ourselves the bitter necessity of having to give up ideals by never acquiring them in the first place. We shrink from the burden of the detour. But the principle that a straight line is the shortest distance between two points is true only in mathematics. Everywhere else in life it is otherwise.

I append here as an illustration an excerpt from the graduation speech of an eighteen-year-old which made a deep impression upon me. Here, too, one catches a whiff of skepticism with regard to ideals. But we note that it is a skepticism that has gone through all the stages and then did not simply liquidate the ideal, but at most de-Platonized it. It is an idealism that is moving away from the cloudy realm of the pseudo-absolute into the sharp winds of life as it is. Its flame is beginning to flicker; the youngster is discovering its relativity, but it is still burning.

"As we now go out into life, do we have any great patterns . . . that could be compared to a lighthouse with solid foundations which we can trust with absolute certainty? I think not; and for two reasons. We no longer believe in the faultless heroes, and the majority of us are no longer capable of the kind of devotion and abandon that simply dismisses as unreal the fierce winds that drive our ship. Are we then a generation that insists upon leading a life that is aimless, rootless, and cowardly? I think not. I wanted only to show that we cannot submit ourselves to any boundless idealism. In using the metaphor of a lighthouse and a ship I have made use of words we find in a poem by Borchert:

> A lighthouse I would be
> In wind and night—
> For cod and smelt,
> For every boat—
> Yet I myself
> Am but a ship in distress!

By what are we guided? I would put it this way: by the light-houses on the beach, which we know are exposed to the winds just as we are, but which shine nevertheless."

F. THE NECESSITY AND THE ART OF DREAMING

If all this is true, then I cannot simply say to the "skeptical generation" of our youth today: You are right in your ironical attitude toward idealism. The precocious wisdom of burnt children (I mean this very seriously) is still not the wisdom of babes and the truth of wise virgins.

In conclusion, therefore, I should like to pose the following question: If the ideal is full of temptations, should we challenge and oppose all idealism? Shall we be quits with ideals? Or would this not be to throw out the baby with the bath? And here I must say something in behalf of standing up for ideals and scorning the tempter. Any suspicion that this can be done cheaply can hardly arise now that we have gone through our critical analysis.

Every creative passion in our life is nourished by the ability to dream dreams, regardless of whether one dreams of "monumentalistic history" in Nietzsche's sense or of an ideal state or of a great man. An educator who does not know how to teach this kind of dreaming, how to evoke the vision of the ideal, hardly deserves the name of educator; he is merely a pedant. "What would the world be without the dreams of fourteen-year-olds?" asked Albert Schweitzer.

Only when one can dream and incorporate one's goals in the image level of the mind, where they become the motivating power of our active life—only then does the spiritual question arise: the question whether I shall learn to combine with my dream of the ideal a decent thankfulness that there is someone who commands my reverence and, hence, someone—God—who bestows authority and credibility in the shadow of death and sin, or whether I shall make an idol of my dream. Only when I dream of the ideal state do I genuinely face the decision whether this means that I am advocating the illusory perfection in which the "dehumanized human being" perishes of emptiness and deadly boredom in the midst of a perfect apparatus of external life, or whether I shall recognize that this kind of perfection can at best be only the basis on which the real purpose of human existence, namely, filling it with meaning, can then proceed.

But how can I ever be confronted with this decision between obedience and idolatry, between thankful reverence and the deification of man if I evade the alternative, if I never venture upon the ideal, if I flee into a zone of ethical security, which leaves no room for obedience but is only an area beyond the decision of obedience or disobedience?

I am willing to admit in this connection that I often try to visualize the image of an ideal professor. Indeed, I must do so, simply because I possess imagination. I must say that this ideal image often gives me a certain strength, but also that it not infrequently makes me miserable because I do not attain it. Here the ideal is a ciphered call from God addressed to our imagination. It becomes for us both a promise and a judgment. It is something like a patrol sent out ahead by the Word of God, but also like a reserve force which is left behind.

The person who never ventures to dream of the ideal never faces the question whether he is willing to be sober and clearheaded. But the soberness which he thinks he possesses is merely sterility. And an a priori chastity of this kind is merely impotence. I take the risk of making this statement: I must venture the drunkenness of idealism in order to gain a holy soberness. The man who tries to attain the detached calm of age by refusing to face storm and stress and bypassing the places where the gales are blowing will pay for this forbidden, anachronistic anticipation by failing to become wise at the right time and by being precocious at the wrong time, by never reaching mature age at all, but rather ending in senility. Then he is not advocating, as he thinks he is, the virtue of clearheadedness; the calorie deficiency to which his real nature has been subjected has only played a nasty trick on him. Therefore, rejection of ideals based on premature skepticism is merely a victory for the world's tribulation; certainly not a victory of my Lord, who has overcome the world's tribulation. But to attempt to base rejection of ideals on faith is only self-deception and choosing one's own way of worshiping God. It is self-deception because what is at work here is not faith, but lack of faith, the timid faith that will not take the risk of idealism, because it is constantly plagued by visions of failure and will not trust that God can make anything of the poor in spirit, of rich young rulers, intellectual skeptics, and imaginative idealists, will not really believe that he gathers his people, not only from the highways and hedges, but also from the mountains of the moon and dreamy summer meadows. Rejection of ideals is self-chosen worship because it cherishes the illusion that there is a form of thinking and feeling (namely, that of skeptical realism), which is conformable to the will of God and therefore does not need grace, because it is by its very constitution *in* the truth. Woe to those who accuse the idealist of idolatry and of setting up false absolutes while they glorify their own impotent lack of enthusiasm, and even boast of it.

Again we say: Man must be able to dream—but he must also be prepared to awaken from his dreams. The imperative "Be sober, be watchful," means: "Be prepared for sober disillusionment and be watchful and wakeful!" The person who makes watchfulness and soberness an end in itself, a virtue, an attribute of his own, and therefore a "work," and does not see that these should merely be attributes of his faith, falls into a permanent state of dull sleepiness and becomes a witness to the kind of boring drabness that makes a caricature of the Lord of Christianity and causes the children of this world to flee from him before they have heard him speak a single word.

G. THE GREATNESS AND MISERY OF THE IDEAL

We may therefore characterize the greatness and the misery of the ideal in this way: Ideals are compressed, visionary images of goals which we pursue with passion and which therefore affect us not only at the level of abstract thought, but also at the image level of our minds. When we cling to them we are like little children who build houses and cities of toy blocks and imagine themselves living in these figments of their playful hands, as if they were in a real world. But at evening their father comes and sends them to bed, telling them to take down the houses and put the blocks back in the box. Then suddenly they realize that they have only been playing. But the dream of the little city they built stays with them to become an element of their world-view, which survives their childhood. It is true that when evening comes the Father will come and we shall have to dismantle our dreams. But does this mean that we should not even begin to build, simply because we know that the night will come when it will all be over? Or is not this the very greatness and gift of our childhood, that we are allowed to play and to dream under the eyes of a father, prepared and ready to hear his call to stop and put away the blocks? "I know of no other way to deal with great tasks than in the spirit of play," said Nietzsche. Does this necessarily mean triviality, does it mean giving up the great goals and dreams of what grace has in store for us? No; on the contrary, the very greatness of the ideal is that we are allowed to play in the name of the Father and under his eyes; and it is the misery of the ideal that it is *only* play and must be discontinued when evening comes. He that has ears to hear will understand that what is meant here is not the absolutized ideal. He who knows that in the morning he is free to unpack the box of blocks and that in the evening he is under command to straighten up the room again will be aware that the ideal, if it is to be in accord with the freedom of the Christian man, must never be a fixed and idolized structure, and that therefore it must not be a stationary monument around which his life revolves.

Without this interim in which such houses are built in play there would be no life. What we mean can be best expressed theologically in the term used by Dietrich Bonhoeffer. I mean his concept of "the penultimate."[6] The ideal too is a penultimate thing.

Here I confess I must say something else that is quite heretical: one should therefore take the ideal, which can so easily become nothing more than a fizzling, fascinating, and unreal Roman candle, and joyfully shoot it into the air, and not allow it to go dead in storage. True, one should be able to distinguish between what is true and what is false in the ideal. But how awful the notion that one must guard one's ideal like a maiden aunt, keeping it tame and respectable. He who fusses about with every blade when it has hardly poked its head above the ground because he is afraid of the weeds will involuntarily root up the wheat too. But this very attitude, which Jesus condemns in his parable (Matt. 13:24 ff.) is often the one we adopt toward our ideals. The person who is afraid of the "weedy" ideals and hence never lets the "wheaten" ideals come up or tears

---

[6] Dietrich Bonhoeffer, *Ethics*, trans. by Neville Horton Smith (New York: The Macmillan Company, 1955), pp. 84 ff. (Trans.)

them up prematurely is not relying upon the Lord of the harvest, who gives to us the calm composure of free children of God, because it is *he* who keeps his sovereign watch over his fields. Such a person falls victim to the worrying care that plagues and cramps fussy, moralistic souls.

Anyone who has a passion for great goals must also be able to dream of his goals. For a man with vision need not necessarily be a visionary. He who is stirred and gripped is also gripped in the image level of his mind. And he who wills to do great things by no means merely "wills" to do them; he is also lashed by his passions and driven by his ideals. However, dreams that are constantly checked, examined, and bombarded with regimentation, and thus cannot flow out freely, are not dreams at all, but only anxious spasms.

He who denies the penultimate (the ideal state and the just society) and the ideal images of the saint and the hero a chance to have that interim in which they are the objects of one's idealizing and dreaming simply turns them into expediencies and robs them of the glory of the creation and the dignity of authority. He who lives only in the name of the ultimate and bypasses the penultimate offends against this world, because he despises it pragmatically and approaches all such God-given things as one's country, friendship, and authority merely as a snob deigning to take advantage of them. But then he also loses the ultimate, in whose name he thinks he is living and by whose authority he thinks he can reduce all the things of this world into mere relativities.

Dietrich Bonhoeffer uttered this profound statement about that attitude: "It is only when one loves life and the earth so much that without them everything else would seem lost and gone that one can believe in the resurrection of the dead [i.e., the ultimate]." This means, after all, that the person for whom the lights of this world and the sparkle of dreams have been extinguished, the person for whom this earth has become a wasteland, reverted to the state in which it was before the creation, no longer hears in the message of death and resurrection the news of God's tremendous miracle that overcomes the world, but is closing his ears to the glorious sound which proclaims that the gospel *surpasses* all the things that we love. How can there be anything left of faith and the defiance that says "Nevertheless" in a person who thinks that the only competition that resurrection and eternal life have is a dead world that isn't worth living in? For him Christianity thrives only in bad weather; he thinks he has to tear everyhing down, change it, and replan it before he arrives at the comforting message. (You know the familiar sermon outline. First point: everything is terrible, wicked, meaningless. Second point: but faith is the rescue-rope in this wilderness of a world.) This kind of competition between the kingdom of God and a wilderness world is too cheap.

> Fair is the sunshine,
> Fair is the moonlight,
> Bright the sparkling stars on high;
> Jesus shines brighter,
> Jesus shines purer,
> Than all the angels in the sky.[7]

That is how God surpasses the gifts of this earth. The firmament and our ideals ultimately topple before his greatness; but until then they sparkle with light. And he who goes on thinking that the only way we can make the light of eternity shine is to darken this earth and snuff out our ideals is really giving very little glory to God. He is throwing away the earth without honoring heaven in doing so. He is betraying the penultimate and still doing nothing more than turning the ultimate into a docetic phantom. But, said Bonhoeffer, "We live in the penultimate and believe in the ultimate." Only he who has loved the sea knows what the Bible means when it says that the sea will be "no more" (Rev. 21:1) when the ultimate has come.

I should like to see our younger generation preserved from slipping too simply into saying that ideals are dangerous, that there is no sense in taking chances with life: play it safe; better to be disillusioned and secure. This is not an utterance of our faith; it's only cracker-barrel wisdom. What it says is that everything is dangerous— smoking, drinking, dancing, loving, and dreaming. But asceticism is dangerous too. If avoidance of all risk and danger is to be the watchword, are you going to go through life as if you were treading on eggs in order to live as a Christian? I have heard that the road to hell is paved with good intentions. But that the narrow path to the kingdom of God is paved with eggs seems to be the *kakangelion* (the

---

[7] Third stanza of the hymn "Beautiful Saviour". (Trans.)

bad news, not the Good News) of many a Christian today who is afraid to walk on God's good earth.

What a pitiful thing it is that for so many of us the gospel has become merely a prophylaxis, a warning sign against all the many fires with which we dare not play. And yet we have that wonderful promise that we shall be "as a brand plucked out of the burning," as Amos said (4:11). Did not Christ come to "cast fire upon the earth"? And what do his Christians do? They set up red lights every-where, warning people: This way leads to the abyss of idealism; this way leads to the demonry of the arts; this way leads to the jungle of worldly wisdom. A world spotted everywhere with red lights—is this the world envisioned by God's redemption? Was the terrible cost of Calvary necessary to produce this paltry fireworks? Does one have to have fish-blood in one's veins—no champagne allowed!—in order to live under the will of God in this penultimate world?

> Despite the ancient Evil,
> Despite the jaws of darkness,
> Despite the fear of death,
> Rage, O world, snarl and spring;
> Calm and confident,
> Here I stand and sing.[8]

From the crumbling walls of this transient world reverberates the praise of Christendom, and in praise, only in the worship of the ultimate, does it find its calm and confidence. Christians have this calm certainty where God watches over them, where they weep and laugh, where they are soberly realistic and where they dream their dreams of the ideal, where they are utterly serious and yet capable of playing. But our self-chosen halting places and artificial sobrieties are not ways of entry into the kingdom of God. The world is a threatening place, and to stand up for the ideal is a venturesome thing. But the real Christian stands in the shadow of God's keeping and he knows how to stand up for ideals and scorn the tempter.

---

[8] Third stanza of *"Jesu, meine Freude"* (Jesus, Priceless Treasure). (Trans.)

III

THE THREAT OF MODERN
SOCIETY TO FREEDOM

MARTIN HEIDEGGER HAS SAID, IN *An Introduction to Metaphysics,*[1] that from a metaphysical point of view both the East and the West are threatening to become identical. Everywhere there is "the same dreary technological frenzy, the same unrestricted organization of the average man."

Man as the object to be organized—this is certainly a conspicuous phenomenon of our world. Thus in the sphere of influence dominated by Marxism-Leninism we hear the thesis maintained that man can be "made," that he can be molded, stamped, remodeled, and manipulated by the influence of his environment. Change man's milieu and you can train him for any purpose you please. But occasionally exactly the same attitude betrays itself on the other side of our globe; for example, when it is said in an American Military school that from a biological point man is a "mistake," because he is no longer biologically equal to the potentialities of space travel which he himself has opened up, and therefore man must also be revaluated biologically in order to show what his real possibilities are.

Having said this, I do not wish to be misunderstood in the sense

---

[1] Martin Heidegger, *An Introduction to Metaphysics,* trans. by Ralph Manheim (New Haven: Yale University Press, 1959), p. 37. (Trans.)

that I mean any cheap equating of the East and the West. No, one dare *not* say that both hemispheres are under the same condemnation, that in the universal night that has fallen upon this world all cats are gray, and that therefore there is no reason to think that the tyranny in the East is a specially vicious form of threat to our freedom. I have no desire to associate myself with this kind of leveling and dangerous oversimplification. To my mind there is a very real difference between the kind of deprivation of freedom and personhood which is an overt part of a political program (because this form of deprivation makes men politically malleable) and the kind of threat to freedom which is cold, unplanned, hidden, and subliminal. This very dangerous, because latent, form of threat to freedom may in fact be making progress among us in the West.

This cold threat may be said to exist in two forms. The first I shall merely suggest and the second I shall deal with in more detail.

The first form of threat to freedom consists in the fact that, with the dwindling of metaphysical substance and the trauma that this inflicts upon man as a person, both his ability and his willingness to be a responsible subject are threatened, and that then the result is something like a *fear* of freedom. In fact, freedom has ceased to be a public ideal in broad areas of the West, and Sartre certainly characterized the general temper of our time correctly when he said that we are "condemned" to freedom and that unfortunately our human dignity will not permit us to be unfree, fixed, dry-nursed, and co-ordinated.

The second form of cold threat derives from a certain autonomous process within our mass era, which, especially in politics and industry, has a tendency, partly conscious and partly unconscious, to produce certain sociological structures which threaten more and more to absorb the personal freedom of the individual.

Instead of beginning with a discussion of principles, which we shall have to face sooner or later, I shall start with a concrete instance of this threat to freedom and then analyze it a bit.

Several years ago, when the European defense community was still under discussion, it happened that the head of a south German state undertook a sudden change of course in his attitude toward this problem of foreign policy. One of his ministers (in other words, a minister bound to his party) thereupon resigned from the cabinet, to the great distress of his party which was then faced with a loss of political influence in the cabinet.

At that time I wrote a letter to this minister, a copy of which I still possess, and I quote from it the following sentences:

There are many people, especially young people, for whom your act constitutes an act of witness. This has nothing to do with the objective details of this political decision. The simple fact that a leading man respects the boundary line between the necessary area of tactics and compromise, on the one hand, and the *status confessionis,* the point where one is bound by one's conscience, on the other, is a benefit and has in it healing strength.

I then went on to say that a certain lack of interest in party politics on the part of our young men was based largely upon the pessimistic conclusion that any such attitude as his even existed any more and that therefore one must keep away from the dirty business.

So you, honored sir, acted politically in a deeper sense, for by your act you have to this extent restored confidence in your profession. We now see very clearly the reaction of your party. I believe that it has much to gain or to lose, depending upon how it respects or fails to respect this attitude.

I

This case, it seems to me, will serve as an apt example for our discussion of the first set of questions to be dealt with and which I would put under the heading of "the problem of the group."

The thing that an outsider as a rule considers to be a particularly deplorable curtailment of personal freedom in a parliamentary democracy (i.e., a democracy which is based upon the interplay of parties and power groups) is indicated in the term "party compulsion" or "party pressure." Now this term "party pressure" is generally, but unfairly, used as a term of abuse, almost an infamy. In reality these things generally are done quite differently. But allow me for the moment, knowing that it is merely a term of abuse and therefore one-sided, to let the word stand without qualification. National Socialism had its magical military metaphor, "Right, *dress!*" for the absorption of the individual into the group, and its electrical-mechanical metaphor, "co-ordination" (*Gleichschaltung*), for the merging of smaller groups into larger groups. So when the same phenomenon appears in parliamentary democracy—or in industry—

no matter whether one calls it party compulsion, group discipline, or the party line, we are very quick to speak of totalitarian tendencies or of the symptoms of collectivism.

The younger generation, of whom I shall say something presently, watches very closely to see whether the voting in the legislative assembly is unanimous and the divisions uniform, or whether certain variations of thought and action are allowed in a party, and thus whether one may conclude that there is a certain freedom of personal decision. Loyalty to a cause, they say, is possible only where there is conviction and individual decision. There is no such thing as party-line loyalty, they say, for then a person merely acts according to the law of least resistance, then he is merely submitting to party discipline and performing a "function." The party apparatus is really nothing more than a "mechanism" and no longer an "organism" based upon personal communication. To that extent, say these young people with an unsophisticated, youthful instinct, loyalty to the party line is only a corruption of real loyalty, because the cadre consists only of the cadavers of former individuals, of individuals who have resigned their individuality. The commonly observable disinterest of young people in our political parties, I believe, has its ultimate cause here.

As for the rest, however, I consider the censures pronounced upon party discipline and the group solidarity, which I have just indicated, to be largely unjust and also immature. One of these mistakes made by youth, with its tempestuous instinct untempered by justice, to reject wholesale everything that looks like party loyalty and party line, I see in the following illustration.

If politics is the art of the possible, this means that it does not merely set up and rhetorically declaim certain aims and ideals, for example, a particular economic and social order. It means rather that politics must also affirm the means which are adopted for the realization of these goals. For the possible is nothing but the realizable. But the realizable naturally includes affirmation of the means of realization. Having said this, it must now be pointed out that there can be no doubt that in the mass era the group is one of the chief means by which the possible can be realized. Today it is largely the group which is the acting subject in historical, political, and economic action, and I might almost venture the thesis that today the group exercises something like the function once assigned by Hegel to the "world-historical individual." Why is it that the group is the really potent factor in historical action? This can be answered with a simple negative observation: When the individual breaks out of line, this has its disadvantages, since, after all, the effectiveness of a political or economic concept by no means lies only in the weight of an objective argument but equally (at least equally!) in the weight and resoluteness of its presentation. For here we are not merely moving in the sphere of argumentation; here we are moving rather in the sphere of the exercise of power.

Winston Churchill, looking back on his younger days in Parliament, said this: "I was so inexperienced as to assume that I had nothing to do except to ponder what was right and then to express it without fear. I thought that loyalty to this principle outweighed all other loyalties. I had no conception of the importance of party discipline and the sacrifice of one's own opinions which one might justly bring to it."

Now, it is true that it is also possible to render this position innocuous by saying that there is really no limitation of freedom in the binding of oneself to the group, to the concerted striking power of the group, since everyone has the opportunity to choose the group he joins and to decide for the views it holds. Hence, there is an element of freedom in this initial act of deciding in favor of a group because, one could argue further, on certain large issues these decisions can be made only by giving one's approval to a group in which one has confidence and to which one delegates one's political will. If one takes into account this initial act of freedom, the so-called party line seems to lose some of its terror, since then it is only the stick by which the individual is kept in line after he has previously made his free, elective decision.

I have already indicated that this argument is one-sided; for it overlooks the fact that in the carrying out of the policy (indeed, in the choice of tactics itself) situations may arise in which even the man who does not wish to abandon the fundamental platform of his party or group may be confronted with the necessity of making an individual decision that skirts the edge of political heresy. And I should consider it undebatable that this room for decision be held open, and not be closed even when for the moment (though, of course, not only for the moment) this entails a certain diminution of the force of the group, just as the minister to whom I wrote undoubtedly reduced somewhat the influence of his party through his resignation from the cabinet, in other words, through his decision of conscience.

The really important thing that I am concerned about may be put in this way. In the parties there must be a clear understanding that the law of concentrated exertion of power, which is an inescapable law of history, has a limit, and that this limit can never be ignored or battered down with impunity. It is a question, if I may define it more precisely, of the limit between what appears to be desirable for tactical reasons and what I would call the *status confessionis,* the point where one simply says: Here I stand (I who want to be loyal, I who basically affirm your intentions), here I stand, I cannot do otherwise.

Permit me now to express this situation in theological terms, even though at first glance its theological character may not be at all apparent. The fact that in our dubious world the truth, the right conviction, does not triumph of itself and by its own self-evidencing power, but rather that the truth, the right conviction, must be fought for and therefore must also be upheld by applying group force—this is a necessity, not a virtue. The fact that I can only live in compromise, that, as Churchill expressed it, I am obliged to make reductions in my own opinions and convictions, in order that the effectiveness of the group be maintained and in order that I may not be reduced to complete political impotence by my ethical and political isolation and even draw the group that sustains me into this impotence, so that finally nothing at all is accomplished because everybody is acting according to his own convictions—I say that the fact that I must live in this compromise with the group is a necessity and not a virtue. And here comes the statement which at first may strike you as being the merest platitude:

There is no more effective way of demonizing the world than to make a virtue of a necessity.

Allow me to try to explain this, simply by adducing certain historical examples which will immediately illustrate this form of demonization. Think of a Bolshevist diagnostician of history carrying on a conversation about the various historical ages with, let us say,

Jacob Burckhardt. Even these two extremely different types of historical analyst would probably agree on one point. They would both say that since the breakthrough of the age of technology something like a tendency toward depersonalization, collectivization, and mass action has entered the picture. I am aware that these are concepts which are far more complicated than this sketchy treatment indicates, but I use them for the sake of brevity. In this diagnosis of a tendency toward collectivization, then, the two would agree. On the other hand, however, their opinions would immediately diverge when it came to the question of how this observable tendency of contemporary history is to be evaluated. For then Jacob Burckhardt (and along with him the advocates of Western freedom, democracy, etc.) would say: Because it is true that this is a very threatening tendency in the mass age, we must do everything we can by way of constitutional safeguards and education to guard personality and to reserve a sphere of privacy, a certain inviolable domain of personal freedom for the individual. We must defend the individual over against the potential omnipotence of the state. We must cultivate and foster the personal as a counterthrust against the observable tendency toward collectivization.

The Bolshevist analyst would argue quite differently. He would say that it is sheer foolishness to oppose a tendency which is obviously a law of history (dialectical materialism, of course, busies itself with laws of history) and to take countermeasures against a trend which is a natural law. This, he would say, would be like fighting windmills. It would mean wasting one's energies struggling against what history will bring to pass anyhow, and in the end losing all one's political and historical effectiveness. It's all right with me, the Bolshevist analyst would say, if you Westerners are so stupid as to want to defend individual personality; go ahead, and fight yourself to death with the trend of the times. If this is the trend of the times, then one should accept it and affirm it. What is going to fall anyhow should be knocked down. If personhood is going to get run down anyway, then it must be shoved under the wheels. One must affirm it in the sense of tragic *amor fati*, i.e., a loving consent to historical destiny. And when one does this, one develops a tremendous dynamic, one multiplies one's own power by the trend and the power of history. This is precisely what is making it possible for us Bolsheviks to conquer the world.

It is easy to see what is being done here. The Bolshevist is making a virtue of the necessity of depersonalization by structuring it into a political program.

We experienced the same thing, exactly the same thing, in our own area at the hands of Hitler. Hitler too made an analysis of history, an analysis that is quite true. He discovered that, as a rule, might goes before right. Nothing could be more correct than this; it is simply true. Here again one can attempt to derive a norm from this observation that as a rule—statistically, that is—might goes before right. Therefore, one can say, we must strengthen the right as much as we can, in order that might may not become uncontrollable and to that extent unlawful. This is one possibility. The other is to argue the exact opposite, that is, in the way Hitler argued. He concluded that after all it was foolish to resist the inevitable trend of history by submitting to this humanitarian nonsense of acting legally and then really coming to grief. No, if it is true that the wolves are howling in this world, then one must howl with the wolves. One must cynically affirm the interests of men as far as one can; for the right and the law are only a handicap when one is dealing with the Machiavellian will to power.

Here again we see at work that fundamental tendency of the will to make a virtue, a program, of the necessity of history, namely, the fact that it is true that might usually goes before right. And this is exactly what we were referring to as demonization.

Every politician and every party or group that is obliged (quite necessarily obliged!) to engage in tactics must be in the clear on this fundamental question of principle. This means that it must decide, and this requires that it determine on principle whether it wishes to make the compromise between the objective conviction of the individual and the strong solidarity which the group demands; in other words, whether it is going to make of this compromise a virtue, i.e., an axiomatic law of political action. This is one decision. If this is accepted, then what the party or group prefers is mere yes-men, functionaries, shadows. Distinct personalities and difficult types would be unwelcome, at least in key positions. The other decision is to take the view that in the long run the only community that has a sustaining historical function or mission is one whose members do not think of themselves as mere termitelike organs performing a function in a collective, but rather as being actuated by the dynamic of personal conviction and responsibility. If one decides for the latter, this involves the great risk of having to put up with certain individual reactions, that is, one must pay the price of renouncing the depersonalizing collective, the will-less instrument; just as the party of the minister whom we mentioned earlier had to pay a price for allowing someone like this in its ranks. The question to be asked here is this: Will such a party be willing to pay the price for the chance that the voice of conscience may be heard within it, for the possibility that a man may really be a "gentleman," not only privately but also on the level of politics? Will it be prepared to pay the price of a temporary setback? If it is, then I believe that in the long view it has won. For the conscience is always a long-term proposition. The mere tactician is blinded by the moment. But the integrity of the individual conscience is not only the most abiding value; when it is meaningfully incorporated in a community it is also something that exerts a stronger dynamic function than the termite-man, who can be utilized only in masses, and is otherwise highly unstable.

II

Having considered these questions of "the problem of the group," we come to the second set of questions. I would put it under the heading of "the problem of the functionary." What I mean here, of course, is not the designation for a particular profession, and my intention is not to wound anyone's feelings. What I mean is a type. Perhaps the term "functioner" would be better than "functionary."

By this term I mean one who merely carries out rules and regulations, one who is merely a "party-liner." In order to illustrate the problem involved I must refer again to what I said before about the instinct of youth. Generally the lack of interest shown by youth in matters of party politics is explained as being a relic of the need for authority that stems in small part from a certain submissiveness to authority in German history and also from the emphasis on authority in the Third Reich. Individual decisions, even those made through the ballot, are dodged by not a few.

For my part, I have always defended these young people and their situation in the face of critical reproaches. And I have done so because I believe that this reserve of theirs betrays a certain instinct for credibility and trustworthiness. They want to listen to someone—a political speaker, for example—who has his own convictions and is not the puppet of another's will, not merely the declaimer of mere group decisions, and certainly not the reciter of reports from the chairman. This aversion and reserve is extremely manifest in totalitarian states in which the patent phrases are kept rolling off the press. "Monopolistic, capitalistic provocateurs," "the Western warmongers," we know the sound of it. This stuff rolls out, as it were, automatically without any personal engagement on the part of the writer. It is remarkable how people put up a kind of umbrella to ward off these mechanized phrases. The catchwords simply run off without touching them. It is this instinct for personal credibility and genuineness, it seems to me, that is the most fundamental reason for the aversion of youth to party politics. They do not want to listen to a ventriloquist, uttering sounds that are anything but his own. They do not care for anybody who says, as I heard a cabinet minister say not long ago, "Well, if I were not a minister, but were expressing my own opinion . . ." They do not have much use for anyone who says one thing *ex cathedra* and afterward, in intimate off-the-record talk over beer and cigars, says, "Well, if you want to hear my personal opinion . . ." They do not care for people with split characters.

Regrettable as is our young people's lack of interest in party politics, unfair as much of what I have just said may be, and even though many politicians do not fit into this caricatured diagnosis, we must nevertheless admit that this lack of interest has its roots, not in apathy, but rather in an honorable motive and a basic substance, for which we can only be grateful.

This became clear to me once in an experience of my own, and since it is very symbolical, I may perhaps record it briefly.

When I was filling the same office in Tübingen that I have here in Hamburg, I often had politicians come from Bonn to the university—big guns whom we set up, as it were, and then fired off. At that time the main question was the problem of remilitarization, rearmament. And the students were very allergic to it. This manifested itself in the fact that there were considerable disturbances in the university auditorium when these gentlemen spoke on the subject. On one occasion I had invited as a speaker an industrialist, a friend of mine who at that time played a leading role in the mining industry; and he was to deal with this ticklish subject. I was eager to see how it would work out. A colleague on the faculty was kind enough to assume the job of introducing the speaker, and he did so as follows:

"My friends, this evening you have the unusual opportunity of hearing a man who has his own opinion. I can prove to you that he has his own opinion. This man has millions. You doubtless have seen his big car outside. So this man has no need to extend or enlarge his influence or his money-bags by assuming the office he now has. When what he does there no longer suits him, he will go back home to his business. You will surely be interested for once to hear a man who is completely independent and therefore has his own opinion, even if it does not agree with yours."

I can tell you that the crowd behaved like lambs; there was no disturbance that evening. The speaker went on to address them in the same vein. He said that, as was proper in academic circles, he was not simply speaking demagogically, since he was constantly calling himself into question. "I know," he said, "that this or that decision I have been talking about is open to question. You could arrive at a different decision by using other arguments; but I believe that for such and such reasons the decision I have outlined is the best. We must make a try, we must make the venture. In a politician, action must always be quicker than reflection."

This incident strikes me as being characteristic and instructive. In any case, I think the politicans should learn this much from the criticism of youth—even though in many details it is unjust and one-sided, and even though above all things we have no desire here to foster the cult of youthful instinct—namely, that the most valuable substance of our people can be mobilized politically only if that which we call the freedom of the individual is given its due place, in other words, when the "anti-functionary" type is given his legitimate place in the political enterprise. The anti-functionary is the one who not only adds up his accomplishments, but who stands responsible for the ethical context of his accomplishments. The functionary— just think, for example, of some of the high military men in the Third Reich—the functionary, without whose help Hitler could not

have carried on his operations, was not, barring occasional excep-
tions, a "war criminal." No, he certainly had an ethos; but it was a
degenerate ethos, an ethos that had sunk from the responsibility of
personal decision to the mere practical responsibility of carrying out
orders. He no longer asked, "Whose wagon am I being hitched to,
whose wagon may I allow myself to be hitched to?" No, his loyalty,
his ethical fidelity, consisted only in the plodding perseverance with
which he pulled the wagon, or, to give his due, even the self-sacrific-
ing spirit in which he pulled it. This is what I mean by degenerate
practical responsibility for carrying out orders.

It should give us pause that men did not ask Christ, "Did you
accomplish great things by healing people, by speaking mighty
words?" Rather they asked him, "By what authority, in whose name
have you done these things?" To them this was more important
than the accomplishment itself.

III

"The problem of the group" and "the problem of the functionary"
engender a third problem, which I would like to broach, namely, the
problem of anonymous deprivation of freedom through the group.
And here I should like, for quite definite reasons, to use as an example the labor unions. But I want to say very explicitly that this is
not going to be a social-political polemic. I could just as well take
an employers' association or a political party.

And in order that I not be considered unfair, may I say that what
follows was presented to a meeting of unionists and discussed with
them. I was gratified to discover how objectively this problem was
dealt with.

The first observation is this: The disadvantaged class can defend itself over against the absolutist state, which represents a
particular social order, only by taking group action, that is, by
organizing unions. Now, as the state undergoes social regeneration
in the direction of what we call, in its extreme form, the welfare
state, certain definite functions cease to be the responsibility of the
unions, and the danger (note that I say it is only a danger) is that
when the apparatus no longer fulfills all the functions for which it
came into being, it will fill the gap with other functions; it will,
for example, yield to the tendency to secure certain positions of

political power. The result may be a tendency to assume the function of a party, which has no parliamentary representation and therefore cannot be controlled, and may ultimately, and sometimes penultimately, lead to a state within the state. In any case, the result may be semi-anonymous monopoly structures which are difficult to control and which limit the freedom of the individual and even threaten his existence as an individual.

When, for example, a union signs a contract with a firm providing that the employer must employ only persons who are in the union, this actually means, depending upon the degree of monopolistic power that obtains in the given situation, the obstruction of a man's career, sometimes even professional bankruptcy.

A certain kind of personal politics influenced by religious, confessional bias, should also be mentioned here as a source of danger. I want very definitely therefore not merely to talk about others but to include myself.

In every case, the restriction put upon freedom by the group tends to be anonymous, that is, it cannot be documented. It makes use of the telephone, it can be expressed with a grunt or a word from a person in a higher position, perhaps only a twitch of the corner of the mouth or an eye movement. In any case, the important thing here is the anonymous character of this kind of restriction upon freedom. Here the task of the state is to defend freedom through the judiciary process.

The democratization of life has developed a great many measures that safeguard the freedom of the individual over against the state. And here I do not hesitate to contend that this development is faced with a latent threat of being shut off because the place that the state has left open for the freedom of the individual is being taken over by the group, and that thus the same question of restriction of freedom becomes acute again, though now in a different way. The difference is that freedoms granted by the state are somehow transformed in the process from the freedoms of the individual (which they were meant to be) into the freedoms of groups and corporate bodies. Since these liberties can be claimed only through the collective voice of the group and since these groups, when they have gained a certain measure of power, are able to influence very considerably the actions of the state—one need think only of the right to strike, for example—the state is indirectly and insensibly driven again into the role which it disclaims when it claims the name "democracy." To my mind, therefore, the state must by all means bring under control this group invasion of its fundamental rights and its democratic ethos.

The kind of personal politics that we mentioned earlier is, of course, a difficult problem. It is not, as one might maliciously think, motivated entirely by the desire to form cliques and the naked greed for power as an end in itself. Rather there are behind it two chief motives.

The first motive of personal politics is always the desire to secure fellow workers who use the same terminology and the same criteria for making decisions. An executive who is obliged to practice personal politics simply cannot afford to engage as a fellow worker a man, no matter how competent he may be, who on principle takes his stand on a different level of conviction or professional opinion. This would mean that every day he would have to discuss everything with him afresh, going back to the very beginning of basic principles. Even the smallest routine decision would always lead to this *regressus ad infinitum*, this endless difference of opinion and principle. Community of mind on the decisive things (and thus a common basis in terminology, in instinct, and also in a certain constitutional unity) creates a basis of confidence and eliminates the constant need for justifying every individual decision. Birds of a feather are reassured by the smell of the nest they come from; this makes the group more capable of action and it saves trouble.

There is still another motive, however. This kind of personal politics generally tends to be active where the law must be wide-meshed, leaving room for free play of action. Here the standard demanded by one's own conscience can be attained only by surrounding oneself with men in whom one has confidence, that is, by filling up the gaps and possibilities of variation with choices made from a personal political point of view.

I may again illustrate with an example, which I think will make very clear what has been expressed a bit abstractly. The example is the section in the German penal code directed against abortion.

Originally abortion was radically forbidden. Later supreme court decisions permitted abortion in cases where "medical indication" suggests it, for example when appendicitis interferes with the carry-ing out of the pregnancy. This means, then, that if the "medical in-dication" is present, the physician is not compelled to interrupt the pregnancy, but he is not punishable if he does perform an abortion. This makes a difference. Here the law allows a certain latitude. But it is significant that the Roman Catholic church, for example, cannot accept this latitude, because for dogmatic reasons it is unable to recognize the "medical indication," and also because it says that this would be a case of killing an innocent child. Using a very respectable argument (and I want to say this emphatically) the Roman Catholic church requires the sacrifice of the mother when there is a conflict between the life of the child and that of the mother. I consider this argument respectable because ordinarily the decision is made on purely pragmatic grounds. The usual argu-ment is that the mother, say the mother of a large family, is more valuable than a fetus; whereas Catholicism says that the value of the mother is not realized by saving the life of the mother, but rather in her sacrificing herself. Consequently, in its opinion the Catholic church can deal with this latitude in medical practice, which is legal but which it regards as illicit, only by pursuing a kind of personal politics, namely, by seeing to it that physicians who hold this attitude are placed in key positions where gynecology is concerned.

Even though this kind of limitation put upon medical freedom through what we have called personal politics may be subjectively understandable and must at least be morally respected (in any case we cannot fairly speak of it as "political Catholicism"), these more or less hidden interventions must nevertheless not be allowed to continue uncontrolled by the state. For if they are not watched and at least curbed, the danger is that the non-Christian or the non-Catholic population will also be affected by measures that touch their intimate private life and their most personal decisions, and on top of this invade a sphere that deeply concerns the life of the family and the life of the mother.

I pass over the many other areas in which this same problem of restriction of freedom becomes acute. (One of them, which I called "subliminal restrictions" of freedom is discussed in another "chapter of this book.")

Let me, however, add these concluding words. Everything I have said above may appear to be more a sociological than a theological discussion, which to some may seem somewhat odd, coming as it does from a theologian. Therefore I am concerned to make it clear that these sociological problems are exposed to a kind of indirect lighting, and that, in concluding this discussion, it makes sense for us to point to the real source of that illumination and briefly indicate how this has determined the whole point of view of this presentation.

What I am saying, as I have said so often, is that the problem of freedom is dealt with in an ultimate sense in the parable of the prodigal son. In this parable the prodigal son is not merely a scamp or an unruly child. Indeed, his purpose in leaving the father and going to the far country may have been based upon an idealistic, ethical motive. He may have wished to liberate himself from dependence upon the parental home and its authority, and assume responsibility for shaping his own life on the free paths of the far country. In other words, the motive of the "lost" son is freedom. Freedom is not realized when one simply continues to be the function of a superior will, say the will of the parental home. A person must have elbow-room, he must have the opportunity to go his own free way. But the strange thing is that this will to freedom leads fundamentally to unfreedom. The son who wanted to be free fell under the dictatorship of his instincts, his passions, his sexuality, the dictatorship of ambition, the will to power, and homesickness, and finally wound up in the pigsty, the symbol of utter lack of freedom. He then turned and went back. And because he turned back, he became, for the first time, really free. In finding the father, he found himself.

This means that mere self-expression and self-development of the individual does not bring freedom, but only slavery, the final threat to freedom. Freedom, the parable is saying, is possible only in being bound to the Father. Only so does man realize his nature. For his true nature consists in being a child of this Father. Human nature realizes itself in becoming a free, mature child.

So man has his freedom only in being bound, but—and this is the crucial thing—in being bound to what? He has no freedom in binding himself to men or groups. This is precisely where he loses it, by degenerating into a functionary. He has his freedom only in binding himself to the Ultimate, by being directly subject to the final court of appeal. I believe it is possible to reduce the whole gospel to this brief formula. Here we are taught that man is immediately subject to God and that this permits him to take all the authorities that lay claim upon him, including the state, parents, and superiors, and see them all under the light of the Ultimate Authority and thus (with all his willingness to serve the authorized, and thus legitimate temporal powers) be free in an ultimate sense from all secondary and creaturely authorities. This is the antitoxin for the disease of becoming a functionary.

It is an axiom of the Christian doctrine of freedom that only he who finds God finds himself. Only from this vantage point can we understand Luther's statement, with which all Christians would doubtless agree: "A Christian man is a perfectly free lord of all, subject to none; and Christian man is a perfectly dutiful servant of all, subject to all."

The healing and helping power which we implore for our generation cannot begin with a reordering of a threatened world, an organized attempt to restore a world gone out of joint, nor with an organized attempt of the welfare state to provide new securities for men and bring socialized perfection to society. Healing and helping power cannot do its work in us by these means, but only by our first being reordered ourselves, by becoming what we were intended to be.

IV

THE ANTITHESIS OF
FREE SOCIETY

A. ATHEISM IN THE MARXIST-LENINIST WORLD

TO WHAT EXTENT DO THE ATHEISTIC PRESUPPOSITIONS OF SOCIALISM
make co-operation with socialistic development impossible, or to
what extent is co-operation possible despite these atheistic premises?

The decision we make with regard to this question cannot be
arrived at on the basis of an empirical impression made upon us
by a more or less crude and open practice of atheism. For this impression may be discounted by the possibility that the atheism practiced may not be an integral part of the doctrine *itself,* but is rather
determined either (1) by tendencies inherent in the times, or (2)
by measures taken by the supreme authorities which are tactical and
therefore conditioned by the situation, or (3) by the arbitrary actions of subsidiary organs of the state. Our practical attitude toward the governmental apparatus of Marxism-Leninism will be
modified, depending upon which of these three possibilities is true.

Hence the impossibility of making our mere "impression" of the
atheism that is practiced the ultimate criterion of our ethical decisions shows that we cannot evade the question whether and to
what extent atheism is an integral part of Marxist doctrine itself
and therefore whether it is constitutive or merely accidental for
the system as such.

The first question we must ask, therefore, relates to a problem of
interpretation.

A certain latitude of variation in the interpretations that are possible here was expressed in a group discussion of this subject[1] and therefore it may be characterized best by a number of notes taken during the course of our discussion.

INTERPRETATION A

Thesis: *The dogmatization of atheism in the Communist movement is historical in origin and can be overcome in the course of history.*

1. The atheistic tendency in the Communist movement arose through an "accidental" constellation in intellectual history which happened to be present in the incipient phase of Marxism—a constellation that was able to develop all the more intensively, since to some extent it still continues to exist today (the emancipation of science, secularism, etc.).

2. A comprehensive word that describes this constellation is the term "secularism." Unlike the Middle Ages, the Reformation, and even the Enlightenment, it made possible for the first time an interpretation of the world that is independent of any concept of God, in other words, an atheistic interpretation of the world. It was in this intellectual climate that Marxism was established.

3. This secularistic inception produced a fundamental antagonism between faith and knowledge. From this point of view the faith advocated by Christianity looks like an obscure, "mythical" stage of knowledge which is automatically liquidated in the mass of scientific enlightenment.

4. *Ecclesiastical Christianity itself is largely at fault* for this misunderstanding of faith which is "in the air," and for the following reasons:

a) A particular understanding of faith as a *fides quae creditur,* a particular form of the doctrine of verbal inspiration and thus a legalistic attitude toward the literal words of the Bible made way for the misunderstanding that the Bible also contains a binding "scientific explanation of the world" and thus presents an authoritative criterion by which modern science can be accepted or rejected. In this way the inevitable result was that the relation between the

---

[1] In a study commission of theologians from both East and West Germany.

two became an exclusively competitive one. On the other hand, the incontrovertibility of scientific results inevitably discredited Christian theology and exposed its advocates to the odium of intellectual dishonesty. This intellectual failure on the part of the church tended to strengthen the Marxist suspicion that the motive of this assumed obscurantism of the church was based not merely on a lack of enlightenment, but above all on a social purpose, namely, to use religion to protect the interests of certain classes while other classes are "kept in ignorance."

b) The conviction that religion was not a "confession of truth" devoted to the cause of truth, but rather a pragmatic weapon in the class struggle, was strengthened by the observation that the church was intertwined *de facto* with certain social structures (throne and altar, citizenship, feudalism).

c) Further, this misunderstanding would not have been possible had not Schleiermacher subsumed Christianity under the general heading of religion and thus made the "objective" Christian witness merely a part of general anthropology. This made possible the counterblast delivered by Feuerbach, which was the same kind of subversion of Schleiermacher as Marx perpetrated upon Hegel. Thus Marx was able to go to Feuerbach and to a certain extent *also* to Schleiermacher and provide himself with the epistemological arguments to demonstrate the ideological invalidity of religion. And when this happened a Christianity which had become a mere "religion" was impotent to defend itself. It must be admitted, however, that this argument has only relative validity, since faith in revelation—no matter what form of theological reflection it may take—is on principle defenseless, and must of necessity be defenseless, against this kind of impugnment.

d.) Finally, Marxism received from Hegel—strengthened by the political consideration that an eschatological goal for history also possesses a dynamic for the mobilization of the masses—the impulse that drove it to political messianism.

5. All these historically conditioned constellations contributed toward the formation of an atheistic tendency. It therefore would seem not impossible that in the course of history there could be a corresponding demolition of this induced atheism. In this connection we dare not forget that Communism—contrary to its own

self-image, which it regards as a constant—is subject to the pressure of changing history. Newly emerging factors, such as a non-state church, a worldly, "non-religious" form of preaching of the kind advocated by Bonhoeffer can lead Marxism-Leninism to a revision of its atheistic position. Figures like Barth and Niemöller have already focused attention upon this.

6. That this possibility of modification exists is also shown by the fact that, alongside the Leninist variants, there has also sprung up from the Marxist root a more liberal, more revisionist, Marxism, which is tolerant of religion and leaves room for metaphysical convictions.

INTERPRETATION B

This interpretation upholds the following thesis: Atheism has constitutive significance within Marxism-Leninism, which, without atheism, would collapse.

1. Dialectical materialism, by reason of its axiom that history, which proceeds and comes into being through the class struggles, is exclusively determined by the economic substructure, has on principle, no place for any concept of God.

2. The localizing of religion in the superstructure and labeling it with the term "ideology" denies it from the start the right to make assertions of truth which may then be tested by their conformity to reality. Religion is therefore, on principle, not to be interpreted as representing the *"truth,"* but simply as representing conscious or unconscious social *"purposes."* These purposes are inimical to the working and exploited classes and thus make religion a determined opponent of Marxism-Leninism.

3. The competition of religion with science and the religious thesis that the ultimate foundation of the world cannot be investigated and discovered, or one might say, the notorious "irrationalism" of religion is a hindrance to scientific knowledge and therefore to intellectual progress. *Religion is therefore not only "untrue," "obscurantist," and therefore incapable of being discussed in the epistemological sense, but is also impossible in the pragmatic sense, because it blocks the progress of knowledge and leads to a fundamental intellectual invalidism.*

4. Putting people off with promises of a life to come paralyzes

all social revolutionary activity and thus also blocks the progress of society.

5. Religion—in any case the Christian religion—preserves the personal individuality of man, makes him the bearer of a conscience and thus furnishes him with inhibitions that make him resistant to the desired functionality of the individual. Religious faith, therefore, immunizes a person against every kind of collectivism and takes away from him the ability to throw himself "without reservations" into advocacy of the doctrine as well as the methods of violence.

6. It is part of the genuine nature of Marxism that it subsumes all the phenomena of life under one simple, universal formula, namely, dialectical materialism. This fixation by means of a single organizing principle, which has the status of an *ens realissimum* (ultimate reality), is part of the essence of the system and as such it possesses the *quality of idolatry*.[2] This produces a fundamental antagonism not only to any general concept of religion but especially to the specifically *Christian* message.

7. From this point of view then, the historically conditioned factors stressed in Interpretation A are admitted, but they are given a different systematic locus:

a) The secularism referred to above not only controls individual motivations of the atheistic tendency but constitutes the total framework within which materialism and its axioms came into being.

b) Moreover, every intellectual phenomenon—and therefore Marxism-Leninism—is an extremely complex formation which results partly from an axiomatic prejudgment and partly from a multitude of individual empirical factors which then perform the function of corroborating the prejudgment. Here the axiomatic prejudgment represents the supreme principle from which all further conclusions, including that of atheism, are deduced. On the other hand, the individual empirical factors serve the purpose of "proving" the fundamental postulate inductively, that is, on the basis of empirical evidence, and thus making it effective for propagandizing the masses. (In this way a great deal of antichurch resentment can

---

[2] Cf. Thielicke, *Theologische Ethik*, Vol. II, 2, § 294 ff.

be aroused with the help of a concrete casuistry.)

8. This constitutive atheistic tendency is rather widely concealed for the following reasons:

a) Reasons of principle: the alpha privative in atheism is construed so radically that even atheistic propaganda itself becomes a dubious thing. To fight against something which is on principle nonexistent and which must inevitably prove itself to be nonexistent makes only a relative kind of sense. It therefore can be tolerated only insofar as it does not by its militancy increase obscurantism or prevent its logical dissolution in the historical process by arousing excessive resistance (or even the desire to publicize itself).

b) Tactical reasons: a direct attack upon the church creates martyrs, and hardens the situation. Therefore the politically dangerous *status confessionis* is to be avoided and instead the method of indirect, smokescreen attack is to be chosen.[3]

These two different interpretations of Marxism-Leninism, namely A and B, lead to different conclusions with regard to our question.

Interpretation A makes it possible to participate in socialistic reconstruction in that one is then able to disregard the atheistic premises and cherish the hope that by co-operating in the material realm (in the Agricultural Production Associations, for example) one may demonstrate that the church member is capable of functioning in a socialistic society and that in this way the system may some day be robbed of its fascination and its messianic character. The freedom to be objective, which is the gift of faith, should demonstrate itself in a qualified co-operation and have the force of being a practical testimony in that it helps to disarm the ideologies.

Interpretation B, on the other hand, does not allow such a separation between the ideological premises and the material realm, but rather insists that the atheistic tendency also affects everything else. (The position hitherto taken by the church in the controversy over confirmation and youth dedication (*Jugendweihe*) is undoubtedly based upon this conception: though the form used for youth dedication contains only a pledge to socialist society, to peace, and similar things which should be quite neutral, the church has insisted

---

[3] Cf. Thielicke, *Theologische Ethik*, Vol. II, 2, § 2245 ff.

that constitutively bound up with it is a profession of atheism. Accordingly the church could not admit the possibility of a separation between the ideological and material spheres, and therefore viewed the two ceremonies as being mutually contradictory and exclusive.) Hence there is no area, whether it be education or agricultural production, that is unaffected by the ideology and the atheism. Thus decision for or against Christ is presented at every moment and in every place within the practical sphere itself.

To be sure, a quantitative distinction must be made here between more and less possibility of co-operation. That is to say that while it may seem, for example, to be impossible to act as a teacher (since here the pressure of the ideology simply stifles the spiritual man), there may still be a certain freedom of movement in other vocations which are philosophically more neutral (the comparative is characteristic!).

The most important argument in Interpretation A, namely, that the Christian through his practical co-operation can contribute toward exorcising the ideology of its fascination loses force when it is confronted with the sociological consideration that since loyal Christians are decreasingly tolerated in positions of leadership or even of any prominence whatsoever and are being shunted into inferior vocations, their influence upon the whole of society, and thus their ability to perform the function of exorcism, can have only a very limited significance.

The aporia or dilemma with which Interpretation B confronts us raises the critical question of whether a *modus convivendi,* a way of living together in Marxist-Leninist society, can be found at all. The fact that flight to West Germany is not a legitimate solution to this question and that the Berlin crisis has made this physically impossible makes the question all the more important.

This contrast between Interpretation A and Interpretation B may make it appear that A is a lax and liberal interpretation, while B is more earnest, sparing itself none of the difficulties. This impression would be fallacious, however, since the advocate of Interpretation A is concretely aware of almost the same difficulties in the making of individual decisions, and by no means views the program he has adopted for making distinctions and decisions as an "easy solution." He therefore does not advocate any form of *laissez faire;* he is not attempting to say that the whole thing is harmless; rather he considers his interpretation as being only a possible solution for the long run, which will not be achieved without an interim period in which many sacrifices will have to be faced.

From this relative closeness of the two points of view, which appeared as soon as we began to reflect upon individual, everyday decisions, there also emerged in the course of discussion a closer approximation of the two interpretations themselves. The following thesis is presented by all who participated in the discussion as a formula of agreement or as a formula of mutual approach:

In its original form Marxism is a complex quantity which permits the emphasis to be put upon various points. Whereas liberal, revisionist Marxism, under the pressure of history—which Marxism itself regards as a legitimate modifying fact inherent in the system —leads to a position in which the metaphysical zone is left open, Marxism-*Leninism* presents an interpretation of the system in which it unequivocally construes the metaphysical and religious as an interim ideology, like that of the place of the state in the system, and thus makes atheism an integrating constituent of the system. But here again the tactically determined toleration of religion and even the cessation of the antireligious campaign at certain times and places opens up certain possibilities of existing as a Christian even in a socialistic society which is so defined and understood.

Starting, then, with this somewhat approximated position, there are some questions with regard to concrete decisions that present themselves to the representatives of both interpretations:

While neither side believes in an "easy solution" in the sense of concrete distinctions between the premises of the system and the realm of practical life, even the representatives of Interpretation B concede that the total ideologization of all the areas of life does not necessarily mean that there can be no *modus convivendi* at all. On the contrary, both sides—quite apart from the remaining differences in their interpretations—are agreed that through the preserving grace of God there are to be found even in an ideologized state legal and civil functions of order which, in the sense of Romans 13, prevent a *bellum omnium contra omnes* (war of all against all). Moreover, the grip of the ideologized state is constantly being limited by the "indelible character" of certain elemental components of existence (the fact that the government is not "totally" lacking in justice and order, that its abandonment in perversion of conscience is not "total," etc.).[4] So Christianity lives "from reprieve to reprieve" and in the gaps left open in the ideological net. For the *modus convivendi* which is possible within these limitations, the following theses are determinative:

1. The Christian must clearly understand that since, as Luther said, we are in reality sinners (*peccatores in res*) we must exist in compromise, and that therefore there can be no such thing as existential perfection. The problem of compromise must be thought through afresh. The law of God—let us say in the radical form of the Sermon on the Mount—here possesses the function of keeping open the wound of our having to lead a "broken existence" and of preventing any false justification that caters to the spirit of compromise.

2. Compromise confronts one with the unceasing necessity of deciding whether this action is "still" possible or that action is "no longer" possible. Since the isolated conscience of the individual is here exposed to a dangerous downward tendency, the *mutua cohortatio et consolatio fratrum* (mutual exhortation and consolation of brethren) becomes important as an exercise in common examination of conscience.

3. Particularly in view of the possible misinterpretations to which our action as co-operation is exposed, here especially the profession of faith which accompanies our action becomes a fundamental part of Christian existence.

4. What is necessary is to emphasize and also to demonstrate in life the real difference which is here at issue: we dare not accept from Communism the opposites which it sets forth, namely, antitheism (of which it is the advocate) and theism (of which it takes us to be advocates). The primary question is not whether the "idea" of God is advocated or not. Rather what is at issue is the real theological question, namely, that the Communist exists under the curse of the law and hence under a nonreligious religion of law, whereas the Christian lives under the gospel and therefore under the forgiveness of God and its liberating assurance. On this basis

---

[4] This must be vigorously emphasized especially over against the controversial position taken by Bishop Dibelius.

then, we must correct the Communist placement of the battlefront by making it clear that we are not affected by its opposition to religion, because we are *not* really advocates of "religion," whereas Communism itself represents a religion, namely, the religion of law. In doing this the advocate of the gospel will not abolish the front set up by Communism, but will correct it. Atheistic domains too are under God (cf. the prophets).

5. Contributory to this correction of the front between Communism and Christianity will be various apologetic tasks which emerge from the historically conditioned factors in Marxist atheism referred to under Interpretation A and which will have to show that a part of the opposition is based on misunderstanding and prejudice. Among these, for example, is the proper presentation of the relation of faith and science (especially faith and natural science) as well as the relation of faith and cosmology.

6. Further, there is the church's task of social self-criticism and along with this the willingness to disengage itself from certain conventional social encumbrances. On this head Christianity must ask itself to what extent its conventional concept of property is primarily Christian and to what extent it may possibly be conditioned by civil custom. Openness to revisions of this kind—including one's own property—will diminish the blockage that makes the Communist unwilling to listen, insofar as this is caused by misunderstandings.

7. The determinative spiritual task, which includes this kind of qualified co-operation with socialistic society, consists in our practicing the essential mystery of love for one's neighbor and one's enemy in individual, personal, and adventurous contacts with the Communist functionaries; in other words, despite all our opposition to the antichristian "front," we must see in the representative of that front our brother and therefore a neighbor for whom God grieves and whom he seeks. Even ostensible faithfulness to one's confession can lose its spiritual authority when it is lacking in love. But it sins against love when it identifies the individual Communist man with the front which he represents and perhaps even represents as a functionary. Jesus Christ did not identify even the soldier-executioners beneath his cross with the "antichristian front"; rather, he grieved most for the lost children: "Father, forgive them;

for they know not what they do." *The first and elementary act in every act of loving one's neighbor is to separate the man from his front.* And for the sake of this task, if for no other reason, the Christian dare not, so far as it depends upon him, merely exist in the aloofness of confession and anathema, but must remain in close contact with men.

This impossibility of an easy solution and, on the other hand, the possibility of living a confident and comforted existence under forgiveness in the midst of the brokenness of our situation can be expressed in a phrase (which at the same time suggests the laughter of those who have been promised that the world will be overcome): "We sit between the stools—under the umbrella of the Most High."[5]

B. IDEOLOGY IN THE MARXIST-LENINIST WORLD

Karl Marx's materialistic concept of history sees the sustaining impulse of all historical movement in the "conditions of production" which in turn are always determined by the particular stage of development which the available "material forces of production" have reached. The totality of these relations of production constitutes the economic structure of society and this in turn produces a "superstructure" in the form of "social forms of consciousness" which present themselves first in legal and political institutions.

The intellectual spheres such as art, morality, and religion, which again derive from these forms of consciousness, are therefore "echoes and reflexes" of the social life-process. They are called ideologies because they are reflected images of this basic material process, derived from it and, as it were, secondary to it in the scale of reality. Thus the conditions of production in the material life determine the whole social, political, and intellectual life-process. "It is not the consciousness of men that determines his being, but rather their social being that determines their consciousness."[1]

The more recent development of Bolshevistic doctrine no longer tends to interpret the relationship of material substructure and

---

[5] The last half of the phrase, from Ps. 91:1, "in the shelter of the Most High," is a play upon the German word *Schirm*. (Trans.)

[1] Marx, *Ausgewählte Schriften*, Vol. 1, Moskau-Leningrad, 1943, p. 359.

ideological superstructure merely as a one-sided relationship of dependence, but rather inclines to see the principle of dialectic at work in this relationship. Thus Stalin's so-called "letters on language," which appear to be prevailing despite the dethronement of their author, show that ideologies, once they have been evoked, begin to acquire a power of their own and reflect back upon the substructure, thus developing a formative initiative of their own.

The superstructure is produced by the basis, but this in no way means that it simply reflects the basis, that it is passive, neutral. . . . On the contrary, once it has come into being it becomes a very powerful force, it actively helps its basis to take on secure forms and consolidate itself, and takes all measures to help the new social order to clear away and eliminate the old basis and the old classes.[2]

It would be wrong, however, to see in this a renunciation of the original principle that the ideologies are dependent. Rather it would appear that in this variation of the understanding of ideology something like Hegel's "strategy of the Idea" is expressing itself, for this thesis that the superstructure acquires a power of its own is itself a kind of ideology, which arises from the material, social progress and reflects it.

This is not difficult to understand since the real material foundation of history—and hence that which at the same time creatively sustains all other spheres—is the "conditions of production." The differing share in the means of production produces antagonistic classes whose struggle determines the face of history. If therefore, according to Marxist doctrine, history is the "history of class struggles," then the course of events is defined by the social forms in which the varying conditions of production manifest themselves. Because of the opposition between the two classes, these social forms contain that creative polar tension which generates the life and progress of history.

This conclusion, however, has always given nightmares to the Marxist-Leninist theorists. For since their goal was the classless society, this eschatology put them in the painful situation of having to envision a state of affairs in which there would be no history. For in that final stage of society the generative impulse, which is

---

[2] Stalin, *Marxismus und Fragen der Sprachwissenschaft*, p. 5.

inherent in the antagonism of the classes and is actually understood as the very theme of history, would cease to exist. Here the theorists had to look for some other way out: since neither revolution nor class struggle can be permitted within the jurisdiction of Communism and since the paralysis of complete stagnation must nevertheless be prevented, they had to search for some new impulses of historical movement.

These new impulses were sought for in a changed form of dialectic. The creative antagonism was shifted as it were to a different point. Instead of an antagonism between the classes it became an antagonism between substructure and superstructure.

Originally this antagonism did not exist simply because (according to Marx) the superstructure was purely dependent and thus could not have in it an antagonistic impulse based upon a certain autonomy. But now, as history moves further toward the eschaton of the Communist fulfillment, this independent power is being conceded to the superstructure. Certain fixed values in the sphere of this superstructure (such as the moral and political unity of the people, the friendship of nations and nationalities bound to the Soviet system, and even the rediscovered concept of "personality") and also certain processes that go on in the superstructure (such as criticism and self-criticism) now radiate formative influences upon social conditions and can have the force of a creative opposition, a corrective of imperfect conditions.

Thus the law of the movement of history is now rooted in changed conditions of tension: whereas in the antagonistic society the propulsion or historical impetus originates in the uprising of the revolutionary masses against the ruling classes and so the initiative comes "from above downward." On the one hand, the impetus comes from above, in the sense that it emanates from the Soviet state as the institutional representative of the classless society. "The masses thus actively *support* [!] the revolutionary initiative from above."[3] On the other hand, the impetus also comes from above downward insofar as it comes from the sphere of the superstructure and insofar as the Bolshevist doctrine—though originally it was

---

[3] The words of the Bolshevist theorist G. Aleksandrov in a publication of the Academy of Sciences of the U.S.S.R., cited in G. A. Wetter, *Der dialektische Materialismus, Seine Geschichte und sein System in der Sowjetunion, 1952.*

interpreted only as a reflex of the social conditions—now performs normative functions upon these conditions. This becomes apparent, for example, in the satellite states of the Soviet Union. For in their case, their co-ordination with the Soviet Union does not come into being in such a way that the ideology grows out of the material-social substructure. Rather the opposite is true: the ideology perfected in the Soviet Union operates from above downward in a missionary and formative way and thus changes the original direction of the impulse of the historical process. In this case the ideology has now become an independent force with a capacity for creating history. Naturally, both kinds of impetus "from above" are essentially related. For the Soviet state at the same time holds the position of being the infallible teacher of the doctrine; it is actually the institutionalization of the doctrine. So ultimately it is a matter of one and the same impetus from above. Its initiator is the Soviet state vested with the office of watchman.[4]

We have had to take the time to describe these newer tendencies in the interpretation of the superstructure because they reveal an important basic characteristic of the ideologies themselves. That is to say, Marxism-Leninism not only in general describes the intellectual spheres as ideologies and dependent reflexes, but also understands—not explicitly, but implicitly and apparently even reluctantly—even its own doctrine as being this kind of ideology. For whether it understands the relation of substructure and superstructure as a one-sided dependent or a reciprocal relationship depends upon the stage of social order upon which this theme is based. In other words, the doctrine of the retroactive force of the ideologies is not simply to be understood as progress in knowledge, but as the reflex of an advance in social development. Therefore Marxism-Leninism itself is subject to the relativity of all ideologies, which means that it cannot live of itself, but must be related to real life as a reflex. Its doctrine not only "contains" a doctrine of ideologies, but "is" itself an ideology. And, paradoxically, it remains a reflex even when the image seems to take on a life of its own, even when it acquires its own sight and voice and is empowered to

---

[4] In the eschaton phase of this Bolshevistic view of history the separation between the party and the state will cease to exist, so that we need not discuss this here.

exert "initiative from above." For as it advances to the final stage of society, Communistic doctrine has to cultivate this latter idea (of the autonomous power of ideologies), in order to invent a new antagonism. And because it must do this, it is in turn only a reflex. Once entered, the vicious circle in which the doctrine of substructure and superstructure is domiciled cannot be breached. The relativity of all intellectual, ethical, and artistic processes and values endures. And here again the old autonomy of all relativism proves to be true: it always draws the one who relativizes and expresses this in the form of a doctrine into the vortex of relativity. Relativization of the mind revenges itself by making the relativizer relative.

Marxism-Leninism tries to extricate itself from this objection that it relativizes itself and is at bottom merely one ideology among others by means of an argument which can only be described as an intellectual fakir's trick. In order to maintain its claim to the absolute validity of its doctrine and, so to speak, protect it from itself, it must force the resulting antinomy into a synthesis.

First it must make the claim to be objective and, as Stalin has expressed it, base itself upon the "objective reality of the material world."[5] For the opposite of "objective" is "subjective"; so, if it were not to claim objectivity for its statements, it would be allowing its doctrine to sink to the level of subjective expression, of mere profession, or even of a nonbinding, notional fiction. It would be, so to speak, "voluntarily" depotentiating to the level of an ideology. And naturally this cannot be its intention.

On the other hand, it passionately rejects objectivity. For its concern is not to understand the world, but to change it. To this extent its doctrine aims not at objective truth but rather at advocating interests. It is, as we shall show in more detail, resolutely pragmatic. But this compels it to reject objectivity. For the term "objective" is not only an antonym of the term "subjective," but is also antithetical to the term "interested" or "self-interest." The person who wants to be objective dare not have an interested prejudice or interested desires, but must selflessly exclude his interests. He must be neutral. He must transcend himself and his

---

[5] *Op cit.*, p. 260b.

subject-object relation. But Communistic doctrine cannot permit this; for objectivity in the sense of neutralism deprives it of its character as action, its class interest, and its will to realize itself. Thus A. Zdanov, for example, condemns objectivity as "toothless vegetarianism" and condemns G. F. Aleksandrov because he is not partisan enough in his history of philosophy. To be objective means to be disinterested and to that extent nonpolitical.

So this is the antinomy that Communistic doctrine must resolve. First, one is objective, that is, one has uncovered the objective reality of history, one represents an exact science and therefore one can claim absoluteness for its axioms. Second, one is *not* objective; for one represents an interest, a party loyalty. So the contradiction can be formulated in this way: first, one is objective, because one is not subjective. Second, one is not objective, because one is not neutral.

The fakir's trick by which this antinomy is resolved into a synthesis looks like this: It is true that political economy is not a neutral, impartial science; but its partiality robs it of its objectivity only if it is allied with a particular party, which is to say, with one party among others competing with it. As long as this is so, there can be no universally binding and unified political economy, but only competing, and irreconcilably competing, claims. If something is to be objective it must be universally binding, but in principle this cannot be had as long as there are various classes in society which are represented by these parties, namely, the upper class and the proletariat as well as the middle class. On the contrary, objectivity as a prerequisite of universal bindingness is sociologically possible only if there is one unified class, "whose interests are identical with the interests of the progressive development of humanity." Since the goal of this development is the classless society or, to express it differently, the society which has become congruent with the victorious proletarian class, then the goal of history is, so to speak, itself doing the thinking when the victorious class thinks.

This, at any rate, is the way one would express it in Hegelian style. However, this is the way to arrive at that objectivity, which is universally binding and yet biased, objective and yet "interested." For here one interest no longer competes with another, as in the intermediate stages of history, but rather here the goal of history itself has an interest in realizing itself.

This goal of history, conceived of as being almost personified in a mythical sense, is therefore interested, without losing its universal bindingness; it is party-bound without losing its objectivity. For the party that represents it is identical with the class which is co-ordinated with the goal of history itself. The present, and hence pre-eschatological, Soviet philosophy is already participating in this objectivity because it does its thinking in the name of this goal of history.

The intellectual fakir's trick evidenced here is performed in this way. First, the objective basis of history is posited in an axiomatic way and then from it is derived the postulate of the classless society. Second, this ideology is proclaimed as a battle slogan, the purpose of which is not to interpret the world (and thus to know it and be objective in this knowledge), but rather to change it in the direction of the classless society (and thus to be interested and not objective). And third, the classless society devised in this way is used retroactively as a means which makes objectivity possible and thus legitimates its own thinking as the product of objective thought.

If anywhere, then surely here it is clear that the ideology of Communism, even more than all the other ideologies of which it speaks so polemically, lives in a twilight, or better, a "trilight," between whatever life-processes happen to be present, contrived pragmatic expediencies, and pseudo-scientific axioms. And in order to make it accessible to knowledge, one must not allow it to remain in this "trilight," but must rather understand its real focal point. This lies, as we will immediately see, in its pragmatic tendency. The ideologies are devices contrived to achieve certain ends. This becomes apparent above all in the fact that wherever they appear in the normative spheres, such as science, law, or ethics, they rob the norms of their authoritative position and degrade them into mere instruments for achieving certain ends.

So there can be no question of the pragmatic purpose of the ideologies. Therefore what interests us more than this conclusion itself is the question of how this pragmatic tendency works out with respect to the normative intellectual and ethical elements, such as truth, justice, or the good, and to what extent it corrodes or destroys these norms.

On pragmatism itself let only this be noted: Marx says that theory becomes a "material force when it takes hold of the masses."[6] Stalin interprets this statement by speaking of "the powerful, organizing, mobilizing, and transforming role" of such political theorems.[7] Hence, Bochenski rightly says, the ideologies are "instruments of life." An idea of society is not regarded as right because it accords with objective reality, but rather because it is a good instrument for the class which has put forward this idea.[8]

Thus the ideologies are responsible not to the truth, but to the ends which they serve. Therefore they are also variable, not only in the sense that they correspondingly alter the material substructure upon which they are dependent, but also in the sense that they themselves change with the changing purposes which they serve. They are placed at the disposal of men as means of realizing ends, whereas the truth disposes over men. Accordingly, the statements made in the ideologies are not determined by the norm of truth; rather the truthlike form of their statements is simply an expression, in Nietzsche's sense, of the will to power. They furnish an intellectual alibi for the collective will to power in that they appear to state truths, whereas in reality they proclaim a program.

Exactly the same thing is true with respect to the norm of the good, which is likewise corroded by being used to achieve an end. We may think of illustrations that come from an entirely different provenance, such as, "Good is what is good for my people," or "Our country, right or wrong," or Machiavelli's dictum that in the pragmatic areas of statesmanship one should not bind oneself to the ideal of the good, but on the contrary merely employ ethical phraseology in order to gain moral credit and then with this credit attain one's political ends.

Georges Sorel certainly saw something that was right when he defined these social ideologies as myths which do not contain "descriptions of things" but are rather an "expression of the de-

[6] *Marx-Engels-Gesamtausgabe*, Vol. I, 1, p. 614.
[7] *Geschichte der Kommunistischen Partei der UdSSR*, pp. 140 f.
[8] I. M. Bochenski, *Der sowjetrussische dialektische Materialismus*, 1950, p. 140.

termination to act."[9] Just because Rosenberg's "myth of the twentieth century" is so banal, by its trivial oversimplification of lives it brings out all the more clearly the real nature of these tendencies. In the first place for him this myth is the ideological reflection of the racial and biological substance, so that here the scheme of substructure and superstructure can be applied very precisely. In the second place, this myth is an instrument for the exercise of intellectual-spiritual power, for which the problem of truth is incompetent. The totalitarian state needs this ideological instrument. For if it relies only upon terror, it creates an opposition, even though this does not appear in the form of a movement, but only as an "inner withdrawal." Inner resistance, which can never be controlled by terror, can only be overcome by winning over the opposing inward being of men which is not accessible to external instruments of power, that is, by convincing it or paralyzing it by means of suggestion (propaganda). Both are possible only through intellectual-spiritual means. These means are "ideologies" or "political myths."

Religions can be employed to this end. And frequently enough Christianity has been thus misused. If no vital religion is available for exercising this kind of control of the masses, it is also possible to fabricate substitute religions artificially. The Rosenberg "myth" is certainly such a synthetic product prepared in the laboratory. In any case, the characteristic that is common to these attempts is that they all claim the whole man and then proceed to realize this claim with the aid of ideologies. These ideologies represent, alongside a surgical treatment by means of terror, an internist-psychological "therapy," which takes possession of the inner realms of man, either by convincing through argument or by evoking enthusiasm and fanaticism through emotional channels.

This also makes it clear why there must be in every ideology a claim to be absolute. If it is to control the whole man it cannot tolerate any competitors. Therefore it never enters into discussion with them, but simply eradicates them. This points to an extremely dialectical relation between power and ideology: the function of the ideology is to legitimate the will to power, to furnish it, as it were,

---

[9] Quoted in W. Theimer, *Der Marxismus*, 1950, p. 240.

with arguments. On the other hand, the ideology itself needs power, in order that it may not have to enter into discussion and thus recognize its ideological competitors, but simply destroy them. The ideology dare not allow itself to be put in question, since in this way it would lose its striking power and sustain cleavages within itself. Hence it must destroy anything that puts it in question. Thus it not only serves power, but also makes use of power in order to eradicate whatever puts it in question.

This distinguishes it from the substance of real convictions. For it is precisely the real convictions which must expose themselves to being called in question. They strengthen themselves precisely by letting down their drawbridges and granting admittance to challenge. The independence and self-determination of the person who holds convictions comes into being as he resists something and in this resistance becomes himself. The advocate of an ideology, however, never becomes himself, because he never faces the challenge of being called into question; he will not even allow such a challenge to get near to him at all. Conviction aims at that which exists; ideology, at that which functions. Conviction makes a man a person; ideology depersonalizes. Conviction allows a person to be an end in himself; ideology makes him a means and an object. The man of conviction asks: What is the truth? The man of ideology asks: Which influence am I going to follow?

For all these reasons it is small wonder—indeed, we have already made several specific references to this—that the pragmatic tendency constitutes the real focal point of ideology, and that it consequently influences or absorbs all other norms. We shall have to be content to illustrate this with only a few examples. For this purpose we choose themes from the area of natural science (an area which is seemingly very remote from ideological influence, because it is "exact") and the area of jurisprudence.

Though in Communism even the discussion of, say, Einstein's theory of relativity is pursued on the basis of the axioms of the ideology,[10] science's function of providing by means of its arguments

---

[10] The crassest example available in the German language known to the author appears in the report of a "Conference on the Ideological Questions of Astronomy, convened by the Leningrad Section of the Astronomico-Geodetic Society of the Soviet Union (LOWAGO)," in *Sowjetwissenschaft* (1949), 3, pp.

subsequent legitimation for the interests of the ideology appears most conspicuously in the realm of biology.[11] The genetics founded by I. V. Mitschurin and developed by T. D. Lysenko implies that "organisms change under the influence of environmental conditions" and hence that they inherit acquired characteristics.[12] The thesis that "man can influence the transmission of acquired characteristics of animals and plants by regulating the conditions of life" is intended to confirm the axioms of the prescribed ideology in three ways. First, in that here man appears as the master of nature who is to "change" the world in the sense of the thesis set forth by Karl Marx against Feuerbach.[13]

Second, the intention here is to furnish biological corroboration of the thesis of the Marxist environmental theory that man is the product of his social milieu and thus possesses acquired social characteristics. The resulting consequence that man himself is changed through the change of his environment is here carried over into the biological realm: plants and animals can be changed by changing their environmental conditions. The characteristics thus applied to them determine their essential nature. The fact that what is meant here is actually a real alteration of the essential nature and therefore the producing of genuine characteristics becomes evident in the fact that these characteristics are transmitted. For only essential na-

291 ff. Discussed were subjects like "The Battle with Formalism in Astronomy" and "The Battle of Materialism with Idealism in Modern Cosmology." The titles themselves indicate the ideological background which is present even in the exact sciences. In this connection the recognition of certain physical hypotheses (such as that of the finiteness of the universe) are rejected as being "servility to foreign views" (p. 292) or with the statement that this is an illustration of "the decadent idealistic pseudo-science of the last exploitative system in history, namely, monopolistic capitalism" (p. 292). Hence, logically, there is no distinction here between right and wrong astronomy, but merely between "bourgeois" and "Soviet" astronomy. And only for the latter, ideologically determined, astronomy is the concept of what is right and correct subsequently adapted.

[11] At this point we are completely uninterested in whether the representatives of this scientific school of thought are at the moment favored by the regime or whether they are in disgrace. They are important to us only in the fundamental sense of being symptoms of tendencies.

[12] D. M. Troschin and J. B. Kogan, *Naturwissenschaft und Religion*, Wissenschaftliche Beilage des "Forum" (1955), No. 25, p. 12; cf. also Wetter, *op. cit.*, pp. 366 ff.

[13] Here the practice of abortion, carried on to a monstrous extent particularly in the early years of Sovietism, should be mentioned.

ture is transmitted by heredity. Essential nature, however, is determined by environment.

Third, the axioms of the ideology are confirmed by the fact that nature and history are dealt with as being exactly analogous. This is possible only because in the doctrine of historical materialism itself history is approached with the methods of natural science (even though it is a very dubious natural science): history does not enact itself in the realm of personal decision, in which man plays the role of subject, but is derived from the material basis. Accordingly, physical analogies are constantly being used—for example, in explaining the revolution—such as turning quantity into quality. Correspondingly, history can also be predicted in the same sense as can the astronomical event of an eclipse of the moon.

Since the purpose of science is to confirm the ideology, it becomes in the same pragmatic sense as the ideology itself an instrument of the power struggle. It is therefore not difficult to find reflected in the relevant Soviet literature not so much the joy in knowledge gained as delight in the practicability of this knowledge and therefore in the *applied* sciences. Einstein said that "divine curiosity" is the motive of research; if Lysenko were asked what *his* motive is, he would probably reply that he desires to serve the Soviet Union and the class it represents.

More important, therefore, than Mitschurin's genetic "discovery" is the fact that with its help increased harvests and giant forms of grains can be produced and that perhaps in the future it may be possible not merely to propagate human beings but to "propagate them upward" into supermen, in Nietzsche's sense. Thus the scientist becomes not so much a discoverer as a champion of the Soviet Union and the countries friendly to it. In his way he seeks to drive breaches in the front of bourgeois "monopolistic capitalism."

All these slogans which are so intolerably repugnant to the Western mind are by no means inarticulate cries. On the contrary, even in the mouths of subordinate functionaries they are the ultimate vibrations of a fundamental doctrine, which in its inception is, to be sure, no less a slogan and a doctrinaire assumption, but is enveloped in a very subtle intellectuality.

If this pragmatization is already working itself out in the "green tree" of the exact sciences, one may expect that it will go to even further lengths in the humanistic sciences with their greater immediacy to human beings and to history.[14]

We content ourselves with these few references to the ideologizing of jurisprudence. After all that has been said above it is hardly necessary to say anything more concerning one negative assumption, namely, that it would be futile to look for any normative idea in Bolshevistic law, such as justice, or for any authoritative court of appeal, such as natural law. It is true that law is never a structure that is exclusively derivable from the idea of justice because on principle it is a relationship of tension between three fundamental values, namely, justice, expediency, and legal security. The idea of law is therefore very complex, since it combines both normative and pragmatic points of view. Although their mutual relationship is very complicated and there are certain borderline cases in which the superiority of the normative over the pragmatic point of view can be questioned,[15] it is nevertheless beyond question, that the Western tradition of law intends justice to be an "absolute value" and regards it as having equal status with the other absolute values, namely, the good, the true, and the beautiful. Thus one can say that law is a manifestation of culture directed to the external order of social life "whose purpose is to serve the value of law, the idea of law."[16] This means that the structure of law focuses upon the organic center of the idea of justice. The normative point of view is a dominating corrective of all pragmatisms, which are also continuing to play a part.

Ideological law, however, possesses the infallible mark of heresy,

---

[14] It is difficult to select a few representative titles from the massive literature. As an example of the ideological tendency in the writing of history we mention the well known work of G. Buschendorf, H. Wolffgramm, and I. Radandt, *Weltall, Erde, Mensch* (1955). For the fundamental principles of ideological historicism see G. A. Gurjew, *Wissenschaftliche Voraussicht—Religiöses Vorurteil* (Berlin, 1956). For an example of a historical monograph which in its very theme reveals a tendentiousness that is immune to all the facts see A. P. Gagarin, *Die Entstehung und der Klassencharakter des Christentums* (Berlin, 1956). On the ideologizing of ethics cf. the essays by G. M. Gack and W. N. Kolbanowski in the volume of collected essays, *Über kommunistische Moral* (1945).

[15] We are thinking of the ironical tone of the motto: *Vivat iustitia, pereat mundus* (Let justice prevail, though the world perish).

[16] G. Radbruch, *Rechtsphilosophie*, 4 ed., 1950, edited by Erik Wolf, pp. 123 ff.

a real legal heresy, in that it makes an absolute of one point of view that plays a part in every idea of law, namely, the pragmatic point of view, takes it out of its position as a member within the whole organism, and makes it the organizing center itself. Law becomes an instrument of the will to power and thus a department of politics. In exactly the same way that science exists in order to justify the pragmatic ideology by making the truth subservient to it, so the law is there to provide juridical justification for the interests of the system by making the idea of justice subservient to it.

In the initial stages the purely pragmatic goals of the ideology still appear unveiled. But the urge to expansion that lies dormant within it not only works itself out into external struggles for power, but also captures, if one may put it this way, the store of normative goods which are laid up in the consciousness of mankind. A use of power which is surrounded with the ceremonial of an orderly administration of justice makes it more difficult to resist this power in the name of law. Hence it neutralizes certain possibilities of opposition and thus is in accord with the secret aims of the ideological power, which are not only to secure external consolidation by means of terror but also to conquer the inner realms of man including his conscience.

Thus it is quite in accord with the style of ideological exercise of power to stage show trials, the results of which are dictated beforehand and which are therefore only legally disguised maneuvers of power. The power interest which does the dictating here could of course gain its end without this interlude, but since it also makes use of a moral instrument and enlists justice as a handmaiden of politics, it pushes its invasions into the inner realms of man. Even the palpable lack of credibility from which these masquerades of justice suffer does not wholly deprive the holders of power of this desired effect. For in any case they make it impossible for the spectator at these trials simply to mobilize the pathos of his sense of justice against the excesses of brute power; the spectator is now put in the position of having to argue on points of law. He is involved in an enervating discussion with himself. He is confronted with a more complicated situation than would be the case if he were dealing with a naked excess of power. It is less easy to grasp and control—inwardly or outwardly—the complicated than the simple. To this extent moral resistance is broken down and paralyzed. But this is the secret goal of every ideological strategy. This was something that Trotsky at the beginning of the Bolshevist road had not yet seen when he proclaimed an open despotism which was to assert and establish itself without concealment and without "recasting the proletarian dictatorship into any kind of involved legal forms."

According to this view, then, the law is "the totality of the rules of human conduct established by the supreme power of the state as the power of the ruling class in society and the customs and rules of common life sanctioned by the state, the application of which is compulsorily carried out with the help of the apparatus of the state, *in order to guard, consolidate, and develop those circumstances and conditions which are agreeable and advantageous to the ruling class.*"[17]

We add several more characteristic statements which illustrate down to the most extreme crassitude the pragmatism of ideological jurisprudence:

The significance of the socialistic concept of law for the Soviet law of evidence does not "consist in establishing facts according to the Roman formula, but rather in judging these facts." (Note that here the judgment, which means the ideological evaluation, of unestablished facts is assumed to be possible and therefore that in the investigative procedure the criterion of truth is set aside in favor of the purpose of the trial!) This "judgment" is of prime importance especially in cases "where it is a question of social and class relations, where society is endangered by the act committed . . . *from the standpoint of the interests of socialism.*"[18]

"In our Soviet state the courts are regarded as a part of leadership apparatus and through appropriate measures care is taken that courts are actually *instruments of policy in the Communist Party.*"[19]

"The court is not intended to eliminate the terror, but rather

[17] A. J. Wyschinsky, *Fragen der Rechts- und Staatstheorie* (Moscow, 1949), p. 84. Italics mine. By the same author: *Sowjetisches Staatsrecht* (Moscow, 1938), p. 645. Cf. Bert Dirnecker, *Recht in West und Ost* (1955).
[18] A. J. Wyschinsky, *Rechtswissenschaftlicher Informationsdienst* (RID), (East Berlin, 1952), Nr. 5. Italics mine.
[19] Professor Polianskij, *"Parteidirektiven und Strafjustiz,"* in *Mitteilungsblatt der Moskauer Universität* (1950), p. 11. Italics mine.

to *justify* the terror in principle, clearly, openly, and without mincing matters."[20]

"Courts are instruments with which one class suppresses another. Toward hostile classes the courts are *instruments of destruction. Their characteristic mark is harshness, not kindness.*"[21]

"Also for the courts as *establishments of the superstructure* it holds good that they must serve the ruling class."[22]

This confronts us with the question how the ideologies are to be interpreted theologically.

A theological interpretation of the ideologies, which we cannot go into here, undoubtedly cannot be identical with an interpretation of what we call in broad terms "world view." For in a world view it is only a matter of taking a created thing by itself and making an absolute of it, whether it be the spirit or matter or some other constituent part of that which exists.[23] In dialectical materialism, however, it is something other than merely making an absolute of matter. In the last analysis its intention is to undertake this absolutization for a definite end. This end is man himself, and specifically man in his capacity as a nonpersonal social creature. As a rule we call this substitution of a created thing for the Creator idolatry, but what we have here is really an intensification of this apostasy. For here this deification of the creature is again merely a means to an end, namely, a means of making man the lord of all things. From this point of view, then, the theological task is to examine this degenerate view of man which does not merely put the self in a false relationship, but actually proclaims that the self has no relationship at all.

---

[20] Lenin, *Ges. Werke*, Bd. 27; p. 296. Italics mine.

[21] Mao Tse-tung, *People's Democratic Dictatorships* (Peking: Foreign Languages Press, 1950), p. 17. Italics mine.

[22] Minister of Justice Hilde Benjamin in *Neue Justiz* (East Berlin, 1952), p. 436. Italics mine. Cf. the compilations in Joachim v. Kruse, *Kleiner Katechismus der Weltrevolution* (1955). Also Alfred Leutwein, *Die Ideologie des Unrechts, Zur stalinistisch-communistischen Lehre vom Wesen des Rechts* (West Berlin, 1954).

[23] I have dealt more at length with the basic concept of "world view" in *Theologische Ethik*, Vol. 1.

V

WHAT WILL WE SAY TO THE YOUNG COMMUNISTS ON X-DAY?

A POSSIBLE MISUNDERSTANDING OF THE TITLE OF THIS CHAPTER SHOULD be cleared up at once. I am not of the opinion that X-Day, the day on which the Iron Curtain will be eliminated, will be a definite date on our calendars. On the contrary, I believe that this will be a matter of long-range processes, of slow moving and almost imperceptible transitions. Nevertheless, despite this stipulation, I retain the term X-Day, because it provides a focus for our imagination; it compresses these slow-moving, indiscernible processes into a hard fact and a sudden transition. In one stroke, as it were, it confronts us with the whole mass of problems contained in the question of reunification.

But this also makes X-Day a very perilous subject that reveals to us all our helplessness. I speak here as one (let me say this quite candidly) who is not sure what he has to say on X-Day and who heartily wishes that others may know it better than he.

Despite our helplessness, however, we must tackle the problem, and tackle it in the name of God.

We are constantly urged to think of our brethren on the other side of the Iron Curtain and keep alive the yearning to be reunited with them. If we do not actually send packages, this remembrance of them remains a somewhat Platonic thing. For what can we really do? Should we go along with the Adenauer policy of Western

109

strength or with the program of the opposition, which regards a one-sided commitment to the Western world as not being a means at all, but rather a hindrance to reunification? Even if we think we are quite clear about these alternatives and then proceed militantly to advocate our choice, we cannot do much more than testify to a mere opinion. The consequence is that all of us go about with a bad conscience. Hardly ever does a solemn occasion pass by without the main speaker blowing a blast on this horn: Remember our brethren in the East! And then we do remember them, of course. But ultimately what is a kindly feeling or even a strong emotion when our neighbor has fallen among robbers? The priest and the Levite also had some stirrings of emotion as they "passed by on the other side." But only the Samaritan really bound up the wounds. And this is precisely our difficulty; we cannot get over in order to bind up wounds. And meanwhile the others are in danger of bleeding to death. Both the managers of the system and its victims are bleeding to death, though each in their own way and from different wounds.

In the face of this situation, the mere mention of which has something painful about it, I should like to be permitted to say a personal word of testimony. My own troubles of conscience about what we owe to our country and our brethren beyond the Iron Curtain have led me to the conclusion that the theme suggested in the title of this chapter contains a very fruitful and promising program for our thought and action. And I am surprised that nowhere in the West have we heard this question discussed in public.

We may indicate a number of points at which the fruitfulness of this question becomes apparent.

In the first place, this question, "What will we say to the young Communists on X-Day?" may cause us to do some thinking, and perhaps also to institute some inquiries through letters, discussion, and literature concerning what is going on in the minds of our brethren across the border, and not only among our fellow believers and friends, with whom we have connections, but also among the young Communists. Anybody who has witnessed, say, the Whitsun meetings of Communist youth or has been told about them, anybody who has heard the militant songs of the young Pioneers knows what a potential of political passion, what a dynamic, what fanaticism the wielders of power have somehow been able to unleash. They preach a philosophy whose simple premise, namely, that man and all his intellectual values are exclusively dependent upon the economic conditions of society, is such that even the simplest and most unenlightened mind can grasp it and use it as a tangible compass in all the questions of life. All religious, cultural, and historical questions can be solved by a fabulous process of simplification on the basis of this premise. The Reformation, for example, loses all the fundamentally theological problems that lie behind it and becomes a simple social problem, such as was manifested in the peasant revolt. The origin of wars can be very simply explained without the hypotheses of the philosophy of history by saying that they are fought over the sources of oil or that they are simply a matter of economically more powerful social classes asserting themselves over the weaker. But at the same time these simple premises give even the highly disciplined intellect an opportunity for some intellectual acrobatics which is so intricate as to be almost artistic.

And this philosophy or world view is, of course, not *all* nonsense. On the contrary, like every ideology, even the most abstruse, it has its elements of truth. We in the West, preoccupied with all kinds of idealistic notions—expecially during the first decade of industrialization—have forgotten that man does not consist only in mind, spirit, and inwardness, but that his social situation and his material living conditions also put their definite stamp upon the individual as well as upon his culture. And what we in the West have disastrously overlooked, namely, this fact that man is *socially* conditioned, Marxism and its Bolshevistic scholastics have taken and, after the fashion of sectarians, set up as an absolute, elevating it to the status of formula for the whole world.

It is true that the rise of sects always points to certain deficiencies or lack of certain vitamins in the church from which they have broken away. They are, as it were, a kind of scurvy on the body of the church. In exactly the same way the ideological sect of Marxism-Leninism points to such a deficiency symptom in the Western world, namely, that it has too onesidedly thought of man as an intellectual being and that unfortunately even Western Christianity has often forgotten the example and admonition of its Lord, who first healed and fed sick and hungry bodies and then forgave sins.

Having said this, I ask you not to think that I now propose for the thousandth time to grub about in the past and warm up all kinds of reproaches and criticisms that by now have grown quite cold. Rather I believe that this retrospective glance at recent German history contains a reference to *future* questions which are really approaching us with great force.

If it is true that Bolshevistic doctrine, despite its sectarian distortion, contains these elements of truth, would it really be the ultimate conclusion of wisdom, I ask, simply to annex the territories and people who have been permeated by this doctrine, simply to force them to make an unconditional capitulation and pitch them into the blessings of the West and the so-called free world without any self-criticism?

Any church that seeks to woo and win over a sect must first repent, that is, it must first purge itself of the deficiency symptoms that led to the formation of the sect. This is an utterly simple fact, but—applied to the West—it compels us to ask a question that can cut to the quick: Is the West justified in simply reincorporating the people of the Eastern sect without repenting and without a thoroughgoing operation upon its own flesh? What, actually, are the blessings of the West? I know what a blessing it is that we can go to sleep at night without fear of being dragged from our beds. But it would be mere make-believe to try to cover up the fact that in the general consciousness Western blessings consist of something quite different, namely, automobiles, refrigerators, and—God save the mark—freedom. Hard as it is for me to mention refrigerators and freedom in the same breath, I nevertheless must do so, because any number of people think that freedom is only freedom to have a certain standard of living and, what is more, their understanding of freedom is devoid of any metaphysical undergirding and any personal dignity.

When I attend student and alumni gatherings and hear the praises of freedom sung with beery verve and false pathos, as if we were still living in 1848, I feel like stopping my ears; for I keep seeing before me the faces of young people that turn blank and bewildered when they are asked: What do you want to be free *for;* or better, What *use* will you make of your freedom?

Here I would rather take Sartre when he speaks of the fear of freedom and suggests that today we would prefer to be mere functionaries, people who are assigned a role which they have to play but for which, not they, but the author or the stagemanager is responsible. Sartre is perhaps a poisonous insect, but his study emits an acid, which, though it does not heal the "old man" of the West, nevertheless makes certain slogans and certain sentimentalities unpalatable. Sartre prescribes, as Nietzsche did in his way, some therapeutic toxins.

We ask ourselves, is not the idea of the blessings of the West that many people have floating around in their heads merely a kind of very banal materialism?

This would mean that on X-Day the young Communists would have to choose between two forms of materialism: dialectical materialism and Western materialism. Need I portray further features of the face of the Western world to corroborate and give more force to this question? The "biologization" of man, for example, as it appears in the Kinsey reports and many other testing processes which have become the vogue? Or the "technicization" of man as indicated by Robert Jungk in his quotation of an American who says that man is a botched construction because, biologically, he is no longer equal to the technological possibilities he has himself discovered? But we do not propose to get bogged down in analysis of our time.

But if the young Communist had only this choice between two materialisms, do we seriously believe that he would surely choose the Western materialism? I am afraid that we shall have to come to the point where we realize that Eastern materialism is capable of releasing quite different ethical potencies and quite different idealistic enthusiasms—not absolutely different from that of Western humanity, (I really would not go that far), but different from the refrigerator–cum–television materialism prevalent among us.

Why? Let us substantiate it briefly. It is true that in the East too we find a materialistic dream-picture, namely that of the classless welfare state and its depersonalized denizens. But, since this dream-picture is projected into the distant future, there are, so to speak, long intermediate stages of struggle to attain this ideal vision and in which therefore there must be appeals to sacrifice and unselfishness. Since this materialism is tied up with an extremely distant vision of the future, at the present time it can be viewed, as it were, only with a long-distance lens. Hence this millennium of the ideal society does not act directly upon the materialistic instinct (for, after all, the present generation does not yet share in those fleshpots), but rather acts as an altruistic appeal, a challenge to an unselfishness which some day will benefit future generations. So here we have a very strange, indeed, paradoxical, synthesis between materialism and ethical enthusiasm, between the dream of the welfare state and ascetic willingness to renounce any claim on "welfare." Wherever this "welfare" has become a reality, as in the case of the immediate beneficiaries of the "German economic miracle," this enthusiastic self-denial is quite abruptly dropped in favor of the outward and inward gluttony of the moment.

So there is a host of questions to ponder here, some of them political and economic, but some of them also of a more intrinsic kind that relate to the issue between a Western culture with the stamp of Christianity and the non-Christian, pragmatic culture of the East.

Even though it is not my task to raise or to discuss the problems that emerge in this area, I may be permitted to make the brief comment that here we are confronted with a question which is very similar in form, namely, the problem whether in the political, economic, and social areas too it is a matter of mere capitulation on the part of the Eastern system, and thus of simple annexation to the West, or whether it is a question of creating, through the meeting and with the participation of both sides, a third possibility to be gained in a synthesis of both.

In order not to become too abstract, I mention two examples, the first of which I shall merely state and allow to stand as a question which—at least for me—is still open. I mean the question of what is to be done with the so-called "people-owned" businesses. It is clear that we shall have to think in terms of reconverting expropriated small businesses to private ownership, in accord with the Western concept of person and property; but it is equally clear that it will be a problem to know what is to be done with the large scale industries and businesses, such as the large estates that have been broken up in the meantime. If one has certain inhibitions with regard to the exaction of "reprivatization" and "refeudalization" and if one sees in many forms of public ownership the beginnings of a more just social order, even though at first they may be severely tainted morally by Bolshevistic influences, does this necessarily mean that these inhibitions derive from one's adherence to a particular Western political party—such as a socialist party? May it not be that people who have totally different political affiliations may also be concerned about how we can proceed to make clear to the young communists of the East the trustworthiness of our social and political theses and assure them that by no means does the Western platform of the dignity of the individual imply feudal rights for individual persons or that private ownership in *all* large-scale operations must be absolutely guaranteed?

I speak here as one who is in no way committed to any particular political party (which, incidentally, need not necessarily be a virtue). Hence I can afford to raise the following questions.

Even in case we should approve personally or for our party the consistent and unlimited maintenance of private property, ought we not be willing to make certain concessions in the case where we would be united with people whose social thinking has been formed in a totally different social order, and what is more, an order which also has its positive elements and which in any case is not to be rejected out of hand because of its ideological abuse? I am merely asking the question, but I continue to ask it because I myself have not yet found an answer to it and because I am troubled at how little we are concerned about it and how greatly we tend to look forward to X-Day with an all too naïve, sentimental Westernism and a pharisaic self-confidence that can speak only in terms of annexation. This self-confidence, untempered by any self-criticism whatsoever, may with perilous ease lose us our credibility in the eyes of the young Communists. It may all to easily happen that we turn out to look like relatives, who have become rich, motorized, and bedecked with refrigerators, but also banal and shallow-pated, whose empty comfortableness may actually harden our brethren beyond the Iron Curtain in their determination to cling to their ideology and make them unwilling to listen at all.

Another example of the kind of question of social policy we shall have to face on X-Day is the encouragement of educational opportunity. This problem too I mention because it is typical and also because during the last several years as an academic administrator I have been concerned with it and have some insights concerning it. To a large extent our German students, because they cannot live on what they receive from their parents, are obliged to work during vacations and often have to continue working during the semesters. In this way they never really get away from their work, and study becomes a bitter drudgery. Only one per cent of highly gifted students are aided by state scholarships. At Oxford the figure is eighty-five per cent, and the number may be still larger in the other universities of Great Britain. Here again the question arises whether we can convince the young Communists of the validity of our cultural policy if after X-Day we were to *abolish*, in the specious name of an individualistic principle of self-help, the handsome generosity of the Communist program of educational advancement, to which they have become accustomed. But here again something must be said about the other side of this matter. The immense cultural contribution represented by this generous subsidization of educational advance is morally corrupted in the East by the fact that it is used at the same time as a terrorist means of political and ideological selection, in other words, that it is coupled with ideological pressure, with the throttling of all cultural traditions and the classes that sustain them, in short, with the planned extinction of freedom.

Woe to us if the self-righteousness of the West should lead us to throw out the child with the bath, that is, to throw out the cultural and social program of the East merely because it is sicklied over with the propaganda of inhumanism, and simply substitute for it our system. This Western social order may impress the man of the East as being more fair and unbiased, in any case it may strike him as being without the ulterior motives of ideological and political tactics; but perhaps it may still seem to him to be far from desirable, because the correctness of our Western social order at the same time betrays a certain note of small-bore thinking with no great idea in it and without the breadth of a foreseeing conception. And if I look at it from his point of view, the question is whether the young Communist will not conclude that the alternative he is being given is either demonic enthusiasm or sterile honesty, and whether his heart will really be won over by the West traveling under *these* colors. I am merely asking, but I go on asking the question. A troubled conscience compels me to ask it.

Then also consider the following, which may at the same time constitute a kind of transition to the inner and intellectual encounter that will have to take place on X-Day.

Walter Freytag has called attention to a circumstance in the history of missions which is very significant in this connection. This should not be at all surprising, because, after all, in all the various dimensions of existence we ought to feel that we are missionary representatives of the West. Freytag points out that as a rule the willingness of the objects (if I may use such a term) of missionary activity stems from a certain skepticism with regard to their own religion. But this skepticism almost never consists—and this is significant—in a doubt of the theoretical part of their own position, let us say, the religious dogma, or in the case of the Communists, the ideology of dialectical materialism. On the contrary, this skepticism which disposes people to listen is almost exclusively nurtured by irritation with the disparity between the idea and its realization, between the principles of their own religion and the credibility of its representatives and policies.

Applied to this case, this means that we may assume that after X-Day the young Communist, insofar as he reflects at all, or insofar as he has recovered from the giddiness of his propaganda-induced narcosis, and insofar as he is motivated by subjective idealism, will see that his social ideal of culturally and socially impartial aid to education was not only not realized in pure form, and thus shared the insufficiency of all human realizations of the ideal, but that this ideal was already corrupted by ulterior, terroristic motives in its theoretical planning. But the very fact that we can assume this makes it clear that for him the West will have moral standing only if, instead of seeing the zealous pursuit of these ideologically corrupted cultural and social goals, he sees the same dedicated efforts being made in the atmosphere of absolute objectivity and thus gets a convincing picture of a society that is truly interested in human welfare. Only then would the West have an answer to a question which is now latent, but which would certainly become virulent after X-Day. On the other hand, if the only answer the West has to give to the demonic cultural and social zeal of the East is its own failure in the area of culture and social justice, then the receptiveness induced by this skepticism will be immediately destroyed, indeed, it will be driven into a hardened attitude that will produce a heightened missionary passion for the cause of the East and lead to political consequences that are hardly imaginable.

So, no matter how we twist and turn, our Western self-confidence is shaken, and we are challenged to get away from this dreadful quietistic, *laissez faire* attitude that so largely characterizes our approach to this fateful question and is gradually reducing us to "impotence."

To repeat once more the crucial point we have been making: We of the West simply are not in a position to rest on our laurels and assume that the East would be happy to be allowed to share in it by means of an "annexation." There is still too much that is rotten in the state of Denmark to permit us to indulge in that kind of sentimentality. Therefore, instead of asking what we will have to say to the young Communists on X-Day, we should first solve the previous question of what we still must say to ourselves.

Meanwhile, the thought of the time when we shall have to stand up and give an account to the young Communists may have in it a strong power to liberate and challenge us to creative self-criticism.

Only after we have thus gone through an exercise in disillusionment, or if you please, desentimentalization, and come away from this self-examination with a few black-and-blue marks will we be honest enough with ourselves to be entitled to ask what the Western world might at its deepest level have to communicate to the young Communists in the way of genuine impulses to freedom.

I want to say quite emphatically at the beginning of this section that I present these considerations as a Christian. I therefore do not simply start out with the idea of the so-called "free" or democratic West. It would appear to me that these terms come close to being mere clichés. Rather I start from the fact that the so-called Western world acquired its intellectual and moral substance in encounter with the figure of Jesus Christ and that therefore the secularized West is like a machine whose motor has been turned off but still goes on turning for a time, though really only for a limited time. It may be that the de-Christianized West is looking for some other sources of motive power in order to gain new impulse. How far it will get with the substitute religion of existentialism or the social gospel idea of the welfare state, I think I know. But this is not the place to discuss that question. In any case, at the present time, if all the signs are not deceiving, we are living in a strange interim: what we consider movement or even vigorous activity appears to be nothing more than this continued running of the machine after the power has been shut off, while the East has cast about for new driving forces of an ideological kind. I speak therefore from a very definite position of faith.

As for the reference to the metaphysical undermining of the Western world, we need here to take note of some things that Sartre has very rightly pointed out. Sartre rebels against the fraud being perpetrated by the secularized world, which, after having denied God, still wants to hold on to the eternal values of which God was the creator or at least the guarantor. The existentialist is more courageous, he says. The existentialist "thinks it very distressing that God does not exist, because all possibility of finding values in a heaven of ideas disappears along with Him; there can no longer be an *a priori* Good, since there is no infinite and perfect consciousness. Nowhere is it written that the Good exists, that we must be honest, that we must not lie; because the fact is we are on a plane where there are only men."[1] Therefore, Sartre likes to quote Dostoievski: "If there is no God, then everything is allowed." And because everything is allowed, one must fear everything.

On this plane (which in any case must be respected as an honest, hard-headed resumé of secularism), on this plane, I say, the Western world could hardly have anything really liberative to say to the people who have lived under the fear of an ideological tyranny.

This leads us to several points of view from which the West—that is, a West which was conscious of its origin, or better, which was really reflecting upon its origin—would have a constructive message to give to the young Communists on X-Day.

1. The first point of view which would have to play a part in our dialogue with the young Communists I would call the message of confidence. It seems to me to be of crucial importance that we should see very clearly why it is that a man under an ideological dictatorship lives in fear, anxiety, and lack of confidence and trust, and why it is that we in the West do not need to fear the night when the rap on the door will be heard. The question thus raised can be made clear by considering the story of the tower of Babel. I believe that one could interpret the situation of the young Communists for them by making use of this story. Certainly it will hardly be sufficient in the face of the young Communists and their

---

[1] Quoted in Roger Mehl, *Kerygma und Dogma* (1955), 2, p. 156. [Translation from Jean-Paul Sartre, *Existentialism*, tr. by Bernard Frechtman (New York: Philosophical Library, 1947), pp. 26 f. (Trans.)]

frightened, untrusting world to invoke the Western ideal of humanity. It can hardly be assumed that this ideal, which has been filtered through long tradition, cooked over and over again on the hearths of many philosophies, and is now rather lacking in vitamins, is really capable of providing a substitute for the robust principles and hard-boiled practices of Communism. We ought to remember the haunting word of warning once uttered by Franz Grillparzer when he pointed out that it is possible to observe in history a descent or retrogression from divinity to humanity to bestiality. What he is saying is that it is impossible to hold on to the ideal of humanity once its ultimate foundations are taken away. Was not Sartre saying the same thing? It is very noteworthy that every word that we would like to address to the young Communists first becomes a call of repentance to ourselves.

2. The second point of view which would have to determine our encounter with the young Communists on X-Day I would call the message of freedom. The so-called free West still finds the best expression of its democratic ideal in the classical formulation given to it by the French Revolution in the trilogy "liberty, equality, fraternity." But respect for the historical dignity of these ideas must not prevent us from declaring that they can no longer be emblazoned on the banner that would be hoisted at the meeting of East and West on X-Day. Is the principle of liberty, which governs this trilogy of ideals, really capable of playing the role of the supreme value? Eduard Heimann, an American sociologist, in a very profound analysis of recent culture, said, "A system in which liberty is the supreme value will easily degenerate into a dominion of freedom for the *strong* individuals, classes, and races, and at the expense of the *weak* individuals, classes, and races." In other words, does not freedom, which is not exercised in the name and within the framework of ultimate obligations, but rather as an end in itself, lead to the freedom of the stronger and therefore to dictatorship over the weaker, that is, to loss of freedom by the weaker? This is precisely what Marxist social theory asserted in its thesis that when a small owner-class has free control over the means of production this enables them to force their will upon the great mass of nonowners and then on the basis of their enslavement they are in a position to exercise their own freedom to an excessive degree. In this case freedom

would no longer be a universal ideal, but would have become the monopoly of a minority.

Even though one is not a Marxist one will concede that this theory is correct except for one qualification, which Marx himself, of course, did not see, namely, that here freedom is understood as being the supreme value and that there is no longer any ultimate authority, no God in whose name freedom is exercised. Then freedom becomes a license for individual or collective egoism, then it nullifies equality and consequently fraternity also. Freedom which is made an absolute, that is, a freedom that no longer serves and is not bound, becomes a power of destruction.

Therefore, Marxism has made a small change in the order of this trilogy of ideals. In its view the order must be as follows: equality, freedom, fraternity. Here equality means the fundamental equality of all members of the collective. Bolshevism breaks up the natural rock, the organic layers of classes and communities, pulverizes and atomizes them, and then rebakes the ground-up molecules to produce the synthetic stone of the collective. So here equality is nothing more than the co-ordination of the molecule in the collective. But does not the whole process have an amazing similarity to what has happened in the West? Is it not true that these ideas then take on a life of their own and proceed to head for goals that are quite different from those that the ideological dreamers envisioned and desired? For the ideal of equality, which now heads the trilogy, is an abstract and unnatural construction which is to be achieved merely as a forced, dictatorial process of leveling. But when freedom thus becomes a forced thing it nullifies itself from the start, or more precisely, it removes freedom from the sphere of the individual to that of the collective. Then freedom is only the alleged freedom of a class, for example, the dictatorship of the proletariat. But ultimately what else is this dictatorship but the selfish freedom of a group (in this case, the proletariat) to whose higher dignity the individual must sacrifice his own rights? What else is this but a degenerated freedom? Or would you say that it is not degenerate, if the collective in the name of its freedom and its privileges tyrannizes over the individual, depersonalizes him, and thus either victimizes him or turns him into a will-less functionary?

What becomes of the third idea, fraternity, in the course of this process of deterioration hardly needs any further mention. (If we had the space, there might be a certain gruesome attraction in seeing how even the idea of quality simply cannot be maintained as an artificial social construct. We know that nowhere else are there such class distinctions as there are in the Soviet Union. It is an ironical vengeance; it is an example of "the strategy of the Idea."[2] So we ask, are not both the East and the West in the last analysis facing the same crisis, in that both in their own way are sacrificing to false gods, whether it be the golden calf of a deified freedom or worship at the ideological altars of a synthetic equality?

It may be, therefore, that we will sit up and listen when we learn that Luther, Luther the *Christian,* was quite familiar with this trilogy of ideas—but with this noteworthy and very striking difference, that here they occur in a different sequence, namely, fraternity, freedom, equality.[3]

How does Luther come to put brotherly love first? You will note at once that I have made a slight change in the first of the three ideas. The word "fraternity" expresses a principle, and in the immediately personal sphere this is always a somewhat forced construction which is remote from real life—which is what happens when I try to turn love into a principle.

The term Luther uses is brotherly love, and it might also be called neighborly love or love of one's neighbor. But as soon as that term is used, then the theological context to which Luther is referring is immediately clear to the initiate; for love toward my neighbor is always grounded upon the fact that I myself am loved by God and am passing on this love. The wicked servant of whom Jesus speaks in his parable can love his neighbor only if he himself appropriates his lord's forgiveness and always remembers it. Love and forgiveness and openness for my neighbor is therefore nothing less than the passing on of gifts which I myself have previously received. Then the neighbor too becomes something different when he is seen from this aspect. Whereas I naturally judge him merely in terms of his usefulness to me or to society and thus consider only his functional value, under this new aspect he becomes transformed in the sense

---

[2] *List der Idee:* Hegel's phrase for the cunning use the Idea (The World Spirit) makes of men and movements to achieve its goals. (Trans.)

[3] Cf. Johannes Heckel, *Lex Charitatis* (1953), p. 40.

that now he is given the accent of infinity: he is one beloved of God, he is dearly purchased, he is the apple of God's eye, he is sacronsanct.

Love of one's neighbor therefore does not result from a moral decision and effort; it can only be had in faith, that is, it comes into being only by my having found contact with the Father through Jesus Christ.

But then at once we also see how the concepts of freedom and equality relate to this sonship to God; for freedom means that I am directly related to God. That is to say, when my conscience is bound to God, then nothing else and no one else dare rule over me unless this other power has received a mandate from God and is able to prove that it has this authority.

As an example of this I mention the following. In and of itself the state does not have the position of an authority and therefore it does not possess, without further qualification, the power to do with me as it pleases. During the time of the Third Reich this question was as acute for us as it is today for the people under the ideological tyranny of Lenin. True, it is written in Romans 13: "Let every person be subject to the governing authorities." But immediately there is added the reason why we should be subject: the governing authorities have the mandate from God to reward the good and also to punish the evil. Hence the state itself does not represent an ultimate norm; on the contrary, it is itself subject to norms, namely, the commandments of God. So, if I am directly related and responsible to God, in this connection this can only mean that I have the freedom to demand of every authority that makes a claim upon me that it prove its legitimation. For I have the freedom to be obedient only to God and to recognize an authority over myself only if it stands within the same obedience (and thus is not a *norma normans* but rather a *norma normata*). Hence even Luther and Paul are not simply authorities for me; rather they must constantly authenticate the authority of what they say in the light of that to which they are bound, namely, the Holy Scriptures, which is to say, the Lord who has spoken to them.

It was this mystery of authority that constituted the ultimate cause of the church struggle: the Confessing Church under the Hitler dictatorship believed that it was facing a perversion of the state. It observed that the state punished the good and rewarded the evil and hence was reversing its original mandate. It therefore refused to recognize the Third Reich as a state. This makes it clear that every ideological tyranny is by its very nature antichristian, indeed, *must* be antichristian, for in order to exercise power it needs will-less instruments who will allow it to dictate to them what is good and evil, right and wrong. Hitler and Stalin each gave their definitions after their own fashion: God is what is good for my people, or what is good for the world revolution. And Goering went so far as to say: Whoever is Arian, I am for him.

Consequently, the freedom of the children of God is the great offense for every ideological tyranny; for their freedom sets limits upon its totalitarian claim. Here the state is required to prove its legitimation. But this undermines the very foundations of its pretentions and shatters the ground rules of its exercise of power. For the children of God are not the kind of wood from which one can carve puppet functionaries.

My conviction is that this message of the freedom of the children of God is the crucial message that must be carried into all areas where the omnipotence of the state rules. It is the unique, special gospel for the world of the functionaries, because it will enable them to recover and be changed from mere depersonalized instruments into free men.

But none of the battle cries of the West about the derogation of human dignity under ideological dictatorship will convince the young Communists as long as their own sense of personal dignity has not grown up within them and thus provided them with a spontaneous immunization against dictatorship. But how can the sense of personal dignity arise except through this message of freedom? And how can this message seriously promise freedom if it is not at the same time the joyful message that we are the children of God? For the opposite of slavery is not freedom from all restraint (this soon leads, as the parable of the prodigal son shows, to new chains and entanglements). The opposite of slavery, as Paul shows us, is sonship. Freedom is not the opposite of restraint and submission; it is a special kind of bondage. Bondage to powers, institutions, and men enslaves. Bondage to God liberates. For freedom does not mean (to quote Paul de Lagarde once more) that one may do what one wills, but rather that one may become what one should. But we are called to become that image which God intended us to be. To fulfill this purpose of God, this destiny, and to leave all else to be added unto us, this is the only thing that deserves the name of freedom.

On this basis then, we could go on almost indefinitely expanding on what we shall have to say to the young Communists and, most of all, to ourselves.

In conclusion we may at least indicate one further problem area, in order that we may get some idea of the infinite profusion of ideas and impulses that open up for us when we take this road. This last problem area would include the freedom of science. That is to say, science too is related to the mystery of freedom and redemption. Christ frees a man to be objective. Surely it is a remarkable thing that science and technology have, besides the root that lives in the native soil of Greek culture, another root in the Christian West. What might be the reason for this? The reason probably is that through Christ the world was stripped of its demonic character, (*entdämonisiert*), so that men lost their fear of it, gained the ability to be calm and objective, and thus were able to look at it from the observer's point of view. A Hindu, for example, could never study the anatomy of the cow, since the cow is holy and he would necessarily fear it. It is true that this benefit of objectivity gained through the redemption continues to survive for a time after secularized man has long since cut himself off from the source of this freedom. But when the ultimate consequences of this secularism are drawn he again abolishes freedom of investigation, and for the very simple reason that the unredeemed man is afraid of the truth. The dread of his boundless loneliness, which Jean Paul once described so vividly in *Siebenkäs*, compels him to surround himself only with creatures of his own making, not only with men who are his submissive functionaries and have given up their freedom, but also with truths which are his creations, that is to say, with truths and principles which are not allowed to call him in question, but only to corroborate him. National Socialism demonstrated this for us in the way in which it dealt with religious truth. It emphatically made religious truth its creature in that it demanded that religion be conformable to man. Bolshevism demonstrates it in the way in which it degrades scientific truth by making it its creature, not only humanistic scientific truth, as it does when it falsifies world history so that it looks like a one-way street to its own ideological goal, but also with the truth of natural science. When a certain authoritative school of thought in Bolshevistic botany teaches the inheritance of acquired characteristics, this is nothing else but an attempt to abuse a biological truth for ideological ends. For the philosophical axiom of Bolshevism states that man's being is stamped by his social conditions, that is, by his milieu. But if it is really his being that is thus dependent upon his milieu, then this must also express itself in his biological substance in that what he acquires from society, from his environment, passes over into the biological process of heredity. Here we see what an unfree, unredeemed science is, a science that is not free to be objective. Here we have a plain illustration of the ideological dogmatization of life.

The one important thing we have been trying to convey throughout this whole multiplex train of thought is this: that it is an open question whether X-Day will be a day of blessing or a day of curse. A naïve anticipation of this day that touches only the level of emotion or patriotic enthusiasm dangerously overlooks the seriousness of the real problem. X-Day will be an unhappy, cursed day, it will lead to devastating historical consequences, if we proceed with smug Western self-confidence to impose annexation upon the people beyond the Iron Curtain and bestow upon them certain blessings which have long since become empty shells in our own hands. It will be a day of blessing if we are willing to face the convinced Communist and examine the credibility of our own foundations, if we undertake some hard revisions, and are ourselves prepared to change.

X-Day will confront us with a host of political, economic, and organizational problems. But all this would be putting the cart before the horse, if this were all that was to be done. The secret blessing and the secret challenge of this day is that it compels us to reflect upon the ultimate questions of our own life. For the real truth is this: in the end it is not a matter of the Christian West— after all, that is only a geographical, cultural, historical concept—but rather a question of myself. And when I have to deal with this question of destiny I can speak only in the first person. For it is I who have been called by name.

VI

FREEDOM AND LOVE OF ONE'S NEIGHBOR: A CRITIQUE OF THE IDEA OF "HUMAN RELATIONS"

ONE OF THE MOST PROMISING FEATURES OF THE INTELLECTUAL SITUATION after the German collapse of 1945 has been the fact that in almost every sphere of life there has been a renewed search for the ultimate foundations of life. The creative urge behind this questioning and searching is undoubtedly the knowledge, or at least the feeling, that the ideological tyranny that lies behind us and the collapse of that tyranny were not caused by any accidental political circumstances, but that both point to a very deep-seated focus of infection in the very foundations of our understanding of existence. Our attitude to the ultimate, essential meaning-giving values of life must have been dangerously undermined for our nation not to have been immunized against the triumph of might over right and the primacy of biological forces over spiritual and moral standards to the extent that would have seemed proper for an old, cultured nation and a member of the Christian West.

In the same way we felt instinctively that the catastrophic end of the totalitarian state could not be explained as being the result of a particular constellation of obvious events (such as the exhaustion of the armament potential, the decimation of human life, or the failure to construct the atom bomb in time), but that this regime had reduced itself to absurdity by ignoring the basic truths of life, and especially the truths regarding the state, the law, and human nature as a whole. There may be a connection between this sense of crisis in the ultimate foundations of life and the fact that the collapse was followed by an almost unanimous endeavor to find a radical reorientation in the most widely varying areas of life:

The *statesmen,* disquieted by the deadly consequences of a political system that considered itself to be its own law, searched for some ultimate standard for their actions; they began to inquire into the competence of ethical and theological categories and therefore into regulative principles.

The *jurists* deeply sensed the crisis created by a conception of justice in which the law was positivistically laid down by the holders of power, and looked for some ultimate court of appeal; they called for a legal authority oriented upon natural law.

The *doctors* recognized that mere biological categories alone are not sufficient foundation for their work of healing. But as they discovered more and more that man is the real object of their profession, the question of the meaning and essence of human existence loomed upon the horizon of their thinking.

The *technologists,* too, observed that their problems were not merely a matter of technological progress, but that they have really terrifying implications for the advancement and the destruction of human existence, so that technology is completely ambivalent and that therefore it, too, is confronted with the ultimate questions.

It would appear, as we said above, that it is a promising thing that these foundational questions should have become so vital to us, and that the collapse of 1945 should therefore represent a turning point of profound importance in the history of thought.

The fact that industry too is concerned about the fundamental questions of existence is expressed not so much in its concern for social reform—rather this tendency which is at work in it has its exact counterparts in all highly civilized nations—as in the attempt to understand the background of these social reforms and to take them into account. But the question with the deepest background of all is the question of the essence of man. For it is precisely this man who is object of all social action and reform.

The alternatives within which this question normally moves may be defined as follows: Is man merely a producer and is his rank and dignity, and thus his role in the process of management and production, determined by the degree of his achievement as a producer? Or does he have a dignity which is quite independent of the volume of his production? In other words, is "man" (*humanitas*) merely the code word for a specifically defined functional value within the social structure, which would make humanity merely the means to achieve an end, namely, production, or is it independent of all achievements, that is, an end in itself? Historically speaking, the Bolshevist ideology decides in favor of the view that man is the performer of functions, while the so-called "free world"—at least in its fundamental program—takes the stand that man (*humanitas*) has intrinsic value. How these two concepts can become intermingled in actual practice despite the program that is adopted we shall discuss later.

But whatever decision is made at this point, it is obvious that this is not only a matter of mere processes within a philosophical theory or within a person's inner attitudes, but rather that this anthropological decision has a determinative and very real influence upon the actual facts of economic and social-political organization.

But that at least the realistic side of the problem has been recognized—even by those who have not penerated to the deeper levels of the problem—is apparent in the fact that the term "human relations" has become a popular slogan. In any case, the term itself predicates the fact that "human relations" play a determinative part in public life and especially in economic life and that therefore they play a part which is on a par with, if not above that of, the technical side of production and management, the factors of raw materials, labor, and marketing.

This purely empirical observation that human relations play an exceedingly real part and therefore must also be very carefully planned and organized is by no means new. What is modern in it is only the systematized technique which has been elaborated to cope with the problem. In fact, the term "human relations" expressly emphasizes the *technical* side of the manipulation by which human relations are shaped in an organizational way. From the historical point of view, it may be disputed whether this technique originated in America; in any case its systematic elaboration into a technique is peculiarly American. Since "human relations" in this signification of the term is an imported idea, it cannot be regarded as characteristic of the German or even the European cultural situation, unless the very fact that it has been imported allows us to draw indirect conclusions of this kind.

But the important and characteristic thing for our inner situation is undoubtedly the way in which we deal with the idea of "human relations." The very fact that this idea is argued about and even more, the way in which it is discussed provide us with important clues to the diagnosis of our spiritual condition. But though we shall give consideration to this analysis in what follows, it would seem to be much more important to look for the deeper criteria which will enable us to cope with this problem both theoretically and practically.

In any case, the problem as such strikes us as an exceedingly profitable one, since it gives us the opportunity to clarify the way in which industry has been brought up against the fundamental questions of philosophical, indeed of theological, thought.

It seems to me to be important objectively, and, above all, fair, for me to put my cards on the table at once and make it clear that I propose to deal with the problem as a Christian. This declaration is very important, because the question of human relations can be viewed only from the particular understanding of man which we always bring to the problem. And though this view that we bring with us may indicate a certain bias, it nevertheless does not have the character of a dogmatic axiom, which the reader must either accept or reject—and in the latter case, stop reading at once. On the contrary, we start from the position that what we have called the Christian bias must either stand or fall on this problem of human relations. To the extent that it proves its validity the reader will feel attracted to give serious consideration to the presuppositions and standards of judgment here set out.

Human relations have to do with interhuman relationships. I may be permitted this rather banal tautology because it immediately leads to a theological problem, since the idea of "neighbor" and "love of one's neighbor" is normative for the Christian understanding of interhuman relationships. In this sense, then, it should certainly be profitable to relate the substance of this idea of human relations to this analogue from the field of Christian thought, namely, love of one's neighbor.

Perhaps we may even go a step further, however, and, in order to dissociate ourselves from all pious instincts and traditional moral standards, subject the concept of love to a more reliable examination in the light of what Christianity calls "love of one's enemy."

The commandment "love your enemies" has always constituted a certain offense to the ordinary human mind insofar as it is taken to be a demand to perform a somewhat forced mental act. In the first place, how can anybody command me to love? Is not love a spontaneous act, which occurs "of itself," quite independent of any external pressure? And if this is so, how can I be enjoined to love, of all people, my enemies? After all, the spontaneous reaction that I have from my enemy is that of immediate defensiveness. So, obviously, when I am commanded to love my enemy, the only way I can fulfill this command is to act contrary to my basic instincts or simply to suppress them. This is the reason why there is a tendency to regard love toward one's enemies as a source of complexes and forced, convulsive behavior.

The fact is that all these objections are justified if we look at love toward one's enemy from the moral point of view. All the more important is it, therefore, to see exactly what Christ meant by this "love for one's enemy."

The crucifixion scene provides us with a very significant model of what it means to love one's enemy. When Christ in the presence of his tormentors prays to the Father, "Forgive them, for they know not what they do," there can be no doubt that this is an expression of love for one's enemy, namely, a concern for their salvation, which they were in danger of losing through their shameful conduct. There can be no doubt, however, that this love was not the result of a kind of victory over himself, in the sense that the Crucified simply "repressed" his instinct for self-preservation, his natural defensive reaction to his tormentors. On the contrary, what determined his reaction was this: Christ saw in his tormentors not merely the representatives of hostile forces arrayed against him, but rather the children of his Father who were pursuing a path that could only lead to disaster. He saw in them the image of what God intended them to be and saw that it was about to be ruined. He saw, therefore, that the real "being" of his enemies did not consist merely in their being representatives of the hostile front; rather he saw through and beyond the functions they were then performing against him and recognized in them the real human design that God intended, namely, children of his Father in heaven and thus his brothers.

When he looked upon them, their destructive functions became, as it were, transparent, and he saw behind these externals the original image of the child-relationship intended and desired by God, his relationship to his tormentors was fundamentally altered. When he prayed for them and thus broke through to love for one's enemies, this was not based upon an act of will that led to victory over himself. It was rather the result of a new way of seeing, a real act of seeing. In that his gaze was directed to the real being in other people he penetrated to that bond with them which is stronger than all the separating factors that originate in the functions they are performing at the moment. Love for one's enemies is therefore not the product of a motor impulse of our will; it originates rather in a new kind of optics, a new kind of eyesight.

We may illustrate what happens here with certain analogies in ordinary human life.

In an account of an incident in the First World War we find a description of the following scene. The author tells us that during an assault he dropped into a shell hole between the front lines, his bayonet fixed for attack. To his horror, he found in the shell hole a severely wounded English soldier, and his first reaction was the almost instinctive one of the battle-trained soldier. Only when he realized how badly wounded was the dying man did his attitude toward him suddenly change. His changed attitude was further stimulated when the other man indicated that he was thirsty, making him realize that here was a fellow human being, suffering the need that is common to all men. He gave him a drink from his canteen and received in return a look of gratitude from his suffering enemy. The wounded man then indicated, more by gestures than words, that he wanted to see his wallet. The German soldier felt around in the man's uniform until he found it and drew it out. As he did so, there fell out a number of family pictures which the dying man wanted to look at, apparently the pictures of his wife and children. The unspeakably tender look on the man's face made it clear that this was so.

In this little incident a sudden change took place in the writer's way of seeing things. His first reaction to the soldier lying in the shell hole was that of his fighting instinct prepared for hostility, seeing in the other man only the representative of the enemy and reacting accordingly. Then what followed made it clear to him that the other man was not to be characterized merely by the fact that he belonged to the enemy front, but rather that he was a human being: he was a beloved husband who would be mourned, he was the father of his children and the son of his parents. And once he was seen as the center of these various relationships, he suddenly became a fellow human being and that put him in a different dimension from that of the battlefield.

So in that shell hole there came into being a human relationship which illustrates an essential point of love for one's enemy: the author of this account did not have to be forced by any humanitarian imperative to be "human" toward his enemy. On the contrary, the kindliness he showed became a spontaneous act simply because his way of "seeing" was changed: behind the image of the fighting enemy, against whom his fighting instinct was mobilized, there rose the image of a man to whom he was bound by a primal, innate relationship and with whom he knew that he was related in an ultimate solidarity of suffering, of love, and of being loved.

This basic observation is of utmost importance for all anthropology, for it teaches us that man always exists in two dimensions. First, he is the bearer of some very definite functions, which he regards to be either favorable or inimical to him. Accordingly, he reacts to the other person in a friend-enemy relationship. Secondly, however, man also exists in another dimension, namely, the distinctively human sphere apart from all his functions. He is the neighbor, who has his highly personal relation to God, who experiences his highly personal sufferings and joys, and ultimately dies his own highly personal death.

This analogy should have made it clear to us what love for our enemy means in the Christian sense. It is not a matter of overcoming spontaneous emotions by moral means, but rather of seeing another dimension in which this other person who is hostile to me *also* has his being. For Christ this dimension was characterized by the fact that the other person was both a creature and a child of God and that the functions he was performing were threatening to turn him into a distorted image of his real self. But in that Christ saw in the other person the original image and therefore the real person within, he was enabled to love and was free to love him.

It is therefore quite evident that the consideration of these two dimensions has a tremendously fundamental importance for our interhuman relationships. This can be illustrated as follows. After what has been said above, it should be obvious that when we find ourselves at variance with others over a cause or a certain function it is very important to see the human being behind the cause or the function he is performing.

Variance and disagreement must necessarily exist. They are constantly occurring, and they express themselves in distinct sociological structures and institutions: there are parties and there are creeds. All these manifestations are expressions of divisions and distinctions. Even Christ himself is no exception to this rule of disagreement. What we have just described as his love for his enemies did not prevent him from delivering diatribes against the Pharisees, nor deter him from casting the moneychangers out of the Temple. Here we have instances of clear dissociation from certain attitudes and functions of the other person.

This "seeing the real man," which is so exemplarily evident in Christ, therefore does not bring with it any blunting of the sharp differences over factual and functional matters. Rather these disagreements must be borne, that is, they must be decided on the practical level of political, scientific, or religious convictions.

It makes a fundamental difference, however, whether I regard the man who is opposed to me as being "defined" by the thing he stands for—that is, whether I think I have said everything there is to be said about him if I describe him as being the representative of this or that cause or function—or whether I am convinced that, entirely apart from what he stands for or fights for, he is a man, that he is a person who is loved by his wife and children, a person who bears his own personal sorrows and also has his own peculiar joys, and that in all this he has his own special relationship and destiny with God, just as I have mine.

In modern society with its division of labor this is a question which we have been aware of for several decades, at least in broad outline. As the classes of society grew farther apart because of the different worlds in which they worked, their different standards of living and thus also their different interests and outlook upon life, even militantly lining up against each other under the banner of the class struggle, the opposing social partners saw in each other only the representatives of hostile groups and selfish points of view. The fact that the worker was also a human being became an idea that was remote from the minds of the employers and property owners, just as for the worker—and this is less often pointed out—it became quite unreal to think of the employer as being a human being. The bourgeois regarded the so-called fourth estate,[1] or lower classes, as merely a mass of insignificant people with primitive pleasures and a red flag which they carried through the streets at the head of an organized mob in order to undermine the foundations of human society. The worker in turn saw on the other side only the gorged profiteer lolling on the soft cushions in his mansion, at the worker's expense.

The resulting tension on the human level naturally had its economic and business side too, for it is stating the obvious to say that an optimum social efficiency can be achieved only if the partners work together instead of against each other. It may therefore have been not humanitarian motives but simply economic self-interest that prompted both parties to remove the tension between them. The employer knows that harmonious relations promote pleasure in one's work and that happiness in one's work results in increased production. And the worker on his part is also well aware that it is only the prosperity that results from this increased production which can raise his own standard of living. So at this point the interests of all parties in the social contract run parallel. The higher the profits and therefore the higher the production that produces the profits, the more secure will be the economic foundations for all participants in the economic system and so much the greater will be the proportion paid out in wages, even though one may be dissatisfied with the ratio between the employer's profits

---

[1] Not the Press, as in modern usage. (Trans.)

and the wages of employees.

We said before that it was probably the idea of self-interest that injected this problem of human relations into the production process. That it is a matter of self-interest and expediency to take the human factor into account is apparent from the fact that Stalin made it one of the favorite themes of his speeches, and that in consequence even Bolshevism speaks of "positive humanism."

Fritz Lieb, the Basle philosopher of religion and one of the foremost West European experts on Russia and Bolshevism, in his book on Russia[2] gave eloquent expression to the opinion that the present trend of development in Bolshevism was toward a new humanistic conception. He thought that it was possible to detect in Bolshevism a definite tendency, despite the increasing power of technology which threatened to destroy the initiative and character of human personality, which showed that it was beginning to place an entirely new emphasis upon man, and was coming to see with increasing clarity the superiority of the human element over the material, mechanical, and technological. Lieb quotes speeches by Stalin from the years 1934-1935 as being particularly characteristic of this trend. We quote the crucial passages here because they compel us to give an interpretation which is the exact opposite of that advanced by Lieb.

In one of these speeches of Stalin the following words occur: "In the period of reconstruction technology decides everything." This was necessary in order to create a broad technological basis in all fields of work for socialistic reconstruction. But—said Stalin—many had interpreted this statement in a mechanical sense, that is, they understood it only in the sense that if as many machines as possible were accumulated this would be all that the slogan required. This is incorrect. Technology cannot be separated from the men who set the technology in motion. Technology without men is dead. The slogan "In the period of reconstruction technology decides everything" does not envisage naked technology, but rather technology with men at its head who have mastered technology.

But it follows from this, said Stalin, that even though it was true that previously a one-sided emphasis had been laid upon technology,

---

[2] Fritz Lieb, *Russland unterwegs* (Bern, 1945).

that is, upon machines, now it was necessary to put the stress on the
men who have mastered technology.

We must protect every capable and expert functionary, protect him and
further his growth . . . , carefully educate and train the men, properly
distribute and organize them in the production process, and so organize
the wage system that it will strengthen the men who play the decisive role
in production and impel them to improve their qualifications—this is
what we need in order to create a great army of technologically productive cadres.

In these words of Stalin's we have an excellent example of a particular way of emphasizing the human element. That is to say, we
must realize that this call for a new humanism is not based upon the
idea that man has a right to any privileged dignity above the material
world of technical apparatus. On the contrary, his value is based
merely upon the fact that he represents the hierarchical apex in this
world of apparatus. Thus man is not emphasized here as having a
unique status over against the world of things, but rather is merely
being, as it were, re-evaluated within this world of things. And this
is done on the ground that the man who controls the apparatus is
more important than the apparatus which he is controlling.

It is possible to express the difference between this anthropology
of Stalin and the Christian view of man in a precise statement by
saying that in the Stalinist view it is not a matter of the infinite
"value" of the soul of man, which follows from his being a child of
God, or is a consequence of man's being in the biblical sense "bought
with a price," but rather of what value can be got out of a man, of his
"utility." And as soon as this concept of utility emerges, the consequence is obvious. In normal cases in which a person is healthy and
capable of performing a function he will be accorded certain social
privileges because of his utility. (We need only think of the Soviet
heroes of labor, and types like Hennecke and Stakhanov and the
social prestige they were given.) But when it comes to invalidism and
old age then inevitably the question arises of how to scrap and
liquidate a life that no longer has any utility. And the corresponding
practice of Bolshevism shows how these consequences work out
almost automatically. Classes of human beings who no longer have
any value to Bolshevistic society, such as the bourgeoisie, the aristoc-
racy, or prisoners of war who are no longer able to work are, quite

logically, put on a starvation diet and allowed to die. Essentially, this has nothing to do with a moral breakdown of character or unusual cruelty; it is inherent in the very structure of this Stalinist view of man.

These two terms "the value of man" and "the utility of man" are therefore the key terms in the anthropological problem that emerges here. We shall be well advised to regard this little illustration drawn from the world of Bolshevism as an unusually crude example, but it does not lose any of its value as an example because of its crudeness. On the contrary, it is a good thing to use this example in order to clarify our own "Western" situation.

As the example shows us, there are obviously two entirely different motives for this interest in, and concern for, human beings, which must necessarily appear in any economic system.

1. On the one hand, this interest in the human element arises from a fear that man's very "humanness" is being threatened by certain developments in modern technology. Here I am thinking, for example, of the division of labor which no longer makes it possible for a man to have the same direct, meaningful relation to his "work" which the craftsman had in the classical sense. I am also thinking of the tendency to deal with people in the mass that comes with technology, and further of the degeneration of recreation which is a concomitant of this dealing with people in masses and is increasingly becoming less a means of gathering oneself together than a diversion and a distraction. Because one fears that this constitutes an ultimate threat to human existence one may feel called upon to provide for human needs and strive for certain social forms of living which will protect the intrinsic value of the individual person (such as a certain standard of living, individual ownership of homes, provision for care in illness, personal concern, all of which bring about a correspondingly personal relationship and thus counteract the tendency toward depersonalization).

2. On the other hand, a completely opposite form of interest in the human element may be motivated by the purely economic interest in increasing the volume of production and sales. For there can be no question that a healthy, integral concern for human beings is a factor in the economic potential.

An interesting example of the extent to which this integral, personal concern for the individual has an economic aspect is given by Professor A. Gasser of St. Gallen.[3] He gives an account of experiments carried out in the American electrical industry under the direction of the Department of Industrial Research of Harvard University, the object being to eliminate everything that would hinder the work process (temperature, lighting, location of work benches, etc.); in other words, to rationalize the whole operation thoroughly and consistently. The shops were literally turned into clinics in which the most painstaking diagnostic and therapeutic methods were employed. The results were satisfactory and the volume of production increased. It may have been a certain psychological curiosity which then prompted them to ask: What will happen if we eliminate all these forms of rationalization which we have introduced? This was done in certain departments, and the level of production remained unchanged. It was supposed, probably quite correctly, that it was not actually the rationalization which led to the increased production, but rather the personal concern for the workers which was involved in these experiments. For all this a complicated, psychological interview technique had been required, which had to do not only with the working operations but also with the personal aspects of the worker's life. The worker saw that interest was being taken in him and his way of working and that he was not being exploited merely as a labor unit or used simply as a means to an end.

In a time when there is this tendency to take methodical advantage of every chance of successs, the logical consequence of this discovery is that now business not only rationalizes the apparatus of production and the apparatus of management as a whole, but also rationalizes these human relations which are so important economically, or, to put it even more pointedly, it cultivates and manages men. This process describes exactly the essence of "human relations."

These observations bring us up squarely with the decisive theological difference which we referred to above.

In the theological view, which is concerned with preserving human existence from the pull of collectivistic depersonalization, we have our eye on what we have called the "value" of man—his value in the

---

[3] *Zeitschrift für handelswissenschaftliche Forschung* (1950), Heft 8, p. 364.

sense of his being made in the image of God and being bought with a price.

In the other view, which is concerned only with increasing the volume of production and economic advantage, it is the motive of "utility" that is operative, even though the ultimate consequences which are undoubtedly inherent in this motive are not drawn in the tamed and more restraining custom of the West.

At this point I should like to make a small reservation. The alternative between value and utility in the form in which it is stated above is constructed theoretically and therefore is oriented upon the "pure case." In fact it occurs only in transitional forms, which can be justified as such. For naturally even the employer who is aware of the infinite "value" of the human being in the sense of personal dignity can also figure that encouragement of this value will be economically profitable. This sidelong glance at the profit to be obtained from preserving human values certainly cannot be forbidden, any more than it is considered wrong by Holy Scripture, which says that "sin is a reproach to any people," or that he who honors father and mother contributes to the ongoing of life on earth and his own life, and thus helps to preserve the orders of existence. The salient point is rather the initial actuating motive: whether this concern for the human element is only a means to the end of obtaining economic gain or whether it represents an end in itself, which then also yields, in the form of a by-product as it were, important economic results. We must therefore be warned against the misunderstanding that we are looking upon respect for human dignity and striving for economic gain as two mutually exclusive opposites. This is out of the question. So much the more, however, should we emphasize that the motivation, the mainspring of our action must be clearly seen in each particular case.

It appears to us to be exceedingly significant that, though this alternative of "pure cases" which we have set up is of fundamental importance, even in a purely realistic and practical sense, it never appears in this direct form in life as we see it. We can imagine a business firm organized upon the cynical principle of the utility of man being described in a picture story in an illustrated magazine, and the same thing being done with another firm built on the principle of concern for human values. In principle, the two picture stories would not be different. In both one would see canteens decorated with flowers and attractive, modern workshops. One would probably also see pictures of the firms' athletic fields, company-owned dwellings, and company picnics. In both one would find smiling, healthy-looking employees who seemed to be perfectly content with their life. So from the point of view of normal, everyday life the fundamental difference would not show up. These two infinitely different attitudes with respect to man could lead to an identical social structure. Nevertheless, we have seen what widely differing decisions and diametrically opposed consequences are hidden behind these identical structures.

This is one of the cases in which that which is written almost invisibly between the lines of life becomes tremendously real. For the result of this kind of rationalized humanity and social management of men is distrust. Although these forms of rationalization undoubtedly bring with them some lightening of labor, they can also express a decided contempt for man. This need not be so, as has been made clear, and perhaps in most cases is not even probable; but it *can* be so. The purpose behind these rationalizations may be sensed, and employees are disgruntled by it.

Some explanation of this can be found in what the rationalization experts say repeatedly concerning the distrust that the workers show toward them. The somewhat skeptical question in the minds of the workers is, "What are they going to do now to exploit us in some tricky way?" However unfair this question may be in most cases, it is nevertheless significant that it is asked at all, for it suggests that there may be a double motive for introducing these rationalizing measures. And again we can construct this double motivation only in the form of "pure cases." But here too this construction can be of some help to us.

In the first place, rationalization can serve to lighten labor. Proper illumination, proper location of the place where a man works, simplification of the work process, all these things save the worker's expenditure of energy, both physical and mental.

K. Pentzlin once referred to this aspect of rationalization in a very striking way when he said:

As far as I am concerned the ideal of rationalization is to be found in that passage in Adam Smith's standard work on social economy in which he describes how a young boy whose job was to tend a steam engine was required to keep pulling a string at definite intervals in order to let off steam. The boy discovered that the movement of pulling the string coincided precisely with the movement of one of the connecting rods which moved automatically with the engine, so he tied his string to this connecting rod and went off to play. This, after all, is the very essence of rationalization! We must do everything that will indulge idleness and this urge to play![4]

If, instead of using Pentzlin's deliberately playful and humorous style, we simply say that we are striving to lighten the labor, we shall have stated clearly one of the motives of rationalization.

The other, opposite motive of rationalization is merely to increase productivity and to justify the raising of "quotas" on the lines of the Stakhanov and Hennecke labor methods.

Here again it must be pointed out that these two motives cannot be separated, but that the worker has a very sensitive instinct that tells him which of these two motives is foremost in the rationalization schemes of which he is the object.

If we now take seriously our conclusion that the rationalization processes affect not only the apparatus but also the human beings engaged in the production process, and if we remember that these rationalization measures are ambivalent, that is, ambiguous and capable of being interpreted in two ways, we come to the inevitable conclusion that the rationalization of human relations is no easy matter. For, because of this ambivalence, it is always possible that the man who is thus exposed to these social reforms and labor-saving devices may feel that he is being subjected to a very subtle kind of human contempt and cynicism. And obviously no genuine communication can be established on the basis of this contempt for human values, which, as we have seen, is always a possible factor in the situation. But this shows that there is no simple way to organize human relations.

I say "no simple way" intentionally. That is to say, human relations most certainly cannot be organized where man is regarded as a means to an end and is then organized as such. Kant said that it is the supreme immorality to use man as a means to an end (prostitution, slavery), since this is to miss the fundamental meaning of his existence and to misuse him in an excess of contempt for humanity.

---

[4] K. Pentzlin, *"Rationalisierung—eine Erfindung des Teufels?"* in H. Thielicke and K. Pentzlin, *Mensch und Arbeit im technischen Zeitalter*, (Tübingen, 1954), pp. 32 f.

For this reason "human" relations can never be organized if men are organized as means to an end and therefore organized in an inhuman way. So we repeat, there is no simple way to organize human relations.

There is, however, another way of organizing human relations which is entirely possible. All education of children, for example, consists of a sum of organizational procedures, ranging from providing clothing and food for infants to co-operation with the school. But the point is that in this case the child itself is the end, and in a clearly defined and proper way, the object of this organization. I even have to organize my marriage on the basis of human relations. This begins as soon as I fall in love. I have to make dates and I have to arrange my work to meet them. I may even have to take the meteorological angle into account and choose an evening when there is a full moon. I have to secure theater tickets, make all kinds of arrangements, get my hair cut, manicure my nails, and so on.

But here again we are confronted with the ambiguous character of organization. It is genuine and "human" when I love and seek to make this love a reality, that is, when I devise ways and means by which it may be lived and put into practice, in other words, when these ways and means are the organized forms of my love. And it is "inhuman" when I proceed to organize a prudential marriage or a marriage of convenience, that is, when the other person is only a means to a nonmarital, inhuman, selfish end. And it is this inhuman purpose, this deceitful side of human relations that has largely caused their breakdown.

The extent to which human relations have become a kind of racket and thus the extent to which an originally sound idea has degenerated into a kind of "inhumanity" is indicated by the large number of institutions which have set themselves up as experts on "human relations," operating with large staffs of managers. They send out questionnaires, one of which I quote from, from memory. In this particular case a group of industrialists were being asked to indicate what kind of a Christmas speech they preferred. In order that this Christmas speech might be properly prepared answers were to be given to questions like these: What type should the speaker be (tall or short, fat and pleasant or ascetically angular—for naturally each type has its own style of speaking). Then further they were asked to indicate whether the speech should be neutral or have a religious tone, whether reference should be made to trade-union relations or not. If so, should it be polemical or friendly, and so on. One can well imagine that this synthetic product of a laboratory of "human relations" did *not* hit the mark and in any case certainly could not touch the nerve of humanity since it originated from an "inhuman" source.

I cite another instance, this time an American example, and I do this only because in America the problem of human relations has been tackled very energetically, both in its positive and negative forms, and also because the experimentation has there been largely completed, and therefore Europe ought to take advantage of this American experience which they have gathered as much on our behalf as on their own. Pentzlin is fond of saying that we should not copy America, but rather understand what has been done there. In a social studies report he says,

We saw factories so constructed that they could only have sprung from the idea that man is a technological means, a mechanism that is utilized and regulated like a machine. In that the human factor is investigated, cultivated, and economically utilized man becomes a mechanism which is constantly being probed, tested, and subjected to questionnaires and opinion polls, good for nothing more than economic and statistical exploitation. And it is this dissolving of personality, carried out, as it were, against its will, in the name of cultivation of personality and in the name of "human relations" that robs it of its power to resist communism, faith-healing, demagogy, and all the fripperies of civilization.

(Compare this with the similar failure to grasp the substance of human relations in the Kinsey Reports.)

After having taken stock in this way it is important to state clearly the theological implications. When human relations are in good order this always has its effect on the community, that is, on the social structure, social efficiency, and the social product. The effect is the by-product of the main goal, which is the preservation of the wholeness of personality. But where human relations are pragmatically managed and manipulated this order is radically changed. For then what we have just called the by-product or secondary result, namely, increase in the volume of production and sales, becomes the real aim, and the conservation of individuality becomes merely a means to this end.

This may seem to be a very subtle and almost sophistical distinction, but again the effect of it is like enlarging a small picture to gigantic proportions with a pantograph.

We can see that this is true, and the extent to which it is true, if we stop to consider the familiar maxim of the Nazi regime: "Good is what is good for my people." This maxim is based on the primary observation that the good is always the shrewdest and the most profitable thing to do. Many of our proverbial sayings, like "Honesty is the best policy," bear this out. Undoubtedly what these sayings were really meant to convey was that the good has value in itself, that it has its own intrinsic and specific importance, but that the utility which goes along with this good, and is perceived by anyone who is shrewd enough to do so, is again a by-product of the real good. If we apply this to the maxim of National Socialist "ethics"—"Good is what is good for my people"—we see at once what has happened in this statement: again the by-product has been turned into the main thing and the good is defined as good only insofar as it is good or profitable to the people. It is obvious that this shifting of a small but decisive nuance results in a total transvaluation of values. For now the good is to be defined in purely pragmatic terms. It loses its constancy and thus renders those who hold this view unworthy of credibility; it disqualifies them as partners in any kind of negotiation and makes them unpredictable. The historical consequences of this we all were able to see in Hitler and the origin of the Second World War.

The same total destruction of all values and the complete reversal of all basic principles can also be illustrated by reference to the following statement of Jesus Christ: "Seek first his kingdom and his righteousness, and all these things shall be yours as well." This statement very definitely and firmly points up this distinction between the focal and the marginal, the main thing and the by-product. The main thing is the kingdom of God, that is, the relation to the Ultimate which is binding upon us all. Once our life has been brought into line with this decisive basic relationship all the other relationships, values, goods, follow of themselves. It would be completely wrong, for example, to say that it has been found that an affirmative attitude to the kingdom of God, or piety or being a Christian, bring along with them ordered relationships, social productivity, and the like, and therefore it is desirable to maintain good relationships with the kingdom of God. This is to turn upside down the relation of chief product and by-product and it can be seen in one of the most pernicious maxims of the modern "manager's religion," which is that "the people must be allowed to have their religion." Here, just as in the National Socialist maxim quoted above, the ruling factor is the pragmatic observation that a religious basis for life tends to have a good effect upon the social and individual management of this life and that therefore religion should be fostered and supported. This postulate that religion should be maintained is one that can be put forward by any cynic and any atheist—in the name of the reversal of values mentioned above. This again shows what a distortion results when the distinction between main product and by-product is ignored.

In any case, we insist that this distinction is the pivotal point in our argument, namely, that it would be disastrous to conclude that human relations should be fostered simply because wholesome human relations are good for the economic processes. This extremely short-sighted logic overlooks the distinction we have indicated. Therefore in actual practice it leads, not to the healing of human relations, but rather produces foci of distrust. This is because the man who is manipulated and managed in accord with this theory of human relations immediately senses its purpose and knows very well that he is being thrown on the scrap heap under the pretext of a procedure that looks on the surface to be a constructive social measure. Perhaps this may be the reason back of American experience that frequently the very businesses which have fostered intensive social programs suffer from strikes, when these are the places one would least expect to find them. May it not be that it is precisely these hidden factors which we have discussed that are operative here?

One thing we can say positively, and that is that this discovery of the importance of wholesome human relations can be turned to good account economically only if it has previously been turned to good account in the personal and human sense, that is to say, if one has first entered into a genuine encounter with the man, with one's neighbor.

The size of many businesses entails a corresponding anonymity of the executives. The more anonymous a board of directors is the less it is able to demonstrate its real attitude to the persons in their employ. This constitutes a real difficulty and ways must be sought to overcome it. In any case, however, it remains true that only where this immediate human contact is evident, beyond all organizational measures, only within the context of individual personalities meeting as neighbor to neighbor, can the genuine human relations, which the mere "human relations" managers seek for in vain, grow.

Actually, it is very promising and fortunate that there are things in life that elude all rationalization and all organization and must provide their own, original proof of genuineness. Only when this has taken place do the tasks of organization begin. One of the most promising signs of our time is that we are being confronted with this ultimate issue of our life, namely, the mystery of God and our neighbor—not merely by concentrating spiritually and meditatively upon these questions, but rather by facing with open eyes the problems we meet in our work, particularly in the management of business and the leadership of men. Here the crucial question is this: Is the fundamental orientation of your human relations the fact that the other person has the infinite "value" of a human soul, or simply that he is "utilizable"? When the Christian answers this question of the mystery of life in the affirmative he adds that the mystery of this infinite value of the human being lies, not in his capacity to perform a function, but rather in the fact that he has been bought with a price, that he is under the protectorate of an eternal goodness, and that therefore—as the parable of the Good Samaritan shows—even if he is a poor individual who has fallen among thieves or an incurable lunatic, he is the object of the love of God and therefore sacrosanct.

VII

FREEDOM OF DECISION: THE IMPOSSIBILITY OF CASUISTRY IN ETHICAL CHRISTIANITY[1]

IN THE ETHICS OF REFORMATION THEOLOGY THERE IS NO SUCH THING as a legalistic system which relieves us of the freedom and responsibility of making our own decisions. According to one dictionary, casuistry is a "method of treatment in ethics which provides authoritative rules for making moral decisions in individual cases, especially when there is a conflict of duties." Then the fact that there can be no casuistry in Protestantism means that there are no clear-cut answers that can tell us how to act in an exactly correct "Christian" way in every specific case.

The impression that a Christian (not a Roman Catholic) ethics makes upon an ingenuous reader who has not been very deeply touched by Reformation theology is likely to be a rather disconcerting one. If I were to attempt to express this impression of uncertainty in words, I would put it this way. On the one hand, this reader would

---

[1] In the following the author frequently refers to his *Theologische Ethik* (abbreviated as *ThE*), Vol. I, *Grundsatzlehre*, 2, 1958; Vol. II, 1, *Entfaltung,* 1955; Vol. II, 2, *Ethik des Politischen*, 1958.

148

be inclined to say that evangelical ethics does not know where it stands; that it therefore reflects all too clearly the institutional disruption of Protestantism, and that probably this is the direction in which one must look for the answer to the question why Protestantism—in contrast with its Catholic sister-Church—finds it so difficult to take a definite stand in the concrete tasks of shaping policy in the political, social, and economic realm. No matter whether the question is that of artificial insemination or atomic armaments, one seems almost never to be able to get an answer from Protestantism "as such." The answer one receives depends rather upon which theologian or which school of thought one happens to meet.

On the other hand, the open-minded reader who is not wholly taken up with the surface aspects will perceive, running through the whole range of possible variations in Protestant positions, a unity of fundamental point of view that makes it impossible for him to say with any fairness that this is only a chaotic babble of voices, but would rather suggest to him the metaphor of *cantus firmus* and counterpoint. The initial melody—the life lived in faith—unfolds itself, as it were, in a theological polyphony, which even in its most extreme tensions, indeed, even in certain atonal phrases, allows us to discern the underlying basic laws of its composition. The thoughtful reader perhaps may say that it is as if here two zones overlapped and created something like a zone of tension, these zones being, first, the commandments of God and, second, the understanding of concrete reality within which these commandments are meant to be respected. And while the commandments demand faith and obedience, concrete reality confronts us with the necessity of interpretation and evaluation. The polyphony of Protestant voices is therefore not inherent in the very nature of Protestantism, but is only a secondary result, which occurs when the boundary between the realm of obedience and the realm of evaluation is transgressed.

Let me say at once that I believe that this reader has noted something right and essential, and in what follows I shall try to make clear what it is that he has perceived. Perhaps we can best state this reader's question in this way: Is this lack of a clear-cut casuistry a fault or a virtue of Protestantism?

When we proceed to find out the reasons why Protestantism lacks a casuistry we must keep in mind above all three points of view, first, the Reformation doctrine of sin; second, the Reformation doctrine of Law; and third, the Reformation doctrine of decision.

1. THE REFORMATION DOCTRINE OF SIN

For very definite reasons the will of God—especially in the supra-personal realm of the orders of the world, in social and political life, for example—cannot be clearly known and fixed because we are alienated from this will of God. We have proclaimed our own will, our "self-will."

This phenomenon, which we call sin, is by no means inherent only in our personal decisions—here it is to some extent curable, when we return in trust and love and conform to the will of God—but is also inherent in the orders of supra-personal life.

What I mean by this can best be made clear by reference to the covenant with Noah (Gen. 9:1-7). When the judgment of the Flood upon fallen mankind was ended, the promises of God were addressed to the newly habitable world: "While the earth remains, seedtime and harvest, cold and heat, summer and winter, day and night, shall not cease" (Gen. 8:22). These promises also contain a new law, which exhibits some extremely significant parallels with, and divergences from, the primeval law of creation. At many points it is merely a repetition of the primeval command. But the repeated command "Be fruitful and multiply" (Gen. 9:1, 7) introduces a decidedly new nuance. For this account no longer speaks of a self-contained, almost tensionless hierarchy of creation in which the higher orders are set above the lower, but rather of violent self-assertion of the higher order of man over the lower orders: "The fear of you and the dread of you shall be upon every beast of the earth, and upon every bird of the air, upon everything that creeps on the ground and all the fish of the sea; into your hand they are delivered" (Gen. 9:2).

Nor is there any longer a natural, unquestionable sense of fellow feeling, of being fellow creatures, which would allow life under the eye of the Creator to become a life in which the creatures lived together in peace. What is left is only a rule of justice that employs the means of punitive power to compel the creatures to live together: "Whoever sheds the blood of man, by man shall his blood be shed; for God made man in his own image" (Gen. 9:6). Here the variation from the original order of creation is obvious. It is true that the created dignity of man, which makes him God's image and therefore sacrosanct, still glimmers through. This is the continuity of the reality of creation. But now in the fallen world the maintenance of this sacrosanctity is no longer guaranteed. Therefore it must be enforced by a law invested with force. This is the variant that distinguishes it from life in the world as it was first created by God.

This variation has a definite structure: it consists in the fact that God specifically uses the evil powers which have broken out in the world in order to curb and contain the evil. He sets force against force, or more precisely, he sets legal force (*potestas*) against illegal force. The wonder of his preservation is that he divides the sinful violence of man within him and thus sets it against itself. It is not to be allowed to destroy, but must hold itself in check. If an analogy is permitted, one can say that God heals the word homeopathically, in that he employs the principle of *similia similibus* (like cures like).

Hence the *orders* of the world are to be interpreted according to this Noachic covenant principle: even the state is not a self-contained created hierarchy of higher and lower orders, but rather a system of powers in which the higher egoism of the community, which the state represents, holds in check the lower egoisms of individuals and groups. It is a matter of unraveling the egoism into two strands, a legal one and an illegal one. It is a matter of a self-assertion of a higher order which guarantees inward and also outward order by means of force.[2] Thus according to the Noachic principle the order of the fallen world is upheld with the means of the fallen world.

So the world as it goes on under the preserving grace of God remains questionable. And therefore there is also no such thing as an ideal state, even for the imagination, since even the perfect state is intrinsically determined by the structural quality of *sacro egoismo* and therefore bears upon its brow not only the sign of creation but also the sign of the Fall. It is a twilight order. It is not the order of creation, but rather an order of necessity in the interim between the Fall and the Last Judgment.

This accounts for the fact that there are no clear-cut zones of good and evil, but that rather the world in all its realms lies in twilight.

---

[2] Cf. the chapter on power in *ThE*, II, 2.

And, corresponding to the ambiguity of this twilight, is the fact that on the level of the ethical there are no clear, objectively demonstrable areas of realization for the will of God. For in the framework of the order of necessity this will of God itself is present only in imperfect form. Jesus points to this imperfection in connection with the problem of divorce: Moses' writing of divorcement reflects God's will only in a limited sense. It does not contain the "real" will of God in creation, but only that will which takes into consideration men's "hardness of heart," and thus introduces something foreign to God's real will (Matt. 19:8).

It is because of this twilight situation then that the will of God cannot be easily ascertained in a concrete situation. One cannot simplify the situation and say: God permits divorce. But neither can one say: He prohibits it. Instead of our being presented with the clear will of God, we must seek for it and venture to do it. Naturally, there are definite criteria for this search and venture, so that we do not have to go at it blindly. In the case just mentioned, the criterion for decision consists in what God's purpose in marriage is and what he wills to achieve through it, namely, that the two become one flesh, that what God has joined together should not be put asunder by man (Gen. 2:24; Matt. 19:5-6), and that the husband should love his wife "as Christ loved the church" (Eph. 5:25). In the fallen world, however, the question can arise whether it really was God who joined together these two concrete persons, or whether this union was based on human self-will, the result of which is disorder and a broken relationship. Here we have to venture, under God and in responsibility to him, interpretations of concrete realities in which there is room for differing decisions and hence in which there are no clear-cut answers.

The same latitude of variation in possible solutions occurs in countless other areas of life, especially in the borderline situations. This becomes clear, for example, in the problem of war. It is perfectly clear that God does not want war, that it is contrary to his plan of creation. Even here, however, may there not be cases in which, because of human hardness of heart, an unjust attack must be warded off by force—just as criminal law employs force in order to protect the order of human society against the lawbreaker? Would not the principle of consistent sufferance actually provoke the evil and therefore—in seeming compliance with the will of God—actually bring about the very chaos which is *not* in accord with the will of God? But even though the Christian tradition generally accepts this line of argument, the atomic age presents entirely new questions[3]: Does not defensive war make sense only if that which is to be defended is not itself destroyed by the instruments of defense? And is not this the case with the use of atomic weapons?

At this point in the argument there comes again that moment when we cross the boundary into interpretation of reality and thus enter the sphere of questions of judgment. Thus it is possible that despite the *concensus* in theological criteria—with respect to the extent to which we may resort to defense by force in the name of God's preserving will—there may still be a *dissensus* in the concrete decisions. For here we are caught in the venture of our judgment.

Connected with this understanding of the fallen world is also the following fact in ethics. The difficulty in all ethical considerations always arises when we face a concrete situation. The moment any ethical norm is given practical application it usually turns out that the norm does not fit right here, that is, *in concreto*. The so-called textbook cases, which are intended to express the universal, are, paradoxically, very rare in everyday life.

By a textbook case we understand the congruence of a practical case, for example, an appendicitis, with the "classical" process, that is, the process which follows a particular law, and therefore the case which is in accord with the norm and to that extent the normal case. But it is odd that normal cases are almost always exceptional cases in medicine as well as in ethics. This also explains why the textbooks, which are so readily consulted when complications occur (that is, in the *really* normal cases!), never discuss the precise case concerning which the reader wants instruction. Understandably, their indexes are not inventories of real life, but a collection of abstractions which lack congruence with the highly differentiated variety of actual existence.

To illustrate this congruence once more with the example of appendicitis: it never appears as a "pure case" when it occurs, let

---

[3] Cf. the chapter on atomic war in *ThE*, II, 2.

us say, in connection with diabetes or cardiac weakness or pregnancy or other deviations from the normal. In ethics the situation is exactly the same: the norm of truth and telling the truth rarely appears in "pure" form. Very frequently it is combined with the claims to validity of other norms and thus becomes acute in a conflict of claims, for example, the conflict faced by a physician when out of regard for the patient he must decide whether to keep the truth from him or even to tell an untruth.[4]

This in itself indicates why and how we arrive at the paradoxical fact that "normally" there are no text-book cases. The answer that life is more complicated than the theory is, to be sure, a very common answer, but it is too simple. Rather we must specify precisely what this greater complication is. It lies in the fact that the areas in which several norms having competence overlap; for example, the norm that determines the course of appendicitis and the other norm that determines the course of diabetes. Likewise both the norms of love and truth can make their appeal to the physician at the same time (and therefore in the same case).

Hence it becomes impossible for the physician as well as the reader of a book on ethics, and naturally, also for the jurist, simply to look up the answer in a textbook or a statute book. Rather it requires two additional acts: first, a hermeneutical endeavor, by means of which he ascertains just how the norms have been actualized in this concrete case, and second, a decision in which he *ventures* to define the central factor and the subsidiary relationships, and thus accepts personal responsibility for the remaining nonsubsumable factors, making of it an act which is his own.

The person who makes a decision does not follow a routine, simply accepting precedents gained from the "pure case"; on the contrary, he is always being confronted with the exceptional situation. To a certain extent he stands alone, and therefore without the textbook, without casuistical props. This is one of the reasons why there is no such thing as a medical, legal, or ethical prescription book, that is, why there are no casuistical precedents for all conceivable cases. It has always been the theme of tragedy that life "never did run smoothly"—not only because it demands the taking

---

[4] Cf. *ThE*, II, 1, § 567 ff.

of risks and therefore the risk of failure, but also because there are in it zones of conflict of values which are fundamentally insoluble. But that to which tragedy points, as it were, unwittingly, is expressed thematically in a theological cosmology. The fallen world exhibits rifts and cracks. Because it is no longer in harmony with the Creator, it is also no longer in harmony with itself. Just as men within the field in which the Fall exerts its force fall out of the communication with one another given to them in creation and are set against each other (Micah 7:5 ff.; Matt. 10:35 ff.), so the individual realms of being fall into conflict with one another, and the chaos from which creation was originally wrested becomes an immediate threat.[5] The technical limitations of casuistry which ethics encounters because the concrete cases cannot be subsumed under the textbook norms therefore point back to the breach between creation and Fall.

This outlines the first point of view which illustrates the impossibility of casuistry, namely, that the twilight between creation and the Fall that lies upon the world and its orders makes impossible any direct objectification of the will of God. This will of God manifests itself in the context of our reality only in broken images. Therefore, when it does allow itself to be directly perceived—as, for example, in the eschatological demands of the Sermon on the Mount—it calls in question the very structure of the world itself.[6] The ambiguity of the world as it is compels us to make an interpretation, which because of this ambiguity can only be a venture, and therefore requires latitude for discretion and judgment. For if ambiguity exists, then the concrete case cannot simply be subsumed—as is done in the case of natural law—under the highest principle, or rather, under the unambiguousness of the will of God.

It is in this understanding of sin and therefore of the reality of the fallen world that the impossibility of a clear-cut casuistry is grounded.

---

[5] Cf. Gerhard von Rad, *Old Testament Theology*, Vol. I, tr. by D. M. G. Stalker (New York, Harper & Row, 1962), p. 144.
[6] Cf. *ThE*, I, § 831.

2. THE REFORMATION DOCTRINE OF LAW

The second reason that explains the lack of a casuistry in Reformation theology, which, indeed, is identical with the reason for its emphatic rejection of it, points in a totally different direction. It is connected with the evangelical doctrine of justification and arises from the polemic against the Law, or better, against a legalistic understanding of righteousness.

The biblical *locus classicus* to which the Reformation doctrine of justification appealed was, of course, the saying of Paul in Rom. 3:28, "For we hold that a man is justified apart from the works of the law by faith alone."[7] What intentions is Paul pursuing—and what intentions are the Reformers pursuing in appealing to him—when he appeals to saving grace against the condemnation of legalism, to the Spirit who gives life against the letter that kills (II Cor. 3:7 ff.; Gal. 4; etc.)? To give a correct answer to this question would require us to develop the whole breadth of the Reformation doctrine of justification. Here, however, we can address ourselves only to that special aspect of it which is relevant to the problem of casuistry.[8]

That which in Paul and Luther is described as the "obedience of the slave" or the "slavery of the letter" and regarded as being in fundamental contrast to the love of the child and to the freedom of the Spirit may be described in modern, sociological terms as the loyalty of the functionary to his function. The functionary is not himself when he acts. He is simply an organ carrying out orders. Something else or someone else is exercising his will "through him." True, the man of the Law does the will of God formally; but he does not do it as his own will. The tremendous Chapter seven of Romans shows us how our own will, the *"nomos* in our bones,"* rebels against the strangeness of the Law and is in permanent conflict with it. For this reason alone the Law can never lead to a total obedience, to an *applicatio ad voluntatem Dei,* a real concurrence with the will of God. For because my own will is never congruent with the demanding will of God and at one with it, there is always

---

[7] Luther's translation.
[8] The following section employs formulations from *ThE,* II, 1, § 1 ff.

a remainder of opposition, and the total self never enters into the act of obedience. At most only "half of the heart" (*dimidium cordis*) stands on God's side.

Only as we see this does it become clear why the New Testament says that love alone is the fulfillment of the Law, that only love meets the real intention of the Law, which is to bring about a conformity with the will of God; he who loves finds himself in harmony with him whom he loves. And an act done out of love is therefore also an act done out of conformity. Since this action is not casuistically performed by laws, but is rather the objectification and expression of this motivating love, it has the utmost freedom to develop. This is what Augustine meant when he said, *"Dilige et fac quod vis"* —love and do what you will. The commandment of love means the end of all casuistry; it is that which enables a man to be free.

Therefore ethics does not, strictly speaking, teach us what we *should* do, but rather what we *may* do. It measures the scope of freedom. In the light of exemplary situations it reflects—at least I think that it must be so understood, if we start from the afore-mentioned approach—upon the question of what it means *to live in freedom and with the gift of forgiveness* in the midst of all the entangling autonomisms, all the conflicts of values and constellations of interests, and all the actual circumstances of this aeon that seek to determine us. It shows us how the prodigal son lives after he has forsaken the servitude of the far country and after he has outgrown the virtuous legalism of the brother who remained at home.

So if the theme of ethics is "the freedom of a Christian man," then first of all it is necessary for us to arrive at a new understanding of this freedom. But for us who live today, to "understand" can only mean that we must learn to understand it, not in the Sartrean sense of being condemned to freedom, but rather as a gift and a new possibility of existence. For the fear of freedom under which we labor comes from the loss of existence. The person who is no longer grounded upon the eternal foundations, and therefore is merely vegetating instead of existing, regards every appeal to his freedom as something that compels him to make a painfully revealing and discrediting acknowledgment of his failure. For, after all, the challenge to be free means first and foremost the challenge to be "oneself," and therefore to become a "subject." If I am no longer "myself," but merely an anonymous element in the crowd (*das Man*) or an organ that carries out the orders of an alien will, and therefore a mere object; or if I am merely an object driven by passions and fears, then the appeal to my freedom compels me to the fatal confession that there is nothing left in me that could be free, and therefore that I am vegetating in my failure to be myself.

Sartre's assertion that we are "condemned to freedom" must be respected because of its honesty. That which is a gift and a fulfillment for the existing person becomes a torment and a shame to the person who no longer exists. Only for the existing person is freedom the shining sign of the overcoming of the Law and a liberation to "be oneself." For the person who no longer exists, freedom itself becomes a condemning and destroying law, so that resistance to it is an understandable and logical reaction.

The appeal to freedom becomes good news only when our existence is given a new foundation and thus we are enabled to be free. It is a law of God's intercourse with us, however, that first of all something is given to us, and only then are demands made upon us, that first comes the indicative establishment of the new creature, and then the imperative appeal comes to us.

In concrete terms this means that before we are commanded to love—in order then to receive in this love the chance to be free, the freedom to "do as we will"—God reveals himself to us, to use the beautiful phrase from the Lutheran confessions, as an *objectum amabile* (a lovable object). As he reveals his heart to us and in this way becomes a "lovable object," *our* love springs into being and with it the new existence, which then—but only then—can be addressed and appealed to on the basis of its freedom. For the non-existing person, which here means the person who has not been made free to love, freedom is something that demands too much of him and therefore causes him to flee. For the existing person, however, it is a gift which enables him to be himself and allows him to be what God meant him to be.

So for this reason too we know what we are doing when we refuse to become casuistical.

3. THE REFORMATION DOCTRINE OF DECISION

To be called to freedom, however, means not merely to choose between alternatives, but rather to be able to find the alternative oneself—and also to be obliged to find it. Decision is not an act wholly apart from non-decisional, purely theoretical deliberations; rather the decision is inherent in the intellectual act of deliberation itself.

This is not so in the framework of a casuistical ethics. Here we have what might be called a prefabricated decision concerning what is required in such and such a situation. Then ethical obedience is no longer demonstrated by including the mind in this obedience and discovering with the mind what should be done in the discipline of responsibility and the determination to do what is right. Ethical obedience is limited to the act which is willing to comply with a given command. Here again there is the "halving" of the person which Luther was referring to in the phrase *dimidium cordis*. For the "mind part" of man is, as it were, excluded from the function of decision; it has delegated its independence (*Mündigkeit*) to the authoritative court whose casuistical rules are accepted as unexamined precedents. It is only the "act part" of man that operates in the areas of decision. And then, of course, the range of possibilities possessed by the mind and within which it must choose is reduced to the narrow compass of a mere Yes or No to the casuistical rule.

But undoubtedly a person can be a subject in the real sense only if his mind is given the dignity of being a maker of decisions and thus is also challenged to be obedient, to be a subject, to be independent and responsible.[9]

An indication that this challenge is in line with New Testament

---

[9] This sentence could sound Pelagian, just as the concept of "the subject" has in it a certain tendency that leads to this misunderstanding. But it is specifically Reformation anthropology that insists that man is not only a *subject*, but at the same time the *object* of divine election and divine grace. He makes decisions because a decision has been made concerning him. Here the subject-object formula reaches the limit of its validity. And yet this is an essentially different limit from that which we found in the *casuistical* limitation upon the human function of decision. We can merely refer to the problem here, thus indicating that far from overlooking the problem, we are indeed aware of it.

thought seems to us to be evident in the fact that at decisive points the ethical directions of Jesus and the Apostles are given in dialectical terms. They do not say "what" is to be done, but rather state alternatives between which one must choose and without giving a casuistical solution and making it ethically utilizable, leave it to the one who has been challenged to obedience to work it out for himself. I mention only three examples.

First, "Render to Caesar the things that are Caesar's, and to God the things that are God's" (Matt. 22:21). Here the openness of a decision to be made in a situation in which a prejudgment has *not* been made finds significant illustration, since the cunning question of the Pharisees, to which this logion is the answer, was tactically designed to make Jesus commit himself casuistical. Had he denied the emperor the right to levy tribute—in the unambiguous casuistical sense of "You should not give tribute to Caesar"—the conclusion would be that he was hostile to the government. And had he approved the right of a heathen emperor to levy tribute, they would then have accused him of unfaithfulness to the God of Israel. So here the Pharisees present the basic idea of casuistry in a form so emphatic that the acceptance of it would mean risk of one's life. Now if one is not to interpret Jesus' answer as being purely tactical (which, of course, would be to degrade it), then one cannot regard it merely as an adroit maneuver to get his neck out of a noose. Rather one will see that here something fundamental is being said concerning the openness of decision, or if you will, concerning the "engagement" of the mind.

A second example: "Be wise as serpents and innocent as doves" (Matt. 10:16). Here too there is no prescribed requirement either to act tactically and pragmatically or to act in simplicity without regard for loss. On the contrary, even this is left completely open. Whether I decide for one or the other in a concrete situation or consider that a combination of both is right is for me to choose in the venture of decision and therefore in the context of *my* responsibility.

Third, "We must obey God rather than men" (Acts 5:29). The openness of choice proclaimed in this saying lies in the fact that it is not stated in advance what the situation is in which this alternative appears. Different individuals will be confronted with it in different ways. One person may conclude that under the pressure of ideological tyranny he can still make this or that compromise, because he wants to reserve the *status confessionis* for some fateful, ostensive situation of decision when martyrdom will make an impact; he chooses—in the name of God!—not to allow his witness to be silenced because of some mere bagatelle. Another person may see something dubious and equivocal in the slightest demand made upon him, and without any regard for what it may cost, will consider that this constitutes a *status confessionis*. In the choice of the appropriate situation the choosing, interpreting mind is engaged. It is impossible to analyze the structure of every conceivable situation in advance in order to make a predetermined casuistical choice of the decision to be made.

This freedom of choice in specific action and therefore the possibility that two Christians may act somewhat differently in a particular situation undoubtedly contains within it a certain relativizing of the action, or better, of the form which the act of obedience takes. The relativizing of the act again has its root in the Reformation doctrine of justification. For the real and fateful decisions are not made through what we *do*—for here is where Augustine's dictum "Do what you will" applies—but rather these decisions are made through the way in which I relate myself to God, that is, whether I love him (*diligere*) and trust him (*credere*). The real decision falls, to use a mathematical metaphor, at the sign I place before the bracket that encloses the terms in the sum of my action. The terms themselves can then be very different quantities.

Luther often expressed in very daring, and for this very reason, clear terms this latitude of action within the framework of faith. Thus, for example, he says in the *Theses Debated in 1520 on Whether Works Contribute to Grace:* "1. Just as nothing makes a man righteous except faith, so nothing makes a man sinful except unbelief. . . . 10. If an act of adultery could be committed in faith, it would not be a sin. 11. If you were to pray to God in unbelief, you would be committing an act of idolatry (and therefore of sin)."

And yet it is still too weak a statement merely to say that this openness of choice of action, unlimited by casuistry, is only an emphasis upon the "engagement" of the mind and therefore upon the necessity of drawing the *whole* man into the act of obedience, since otherwise only half his heart would be in it and besides, he would only be the executor of some will other than his own. Much more than this is involved, and Kierkegaard stressed repeatedly that it is precisely the objective uncertainty concerning what I should do that mobilizes the "infinite passion of inwardness." I must *venture* a decision; and in doing this I venture *myself*. This means that I am wholly "in" it, utterly engaged. Then everything depends, as it were, upon me; and this forces me to be extremely wide-awake. On the other hand, if I allow myself to become involved in the net of casuistry, I can delegate responsibilities. Then I have something reassuringly objective, which sustains me and, besides, possesses proved authority. As long as I rely on it, nothing can go wrong. Herein lies the possibility of a certain indifference, a certain unconcern, which, of course, is very difficult to discern outwardly because the "engagement" is concentrated solely upon the right action as being the only sector of responsibility and because in this way the visible side of a person's obedience and concern comes impressively to the fore. In the noncasuistical, open choice, however, both obedience and concern are also concentrated upon the "engagement" of the mind, upon the self: that is, it evokes the "infinite passion of inwardness."

Kierkegaard says in his *Concluding Unscientific Postscript to the "Philosophical Fragments"*:

An objective uncertainty held fast in an appropriation-process of the most passionate inwardness is the truth, the highest truth attainable for an existing individual. . . . Objectively, then, one has only uncertainty; but this is precisely what increases the tension of the infinite passion of inwardness, and the truth is precisely the venture which chooses an objective uncertainty with the passion of the infinite.

That which Kierkegaard here means by the objective uncertainty of God we can appropriately apply in our train of thought to the objective uncertainty of the good, to the fact that it is not given (in the casuistical sense).

The fixed pole around which everything revolves in Reformation theology is therefore the act through which God wrings faith from us and with it an existence oriented upon God. The kind of action that springs from this faith is certainly *not* merely optional or arbitrary insofar as the person who is compelled to decide always sees only *one* possibility in which he is compelled to prove his obedience. (After all, the very concept of decision implies that I am not confronted with a situation in which I can make any choice I please; this would make impossible any responsible decision.) But the kind of action that springs from faith is subject to a relative arbitrariness insofar as in many cases—especially in the borderline situations[10]—there are no objective casuistical norms which would prejudice my decision.

One could perhaps object that the venture of choice in which the mind too is ethically engaged is limited by the fact that then it is the reason that is the chooser. But, the argument might continue, when the reason inquires into an act that is commanded it is bent upon insight and not venture, it seeks to get away from uncertainty and arrive at a well grounded objectivity. Therefore what we have said about the "engagement" of the mind in the choice is at least overstated.

This objection, however, would have to be examined in the light of the question of what it is that the reason itself is based upon, or more precisely, whether the possibility of being reasonable is not itself based upon acts of decision, and in this way also has something to do with the decision made in faith. For even though the facts of reason are not altered by faith, a man's attitude toward reason, the very possibility of his *"being* reasonable," is nevertheless affected by it. Objectivity as an attitude which is in accord with reason and appropriate to the things that are known by reason represents a human mode of behavior and therefore underlies the constructive forces that constitute a human mode of behavior. Since faith is one of these forces, we can only conclude that objectivity has something to do with the redemption in which faith believes, and therefore that possible faith and objectivity do not represent two dimensionally different attitudes, but rather that they merge in the liberation of faith from false enslavements to reason and therefore liberation to objectivity.

That this is actually the case becomes clear as soon as we stop to think what this redemption to reasonableness is. It consists in the

---

[10] Cf. *ThE*, II, 1, index.

fact that reason is screened off at the top and at the bottom and, as it were, kept within its own bounds.

First, it is screened off "from above." Anybody who has understood the dialectic of Law and gospel (for Luther this understanding is the alpha and omega of all theology) learns to separate the two kingdoms from each other and to use the reason in the kingdom on the left.[11] It is a "heteronomization" (giving reason competence in an area in which it has no competence) and at the same time a distortion of the gospel into Law to turn the gospel into a kind of constitution for the kingdom of the world and thus also for the political realm. Therefore there can be no theocracy, but only an order which is worked out in accord with the law of God-given reason and in the name of man's "coming of age" (*Mündigkeit*).[12]

A pseudo-theocracy, in which the reason is "heteronomized," can also be an ideological tyranny or the domination of any kind of political or social utopia. For here too the reason is not kept within its own sphere where it has mature competence, but rather becomes a functionary of pragmatic ideas, which it is expected to authenticate by means of its reservoir of arguments.

The goal of man's redemption is therefore his "coming of age," the liberation of reason to be itself. Or we can also put it this way: Redemption frees it from servanthood into sonship. Insofar as we are thinking of the screening off of reason "from above," we mean the subjection of reason to authoritarian divine laws, to dependence upon divine directions which ignore the mature independence (*Mündigkeit*) of the reason and thus turn the gospel into Law, giving rise to all kinds of theocratic fanaticisms.[13] But we also mean the subjection of reason to the kind of casuistry which is merely the expression of someone else's will.

---

[11] Cf. *ThE*, II, 1, § 1344 ff.

[12] That "coming of age" (*Mündigkeit*) does not mean an emancipation of the reason, but rather the mature independence of a son who is bound to his father; this has been shown in a profoundly incisive way by Friedrich Gogarten, "*Theologie und Geschichte,*" in *Zeitschrift für Theologie und Kirche* (1953), 3, pp. 339 ff., especially pp. 349 ff. On the concept of *Mündigkeit* cf. also Dietrich Bonhoeffer, *Prisoner for God* (New York: The Macmillan Company, 1954), pp. 145 ff., 156, 166 ff.

[13] Here we cannot avoid thinking of the fanatics who, like Thomas Münzer, tried to turn the Sermon on the Mount into a constitution for the world.

ffion

Second, the reason is screened off "from below." For it is exposed to domination by the emotional levels of the self; it is motivated by fear and hope. "Thy wish was father, Harry, to that thought"[14]— this expresses one of the perils to which reason is exposed; and the other peril is that of fear; what I fear I will not admit to be true.[15] My objectivity, and therefore my impartial view of the facts, is threatened because I am not disinterested, and because I then seek to confirm by means of reasons, by means of "thought," that which I am interested in (either negatively, in the sense that it may not be so, or positively, in the sense that it may be so). Luther was referring to this when he called reason a whore, a woman who sells herself. More precisely, however, it should be said that it is the person who has sold—and continues to sell—the reason. Only as a man is liberated from fear and hope, or better, only as a man is liberated from the things he fears and hopes for, and finds his freedom in Him who liberates us from the fear of the world, in Him who would be the sole object of hope, does he gain real objectivity. Only as a person is liberated from the things that bind him does he become objective.

Since this transformation of hope rests upon a venture of the reason that gives it a new foundation, the risk of choice extends into the realm of reason itself. Reason which is uncontrolled by existence can itself become a dictatorship; it can become the object of rationalized superstition and thus a means by which a person loses the mature independence of sonship (*Mündigkeit*), a means by which he falls under a heteronomy.

This view of things may at first be rather startling to post-Kantian thinking, but this does not exclude the claim of truth that is in it. The theological form of this autonomy of reason for which we make these claims is only another way of saying that the person who acts ethically should be a responsible bearer of his action, that he should be a "subject." To that extent it contains within it the profoundest Protestant protest against casuistry. At most the casuistical tutelage of men which keeps them in leading-strings can only

---

[14] Shakespeare, *King Henry IV*, Pt. II, Act IV, Sc. 5, line 91.

[15] In this category also is the suppression of the God whom we fear and then make over in accord with our own desires. Cf. Romans 1:18 ff., "men who by their wickedness suppress the truth."

be a pedagogical interim which must eventuate in the goal of mature, independent sonship. By mature, independent sonship (*Mündigkeit*), however, we do not mean any kind of unbridled, unbound freedom, but rather the freedom that accepts new bonds, the freedom of the children of God.

I hope that this has clarified at least a little of the element of contradiction that is inherent in all noncasuistical thinking and that it will now be clearly seen that it is not merely a "lack," but the "virtue" of the evangelical approach. The statements of an evangelical ethics cannot be simply appropriated, taken over, as is possible in casuistry; rather one must realize that evangelical ethics confronts us with the question whether we are willing to put ourselves under the claim of its basic point of view.

VIII

MAN'S FREEDOM AND GOD'S RULE: ON THE MEANING OF HISTORY

JOSEPH WITTIG ONCE SAID THAT A BIOGRAPHY REALLY SHOULD NOT begin with a man's birth, but with his death. It can be written, he said, only from the vantage point of his end, for only there can one see the whole of his life in its fulfillment. If one views history, or at any rate, the writing of history, as a kind of biography of the world, one arrives at a similar thesis.

Before we examine to what extent this thesis can be exemplified in the Christian view of history, it would seem advisable to point out that certain observations of developments within history also suggest the applicability of Wittig's thesis to history. That is to say, if one takes smaller segments of history by themselves or even if one isolates certain phases of a man's life, one does not arrive at a connected meaning of the whole. Thus we speak of a success of "the moment." The expression implies that momentary success still does not prove that a piece of work, a venture, or a struggle will pay in the long run, that it will endure, in other words, that there is any significant relationship between performance and result. That is to say, "at the moment" it is still not apparent whether a worthwhile act will receive its reward or whether an evil deed will have to be paid for.

167

The system by which a thing is rewarded or punished, or, to put it in more theological terms, the higher will that assigns reward or decrees punishment can be seen—if it can be seen at all—only in extended areas of observation and longer periods of time. "At the moment" it is "chance" that rules. Indeed, chance is actually a category of the "moment." That is, in our usage "accidentalness" generally does not imply a statement concerning the *content* of an event—in the sense, for example, of Schiller's phrase, "Haphazard strikes the lightning," or in the sense that we are on some hopelessly uncontrolled "aimless journey"—but rather implies a statement concerning a very definite *point of view* from which I approach the event, namely, the point of view of the moment.

The moment is therefore also the time-area in which the question of theodicy becomes especially acute. Thus the writer of Psalm 73 observes the momentary success of the mighty, the rich, and the wicked, "whose eyes swell out with fatness" and who—unlike the upright and therefore in apparent contradiction to all justice— always have good luck, until, yes, *until,* one "perceived their end," that is, until one broadened one's view beyond the moment and surveyed the whole of their life's course: "I went into the sanctuary of God; then I perceived their end."

Here the aspect of accidentalness is changed in two senses. First, the psalmist surmounts the moment by viewing "the whole" of their lives, by placing himself at the end of their lives and looking backward; and second, he surmounts the moment by going into the "sanctuary" and thus viewing the success of the moment *sub specie aeternitatis.* Both acts create perspective and then one sees the end, and at that vantage point one sees the laws that bind these accidental moments into a continuous chain. One of the laws that makes its appearance here is the law of guilt and retribution. To be sure, even here this law remains largely hidden; from the theological point of view one must say that even where it seems to be apparent it always remains hidden in its real sense. Nevertheless, one will have to say that certain contours of a law of guilt and retribution are apparent here. It was in this sense that Bismarck once said that history's settlements of accounts are more exact than the audits of the Prussian exchequer.

It is important to remember this; for especially since the collapse in 1945 our German historiographers have tried to operate with this law of extended periods of time and by this means have tended to see the German collapse, not as dependent upon the contingency of the moment (such as the exhaustion of the armament potential or of biological reserves or being a little too late in discovering the atom bomb), but rather in terms of the law of guilt and retribution. The recognition that such an attempt to interpret history must go very far back in time, which is in itself quite correct, has led some to make not only Bismarck but also Frederick the Great, and even the Reformation responsible for wrong developments which have reached their culmination only within our decade. The illusion of having a total view is purchased, as it were, by going back farther and farther in time. But the totality of history cannot be arrived at in this way; what it comes to is a kind of historiography which I would call "crime-story history." The landscape of these writers and observers of history teems with troops of scouts and spies, all of them bent on catching the original culprit, since the obvious villains in the foreground of history who have already been arrested (including the condemned at Nürnberg) always seem to be the cat's-paws and accomplices of an evil, long-since corrupted *Zeitgeist*. This "whodunit-historical" effort to nab the head of the great conspiracy and its concomitant urge to keep widening the radius of its historical research indicates the awareness—though it is a degenerate awareness—that once one has adopted the thesis of guilt and retribution one must advance all the way to the "horizon" of history. Only at the ultimate limit does everything become a law. But where is the limit of history?

We may be reminded of a parallel in physics, the so-called law of great numbers. Contingency appears to be present only within small fields of observation, such as the individual electron. But statistics, which deals with great numbers, sees that the irrationality of the smallest individual occurence is incorporated in a law that governs the whole. Obviously, the same obtains in history too: things that, taken individually, seem to depend upon imponderable freedom, like suicide, for example, turn out, when the average is taken in whole countries or even continents, that is, in the framework of large numbers, to be a predictable constant.

Manifestly, in history, too, large numbers are required before the governing law becomes apparent, which in this case is the law that certain things are always punished "in the long run" and other things always pay "in the long run."

The whole field of observation would have to be available in order to find this law with exactitude. But the claim to have the whole field of observation in hand would be identical with the claim to know the limits of history, or more precisely, with the claim that one stood at the vantage point of transcendence.

Every illegitimate attempt to achieve this transcendence within history is avenged by the fact that at the end of it lies, not sight, but its opposite, delusion and blindness. No sooner do we catch a glimpse of the law of guilt and retribution in a broadened field of observation than in the next moment it becomes more recondite than before. For what we get from the bird's-eye view, that is, from the largest attainable field of observation (and this is really the field of the "observer," the *mere* spectator) is not the law of guilt and retribution, but rather fate, neutral necessity with no regard for values.

This can be observed in Oswald Spengler's morphology of world history in which moral or religious categories like guilt and fate no longer have any relevance whatsoever. Ultimately Spengler's morphology of culture can do no more than interpret history in analogy with nature. Indicative of this turning of history into nature and, by the same token, this divorcing of history from all morality, is the fact that Spengler interprets the millennial succession of cultures in terms of the natural rhythm of the seasons of the year, and thus in terms of a completely amoral, value-free process. Therefore freedom and responsibility, which are all that make guilt, and hence judgment too, possible, are emptied of all content. No sooner does one catch a glimpse of law than its substance is changed; it is no longer a law of history, but only a law of nature.

What we observe here is not merely an empirical observation; it also is indicative of a theological process. The method of employing the bird's-eye view grew out of the necessity for gaining a maximum field of observation. But the whole field can be seen only from the end, from the vantage point of transcendence. The bird's-eye view is therefore, theologically speaking, nothing less than an illegitimate usurpation of transcendence. It is an attempt to elevate oneself above history in order to view it. It is an attempt to cross the ultimate boundary of history from within. And this entails the consequence that follows upon every transgression of boundaries: sight is darkened instead of illuminated. The primeval human beings who transgress the limit between them and God in order to become like God—*eritis sicut Deus*—do *not* become like God; they simply find themselves banished from the father-child relationship, and are cast out of paradise. And doubtful as is Goethe's dictum that the one who acts is always right, it is certain that the observer, that is, the one who crosses the limit, the one who observes from the bird's-eye perspective, is always wrong.

In any case, in the formation of a Christian concept of history it is of absolute importance that the transcendence, which is necessary in order to observe guilt and retribution, cannot be achieved from within history by an illegitimate crossing of the boundary, but rather that transcendence breaks into history from the outside and then emerges within it. This presence of transcendence in history is Jesus Christ. In him is fulfilled the postulate that one can say something about guilt and retribution, and thus about the judgment, only if one sees the whole and stands at the boundary. One may rightly call him the "center" of history. This concept can serve as an excellent parable of our idea of the whole of history if we think of this "center" as being that elevated, central point of view from which one surveys the horizon of history both forward and backward. And as a matter of fact the New Testament does set forth this view of history in many different ways.

First, the New Testament shows us the horizon of history, looking *backward* from Christ the center, when it declares that the world was created through Christ. Manifestly, what this means is that in him it is apparent that from the very beginning the history of the world was designed for salvation. Or one might say, again to vary a saying of Goethe, that the secret of history is not so much the struggle between belief and unbelief as it is the struggle between salvation and evil *(Heil und Unheil)*. History is the realm in which man is summoned to turn back from the far country to fellowship with God. This and nothing else is the secret of the multitude of individuals and nameless people, who nevertheless are known to

God; this and nothing else is the destiny of kings and dictators and "world-historical individuals"[1] and all their empires, all of which, as Blumhardt once said, are under the sign of the "passing," while the kingdom of God is under the sign of the "coming." From the very beginning history is designed for something of which Christ—again from the very beginning—is representative; it was designed for salvation.

But the New Testament also shows us the horizon of history, looking *forward* from the perspective of its center, "Christ." Christ will come again to judge the quick and the dead; he will draw the final balance and close the books on history. Negatively, this means that this final balancing of accounts never occurs within the continuity of history itself: the real "end" of the swindlers and rogues, of those "whose eyes swell out with fatness," never appears within history. On the contrary, illegitimate happy endings are constantly occurring. But at the end of history, when the wheat is gathered into the granary, when the end of all things comes and the yawning chasm swallows up the cosmos, then everything will be plain, because at this ultimate boundary stands the King with his sickle and crown, the King who "knows a man's thoughts" and has never lost sight of this secret of man, of *every* man.

But the judgment of history also appears in the midst of history, not only on its horizon. Because the "resurrection from the dead on the third day" occurred in history, death is no longer understood as a biological law, and thus as a value-free phenomenon of nature, but rather as contrary to nature, as enmity, as a rift in creation. Because here in history the sick are healed and suffering assuaged, the world is manifested in all its sickness and need for healing, waiting for the great day of redemption. Because sinners are forgiven, because this forgiveness is bestowed as a miracle breaking into this world with power, the world's iron, unbreakable enslavement to the destiny of death and ineluctable law is made manifest as nowhere else.

Here what Schiller said suddenly becomes true—though in a way dreadfully different from the way he meant it—"The history of the world is the judgment of the world." I ask you now to take this quite literally. World history does not bring judgments and retribu-

---

[1] Hegel's phrase. (Trans.)

tions in the form of individual events, in the sense, for example, of the words of the aged harper in Goethe's *Wilhelm Meister*, "All guilt is punished on this earth." How often it is not punished! Rather history is both the judgment and under the judgment; it is totally enslaved to a destiny that no man can alter, a destiny in which, ever since that mysterious caesura which is called the Fall, every man is constantly incurring guilt, imprisoned in what Frank Thiess has called the "torture-chamber of history," in the ghastly process of war and rumors of war; a destiny governed by the immutable law that "some must live in the dark and others in the light",[2] that man must incur guilt and must die.

But we shall still not have said all there is to be said concerning the relationship of history and judgment if we stop with this general characterization of the judgment. We must now particularize and ask ourselves whether, from this vantage point, it is possible to apply the term "judgment" to some very definite events (e.g., the German catastrophe) and whether this does not put the question in a completely different light.

If what we have said concerning the Christological center of history is correct, that is, if the secret of history lies in a Figure, who cannot be dealt with merely in intellectual terms, but rather is incognito and can be apprehended only in the venture of faith, then we shall have to say that judgment too cannot be "seen," but is rather an object of faith. I can speak of judgment only if I know the judge, the "person" who decides. At this point the analogy with the earthly judicial process breaks down, since in the latter I must know, not the judge, but rather the laws according to which the judge makes his decisions. Here in the earthly judicial process one must be familiar with the *ordo* in which the judge himself is incorporated and whose functionary he is. But God is no functionary of an *ordo* that is superior to him; on the contrary, every *ordo* is itself grounded solely in his sovereign will. Just as I cannot reason *a posteriori* from the creation to the Creator—as if it were really true that "all things corruptible are but a parable"[3]—but can only know the secret of the creation if I know the Creator and his heart, so I know the secret of judgment only if I know the Judge. And all this means quite simply that the judgment is "invisible",

---

[2] Berthold Brecht, *The Threepenny Opera.*
[3] Goethe, *Faust*, II, v, 7. (Trans.)

just as surely as the Judge and all matters of faith are invisible.

We may now briefly illustrate this hidden judgment which is illuminated only by the person of the Judge.

1. The fact that judgment cannot be objectively ascertained is already apparent in the fact that on the secular level it remains fundamentally ambiguous.

a) Take, for example, the song concerning the shattered armies of Napoleon in Russia:

> With man and horse and caisson
> The Lord of hosts did smite them

Is this really an "unambiguous" case of a judgment of God upon Napoleon? A Frenchman might fairly argue that it was just the other way round (even if one wished to speak in terms of judgment and not simply apply the category of the tragic), that it was Europe and not Napoleon which was the power smitten by God, since, as it turned out, it was Europe which was in this way deprived of the Napoleonic principle of order and its benefits. Europe had the opportunity, the Frenchman might argue, to enter the stimulating orbit of a great political concept, whereas, after Napoleon's downfall, it sank into the epigonous sterility of its own outworn traditions. And, further, in this judgment upon Europe was not Napoleon merely an instrument, a mere executor of the judgment? It is not only the picture we have of the character of great figures that fluctuates in world history; their metaphysical role is also ambiguous and changing. But then does not this mean that all statements about judgment in particular cases are merely relative?

b) Then, too, when it comes to the unusual catastrophes in the life of the world and of individuals where the victims are far more unambiguous than in the case of Napoleon (e.g., the German catastrophes of 1918 and 1945 or lifelong illness in the case of an individual) our diagnosis that these are "judgments of God" is constantly running into an ultimate limit which makes it questionable: Must this suffering necessarily be interpreted "causally" and attributed to a previously committed sin? May it not also be possible to explain it on the basis of its purpose, namely, God's educative purpose? And would not these two interpretations cancel each other out, since in one case the catastrophe and suffering would possess the character of evil (judgment) and in the other, the character of salvation (education)? These two interpretations clash dramatically in Jesus' dialogue with the disciples in the story of the man born blind (John 9, especially vss. 1-3). The disciples proceeded from what was to them the self-evident assumption that the cause of this congenital blindness must be a sin, that it therefore had the character of a judgment, whereas Jesus turned the disciples' "causal" explanation into what seems to be its total opposite and said that the blindness served a "purpose," namely, "that the works of God might be made manifest in him."

So in this case too we appear to be confronted again with the insoluble ambiguity of the catastrophe-situation. For where is the man who would dare to explain this situation as authoritatively as Jesus did and thus force it to disclose an unambiguous message of God? Indeed, it is conceivable—and we shall have to pursue this thought further—that this seeming ambiguity does not discredit the concrete message of judgment itself, but that back of it is concealed a genuine and permanently valid question, namely, the question of what the judgment of God itself really is, and whether the very thing which at first appears to be ambiguous may not express in a very demonstrative way that the judgment itself consists of two integral parts, in other words, that judgment is both punishment for sin committed and education for the future, rejection and visitation, evil and salvation.

But it is this thought that keeps leading us back to the decisive conclusion that the secret of judgment (i.e., whether it is retribution for the past or a visitation for the future) is disclosed only by reference to the person of the Judge, which means, only on the basis of faith.

2. There is another theological reason why judgment cannot be objectively ascertained and that is the fact that the judgment of God may consist in his silence.

The fact that we cannot establish a connection between a sin and the punishment, the fact that God remains silent and passive, when we would expect him to make his will known in a storm of judgment, constitutes the severest kind of test of faith and confronts us with the full force of the problem of theodicy. But it is by no means true that "nothing" is happening when God seems to be silent and passive. The judgment itself may in fact be taking place in his very silence and passivity; indeed, it may even consist in his silence. In the language of faith this means two things: that God is withdrawing his arm and leaving men to themselves; that he is abandoning them to the consequences of their actions and thus delivering them up to their own judgment. The very moments in which the silence of God causes the godless person to feel safe and to mock at divine judgment, because he equates the dreadful act of divine permission with the nonexistence of God, can be the very moment when the man of faith sees the judgment of God bearing down upon the world like an oppressive nightmare, so much so that he would actually feel an outburst of an open storm of wrath to be a relief from the weird and sinister oppressiveness of this silent judgment.

We see, therefore, that the seeming silence of God, his seeming failure to wreak judgment upon the world, cannot be explained by saying that we men lack the antennae to perceive these relationships or that the impression that God is silent is merely a false acoustical impression produced by our unhearing ears and hardened hearts; as if, in other words, the silence of the Judge were merely a matter of some nonreceptivity in our subjective structure.

No, the silence of the Judge is an objective phenomenon; it is inherent in the real nature of divine judgment. Even the angels who stand about the throne of God can testify that God's silence is real; so far is it from being merely a figment of man's deluded and hardened heart. God really can be silent. He by no means judges, or better, he hardly ever judges, merely by smiting the transgressor with a stroke of lightning or some other "catastrophe *ex machina*." On the contrary, he judges men by letting them go in silence, as he allowed the people who built the tower of Babel to wreck themselves upon their own godlessness. By doing what seemed to be nothing, he allowed the dispersion to fall upon them in their godlessness. Hence his silence was extreme activity. What he "allowed" to happen there was the equivalent of coming down and confusing their language. God was at work in the self-confusion merely by standing aside and "looking on." So he also "gave up" the heathen to their own ungodliness (Rom. 1:18 ff.).

This giving up (*paredoken*), that is, leaving one to the consequences of one's own acts, is actually the way in which silent judgment operates, though at first sight one may think that here is an instance in which the law of retribution is obvious to everybody. We can illustrate the manifestness and the hiddenness of judgment by reference to Rom. 1:18 ff. Here the disorder in the vertical dimension—namely, self-assertion over against God—finds its parallel with perversion on the horizontal level. Clear as these consequences of retribution seem to be, they are at the same time *hidden*; for the perverse men referred to in Rom. 1 would probably be much surprised if they had been addressed as being unfortunate: they felt quite well, thank you.

The same is true of the people who built the tower of Babel. They probably would have said: War and conflict, the force of decay and mutual struggle, everything that caused us to be cast out of the original human peace and deprived of "one language and one speech," this is "the father of all things," this is the fundamental impulse of life. Perhaps they might even have replied that a certain amount of wickedness, even of Satanism, serves as a stimulant to the world:

> Man's active nature, flagging, seeks too soon the level;
> Unqualified repose he learns to crave;
> Whence, willingly, the comrade him I gave,
> Who works, excites, and must create, as Devil.[4]

This is hidden judgment: that the ultimate necessity of a world gone out of joint should appear to men to be a virtue.

Everything we have said so far concerning the way in which judgment appears has really been nothing else but an exposition of this one statement, namely, that the secret of judgment reveals itself only as we know the Judge. As long as we do not face this Judge as a personal thou, who, paradoxically, reveals himself in Jesus Christ as our Father, we are hopelessly delivered over to the question of how the world order functions and whether it functions properly. It is actually "hopeless" in the strict sense of the word, because the tormenting question "Why?" not only never ceases to be asked but also is never solved, since it remains unresolved. The great and representative forms of this failure to find a resolution generally take one of two directions:

Either the question "Why?" ends up against a stone wall, that is,

---

[4] Goethe, *Ibid.*, Prologue in Heaven. (Trans.)

in the bleak and comfortless conclusion that the whole thing is unfathomable, whence the next step is the nihilistic conclusion that the seemingly unfathomable has no basis at all and that therefore the world is without direction and utterly fatherless—

Or the question "Why?" ends in the statistical perspective of "great numbers," in this case the conclusion that the whole thing is nothing more than ice-cold mechanical laws and the utter silence of nature. A combination of the first and second answers is found in the attempt to interpret the finite world "tragically"; in other words, to posit an order which is a fate that neither gods nor men can question and of which one never knows who has ordered it or what its purpose is. This situation, in which there is no longer any concept of judgment whatsoever, is itself a judgment.

The deliverance which the biblical message proclaims in the face of this undecipherable problem of meaning, this painful mystery of history with its hidden judgments consists then not in solving the question "Why?" but rather in transforming it into the question "Whither?" and "To what end?" We come back again to the story of the man born blind. The disciples asked, "Why was this man born blind; who sinned?" But Jesus asked, "To what end was this suffering appointed?" and then went on to answer, "That the works of God might be made manifest in him."

The question "Why?" is directed to the "cause" and the answer it is looking for runs like this: Because such and such a thing was done, God did thus and so. But this answer is never found. It is hidden in the counsel of God.

The question "Whither, and to what end?" does not seek such an answer, but is comforted in the certitude that we may confidently allow ourselves to be surprised, because we are being guarded, and the Midgard serpent is not lurking on the horizon; for the foundation of the world is friendly and fatherly. So the Christian, facing the enigma of history, does not formulate a syllogism, but rather says, "Nevertheless, I am continually with thee" (Ps. 73:23). But the Judge is none other than the Father whom we may call upon, and Jesus Christ has assured us that we are his children.

IX

THE FREEDOM OF PREACHING IN THE AGE OF THE MASSES

I BEGIN WITH THE FOLLOWING PREMISE: THE CHURCH OF JESUS CHRIST is not only characterized, with respect to the intellectual sphere within which it "lives and moves and has its being," by the fact that it has a *direct* relationship to the Word of God and thus is called to be contemporaneous with this Word; it is also characterized by the fact that its relationship to the Word is not immediate, but rather *indirect*. And this is so because it exists within a definite intellectual tradition; one might also say, within a definite intellectual climate. With respect to its origin, this tradition or climate is determined by the Greek spirit; with respect to its present form it is stamped by the Christian West, whose mind and spirit is nourished by two springs, Greek antiquity and Christianity. Our message, in the concrete form it takes in theological work and practical preaching and teaching, is being addressed entirely to a world which, even in its secularized structures, is still determined by this spirit. I mention only one of the many symptoms that indicate that this is true: the fact that the theological education of ministers of the Word is completely determined by this dual tradition. The tension between *humanum* and *divinum,* the world and the kingdom of God, which is so obviously constitutive in the Christian concept of revelation, makes, as it were, the encounter between Greek thought and Christianity, between "humanism"

179

and the Christian kerygma an abiding reality that must constantly be restudied in the classical models of Greek thought and the New Testament as well as in the encounter between them. The confrontation of these two thus acquires the rank of an almost timeless model—and the more so as the surrounding intellectual world, and consequently the concrete scene in which the proclamation occurs, is still largely determined by this model, since this scene happens to be what it is—the Christian West.

But while we have largely won our way through to the conviction that the Constantinian age has reached its end and that this results in some very definite consequences with respect to the relation of church and state and the legal structure of the church, there is a further consequence that hardly appears to have entered our consciousness and that is the inevitable question whether this whole intellectual tradition is not also to be called in question and whether its possible collapse does not present some very definite implications for the preaching and proclamation of the Christian message.

In order to understand this, we shall have to bear in mind that in the landscape around the church a whole new world has arisen, a world which has by no means received its stamp from this tradition: I mean, in a word and in common parlance, the *world of the worker*. The compass of this world is by no means confined any longer to the so-called fourth estate;[1] on the contrary, its tremendous material and ideological suction has, over a period of many decades, forced the other social classes into its sphere of influence. The man who is at home in this world is the type of man who is not only *not* at home in this church tradition, but also does not even understand its language. The problem is viewed far too narrowly when theologians are content merely to say that the "language of Canaan"[2] has become unintelligible. The other line of tradition, the language of Greece, has also become unintelligible. Not only the Bolshevist, but also a thoroughgoing Westerner would look at us uncomprehendingly if we were to talk to him, say, about *humanitas* or the "infinite value of the human soul" and meant by this anything more than the technological, economic utility, the mere productive labor power of a man. What we sum-

---

[1] See note on p. 135. (Trans.)

[2] I.e., the language of the Bible and the church. (Trans.)

marize in terms like "liquidate" and "euthanasia" is not only a symptom of defection from God in the Christian sense but also a symptom of the fact that we have long since abandoned the Greek line of tradition and its humanism. This break is so radical that even a new language is beginning to come into being, a leached, mechanized, standardized, soulless language in which the "old" world (not only the Christian world) can hardly make itself understood. As Jacques Maritain has pointed out, in the Greek line of tradition philosophy has "revolved" about the Logos-concept for centuries and within this preparatory realm one could utter the phrase *Logos sarx egeneto* (the Logos became flesh) with the expectation that it would be understood at least "conceptually." The new world has built itself *outside* the gates of the Logos-concept. Indeed, even the term "gate" is no longer appropriate, for this is a closed, a walled-up gate. We are not only de-Christianized, but also de-Platonized.

This faces us with the critical question, which has probably been asked on the mission field, but which still appears not to have been seen as a theological problem that confronts our own mission at home, namely, the question whether and to what extent the message of the gospel can be separated from this other Greek line of tradition. This question goes far beyond what Bultmann is attempting to do with his demythologizing. For Bultmann is concerned merely with the question of the extent to which the kerygma can be separated from the temporary cosmology and the late-Jewish apocalyptic and Gnostic myth of redemption. But here the question is whether Western language can still be the vehicle of the kerygma at all. I ask you to take that statement as a question and to overcome the shock that it may cause.

It may be well to stop and illustrate the theoretical problem with a practical example.

Already certain attempts have been made to draw the consequences of this statement, in the movement called Moral Rearmament and in the Salvation Army. Here the Western style of preaching has been radically abandoned, apparently because it has been concluded that the neo-Western man can no longer be appealed to at the point of his sinfulness, his conscience, the meaning of life, the problem of theodicy, or any other manifestation of the spiritual world and environment of Christianity. (I am intentionally expressing myself in these general terms.) They assume, or think they must assume, that he is nothing more than a complex of nerves, an organism, receptive only to optical and acoustical impressions, especially to rhythm, as his predilection for jazz indicates.

Permit me to give a brief account of an experience I had. While visiting a youth camp on a lonely island in the North Sea I witnessed the following amazing incident. As they were peeling potatoes, about a hundred boys sang with extraordinary vehemence the old Nazi songs, the whole repertoire from the Horst Wessel song to the song of the Hitler Youth, "Our banners wave before us." Every once in a while one of them stood up and gave a remarkably good imitation of Hitler and this evoked almost orgiastic shouts of "Heil, heil!"

What happened here was profoundly symptomatic; for in numerous conversations with the boys I learned two things:

First, as far as ideology is concerned they were as far away from National Socialism as it is possible to be. And I do not mean this in the sense that they had overcome it, for they were too young to have had any need to get rid of it, since the poison had never infected their conscious minds. Simply because of their age and probably also because of their family tradition—most of them came from Christian families—they were outside the sphere of influence of this ideology. In their conscious reflection upon these things they exhibited a thoroughly ironical attitude toward that whole world, and their remoteness from it was also expressed in the style of caricature they portrayed, which would have been offensive to anybody who took it seriously.

Second, at the same time, however, their singing betrayed a fervency that rose repeatedly to a tremendous crescendo, reaching almost to the verge of the ecstatic. As one listened to it, the question that kept thrusting itself upon one was this: Is this the modern schizophrenia of the conscious mind working itself out here—in the sense that the total dynamic of this passé ideology has been overcome only in the *rational* sector of consciousness, but that it goes on living its own life in the subconscious levels of the mind and is far from being subdued?

I believe, however, that we do not need psychoanalysis to explain what was going on here. It requires only an insight into the dynamism of National Socialism itself. National Socialism was able to enter upon its triumphal progress through the German nation only because it did not present itself as a "conviction" (or did so only secondarily), but rather as a psychological dynamic which, by means of rhythm, megaphonic sound, and the stimulation of ecstasy, addressed itself to the most primitive psychic levels, which are exposed in this mass era and are no longer covered up and held in check by the restraints of religion or Greek ethics.

The decadance of the mass era brings with it a mysterious recrudescence of the primtive, which is as different from the genuinely primitive as is the childishness of senility from the childlikeness of a child. In any case, both exhibit an identical phenomenon, which, admittedly, has undergone considerable modification, but which nevertheless compels us to recognize that here we are confronted with a subterranean combination of the asphalt world and the primitive world.

The impression made upon these boys is explained very simply by the fact that, as typical products of modern society, the rhythmical dynamism of the Nazi songs had an immediate appeal for them, regardless of what the "words" of the songs were saying, and that by means of an ironical attitude they immunized themselves against the possible infiltration of any intellectual content that might occur while they were singing them.

They would certainly have sung Salvation Army songs with the same fervency, and the only difference—which, however, might be a very great one!—would have been that they would have omitted the act of immunizing themselves from the text and that their camp counselor would actually have helped them to accentuate the "Word" by preaching and explanation.

In any case, here we have an impressive illustration of the fact that the man of today, and especially the young person, is primarily receptive to sensual, rhythmical, dynamic stimuli, that he is affected by "speech" only incidentally, that his nerves possess the responsiveness of an "Aeolian harp," but that his conscience no longer has the sensitiveness of "gold scales." (Here we are already confronted with our central question: In our preaching will we be able to think in terms of this "Aeolian harp," or will we have to heave great boulders upon what were once sensitive gold scales, but now have become decimal scales, if, indeed, the demolition process of secularization and de-Platonization has not already left nothing but an empty, rubble-covered lot?)

The fact that the man of today is domiciled in this realm of the nerves and is no longer at home in the orbit of Greek thinking and Christianity is the result of his subjection to propaganda. For propaganda, of course, does not operate with the appeal to conviction but rather with sense impressions, with eye-catchers, posters, and the mechanical effect of the repeated cliché or slogan, the intent of which is not to speak and convince, but simply to hammer the nerves and, instead of building up the mind, to provoke mechanical reactions like those produced by animal trainers. That he is at home on this level is also the result of the fact that he is generally content if he has enough to eat and drink, if he earns enough to go to the movies, and is able to satisfy his sexuality.

The theological question that this poses for preaching may be stated thus: Is it possible and permissible to proclaim the gospel within the intellectual, or better, the nonintellectual, framework of this world? Can it really employ what we have called the "Aeolian harp," can it resort to the sensual means of the popular song, of rhythm, or even the optical-acoustical combination of "impressions" produced by a revue? (Cf. *The Good Road* staged by Moral Rearmament.) What if the "outsider" can be reached only here? What if "A Mighty Fortress is our God," what if the very hymns whose strong texts and music we have rediscovered, learned to appreciate and reintroduced into our hymnals, are to him nothing but Chinese music, both textually and musically? Who comes to our churches? I do not mean merely the churches that still employ the "language of Canaan," attended only by a few old women and children; I mean the churches with a strong preacher, or, let us say, only an attractive rhetorician who operates with a few remnants of kerygmatic substance (which, for the rest, may be intermingled with all kinds of literary plums and other bait). Who goes to these churches? Perhaps the man in such a pulpit is happy that so many outsiders and fringe-dwellers come who are never seen elsewhere, all of them willing to expose themselves to a Christian sprinkling. But who are these fringe-dwellers? Generally they are perhaps not much more than secularized advocates of Western culture, chiefly intellectuals, but in any case people who still understand at least the vocabulary of the Greek tradition and therefore, though secularized, have not yet been completely de-Platonized. The real "outsiders" are never seen here at all, or at least very rarely.

When I was a pastor during the war I had in my confirmation class a number of evacuated children who, unlike the South German children in the class, came from the North German metropolitan areas. They could not understand even the most elementary terms, which were immediately intelligible to the simplest of the native children.

To give an opposite example, one time in East Berlin I observed a haphazard group of young boys drummed together from the corners of East Berlin. The mission service began with a hymn in which each stanza ended with the refrain, "Lord, make me pure," chosen to harmonize with the theme of the evening, which was the ethics of sex.

Though I am not a *Berneuchener*,[3] you may well believe that this gave me what might be called liturgical goose pimples. I must confess, however, that, a little while later, I had reason to be ashamed when, after the tenth or fifteenth stanza—the hymn was unendingly long—I observed this saucy gang growing more and more quiet as they sang (one could hardly resist the rhythm and for days afterward it kept coming back to me) until finally one saw something like a yearning for redemption shining in eyes that had grown dim from living on the dark side of life. But then, after the "Aeolian harp" had done its work, when someone spoke and touched their conscience through the medium of words, it so happened that some twenty of them remained for a personal conference with the leader of the evening's program. It should also be said that at that time CARE packages were not yet available. Which of us pastors in the church has ever had twenty such youngsters in his conference room?

As we examine this model situation more closely, we begin to see the theological problem more clearly. The question is: Was the venerable Martin Kähler right when he put forward the motto, so warmly seconded by Julius Schniewind: *Sanctum Sancte?* That is to

---

[3] I.e., a member of the Brotherhood of St. Michael, founded at Berneuchen, a high-church movement interested in liturgical revival. (Trans.)

say, was he right in saying that the Holy also requires a certain holiness, discipline, and dignity in the form in which it is communicated, that it therefore requires, not necessarily a super-solemn kind of speech, but still a language that is worthy and appropriate?

To be sure, the liturgically minded theologians would be inclined to agree with this statement, since they are the ones who are seeking to carry out this principle most consistently. But surely a great many others, too, regard the outward forms which the Word of God has taken on in certain words, forms, customs, and places of worship, not only as being expressions of a style that is appropriate to holy things, but above all as being a required expression of the congregational *response,* as an expression of its reverence and discipline, its worship and praise in the sight of the majesty of God. It would be highly unreasonable to cavil at this; indeed, one must say that it would be theologically impertinent to do so. For it is one of the axioms of the biblical and Reformation doctrine of justification that God's Word and man's response, that God's action toward *us* and our answering action toward *God* ("as to the Lord and not to men"), that justification and sanctification, must correspond, and that therefore the holiness of the majesty of God that is present in the Word must be answered with holiness, fear, and humility in man's approach to it (cf. Isa. 6).

The question I now raise has nothing to do with any doubting or disputing of this holiness in the form which proclamation takes, but rather with what kind of holiness is appropriate to the content of the proclamation, and whether it may not be one-sidedness to regard the majesty of God on the one hand and the dignity and reverence of the form of preaching on the other as the two "contractors" in the relationship of worship.

The days before Christmas during which I write this remind us in a special way that the Logos-made-flesh gave up the heavenly splendor of his majesty and came down into the depths of humanity, in order to restore the lost relationship:

> He a servant, I a lord became;
> What a marvelous exchange was that![4]

---

[4] From fifth stanza of Nikolaus Herman's hymn, *"Lobt Gott, ihr Christen allegleich."* (Trans.)

This was why Luther believed that one cannot "draw Christ too deeply into the flesh" [one cannot overemphasize the incarnation of Christ]; in other words, it is impossible to be too much in earnest about Christ's renunciation of the glory and the majesty, and it is precisely by thus drawing him into the depths of humanity that we honor him. Does this not compel us to face the question whether this renunciation of his must not also in some way express itself in the form which preaching takes?

Let us put it this way to begin with, in order to gain a first rough outline: Should not this manifest itself in the way in which our proclamation is "human," simply because Jesus Christ became a man? In more concrete terms, this would mean that it does not need to be "elevated," with an exalted "Sunday tone," and therefore beyond and above the everyday, solemn, unctuous, emotionally heightened, since all this might be the style of apotheosis, whereas the style of the incarnation is the human, the natural, indeed, the everyday. For Jesus did not speak with his human brothers in a voice from heaven; he sat down and talked with them at their wells; he did not scorn to join the table-talk of sinners and he entered the homes of publicans. Though there one would be struck by the glory of his majesty (how could it be otherwise, since all the fullness of the Godhead was present in the carpenter of Nazareth), nevertheless it certainly was never shown by his having spoken from heaven. (Speaking down from heaven is in itself a mark of pride, of the idols, of apotheosis; cf. Ps. 73:9.[5]) And if he spoke with more authority than the scribes, then surely it was because in the words which he spoke, and which everyone had heard before (i.e., from the rabbis), there broke forth a totally new *ens realissimum*, a new, supremely real being. But this *nova*, this new thing emerged precisely *because* it emerged in the context of the *antiqua*, the familiar, and because it was therefore given its *own* opportunity (and consequently quite independent of the dynamic or liturgical *co-operatio* of the preacher) to demonstrate its "qualitative otherness."

May not this suggest that there is a principle that governs the

---

[5] The reference is intelligible only in the German (Luther's) translation of this verse: "What they [the wicked] speak, is spoken as if it were spoken from heaven." (Trans.)

style of preaching which is completely different from that of "elevated dignity" simply because the *sanctum*, the holy, is not only the message from the right hand of God and about the majesty of God, but also about the message of the condescension of God?

However many theologically essential concepts may be contained within this one word "condescension," for example, compassion in the sense of "suffering with," vicarious suffering, atoning death, what does it mean basically and at the heart of all these terms, except that he came down to find us and bring us home? What else does it mean, except that Christ does not speak from "base headquarters" in heavenly glory, but that he comes down to us in the front-line trenches where the battle with fear, guilt, death, and suffering is being fought, and that his own breast is literally riddled with the missiles that hail upon us all?

This brings us to my question, and I propose to leave it simply as a question: May it not be that this event of condescension, this act of God's coming down to meet us, constitutes *our* commission to go out and meet our brothers outside the gates, those who are secularized and de-Platonized?

By this we mean not only those who are outside the doors of the church, but also those who are outside of what was once called the "Christian" West. May this not mean that we must undertake the venture (or that at any rate a few who are capable must undertake the venture), not merely of continuing to sing the Reformation and ancient church hymns in our church buildings (simply because for the church these have in fact and quite rightly become the legitimate expression of the "holy"), but also of playing upon the "Aeolian harp" on the street corners and hedges for the sake of the poor folk who are susceptible only to nervous reactions, playing Gospel hymns with their peculiar rhythm, and perhaps not even despising the optical appeal of the revue, quite apart from a completely different and revolutionary kind of speech? Ths may be *"kitsch"*,[6] but what of it? May there not be an aesthetic and liturgical form of Pharisaism and therefore of lovelessness, which is unwilling to give up the form of *sancte* that is compatible with the church people, which is unwilling to make any aesthetic, or even any intellectual, sacrifice,

---

[6] Anything in art or music which is cheap, sentimental, "corny." (Trans.)

and therefore evades carrying out the self-emptying of Jesus Christ? May not this lead to presenting modern man, not with the offense of the Gospel itself, but with a false offense? May this not be the offense of serving up the kerygma to the "outsider" in a form of words and music which he does not know what to do with and which does not touch his understanding or his faculty of cognition—much as if it were a message in an alien language or music couched in Chinese dissonances? May it not be that the incarnation means that Jesus Christ is prepared, not only to enter the flesh, but even the flesh we would call *"kitsch,"* and thus is willing to condescend to the nethermost level of human nature? And, if we agree, does not this confront us with certain consequences in our carrying out of this incarnation, in an extreme form of entering into the flesh?

Is the reason why we have not yet faced this task, or at least are not much troubled by the problem, that we have not yet really seen these people outside the church at all? But why haven't we seen them? Is it because they do not come to us—or do they fail to come because we have not yet seen them? Is it because the old tie between the church and middle-class respectability still remains, and still remains despite all our honest self-criticism, has produced a definite blind spot in our perception, in our very faculty of sight? Or because we are *afraid* of what we may sometimes see and what might compel us to make an unprecedented and frightening use of our Christian freedom? Not only the wish but also fear is the father of our thoughts—and the slayer of unborn thoughts. Both are fathers of what we see and what we refuse to see. In any case, which is cause and which is effect here?

I know that to many it may seem odd that a teacher of systematic theology, of all people, and not a practical city missionary should be raising these questions, and I know that by doing so I am exposing myself to the reproach of being out of place. It may, however, be a form of obedience to stand up to this reproach. The reason I have felt compelled to make this statement is not only that I have been moved by many contacts with people (including non-Christians) to have "compassion on the multitude" because it is a flock without a shepherd, but also because I have really been forced to ask the same questions from the point of view of the other side, namely, by theological work on the doctrine of the incarnation. After all, what does it mean to "draw Christ into the flesh"? Does this mean that he must be incarnated in a particular kind of "flesh," a "legitimate" flesh, so to speak, or let us say, the flesh which is within the orbit of what we summarize as the humanum in the Christian-Western sense, and thus a very definite sphere of "dignity"? Or does this flesh mean man's "fleshly being" (*sarx*), which in its concrete form may actually possess all the configurations that can emerge in the whole range of the tension between beast and angel. (As is well known, Pascal saw all human existence is lived within this tension.) In any case, I ask the reader to think the problem through from both of these points of view, not only from the point of view of the practical city missionary but also from that of the theological content and meaning of the incarnation.

How really important this second point of view is may perhaps be made clear from another angle. The condescension of Jesus Christ not only causes him to empty himself of the divine glory, but on the other side also leads to the hallowing of human nature. That which we may call the "infinite value of the human soul" is not based upon the immanent value of this "soul," but rather upon the fact that it has been purchased at great price, that it has Jesus Christ for its brother, that he died for it. Man is what he is through this participation in the *alienum* of grace which God bestows upon him; through this he is sacrosanct, inviolable, and not merely "utilizable." (The basic intent of Lutheran doctrine in stressing the locus concerning the *communicatio idiomatum,* though overemphasized and verging upon the grotesque, was to express this hallowing of human nature through the incarnation.)

May it not be true, then, that even the cheap, trashy "flesh" represented by the *"kitsch"* of popular hymns and revues is hallowed through him who tarries with his divine glory in the lower level of human nature, who accepts and associates with those who react to nerve stimuli and does not despise the "Aeolian harp" (Luke 15:2)?

At any rate, when I saw the yearning for redemption released by that *"kitsch"* gospel hymn in East Berlin, then this song was changed for me—changed in just the same way as a Neo-Gothic church or a parish hall in the plaster-and-*kitsch* style or a movie theater or storefront room used as a church is changed as soon as the Word is preached and an active congregation prays within it. Then generally the moment comes when quite rightly one senses that the category of the aesthetic is out of place, indeed, blasphemous.

And does not this hallowing of words, musical sounds, and places mean further that even these formless forms may well be transformed from within and hence do not remain *kitsch?* In any case, if the church should be forced, not necessarily to a revolutionary liquidation of its previous forms of proclamation, but to a revolutionary expansion of its ministry of the Message, it would have to keep constantly in view the goal to which it must lead people. It would have to know that it must not only go out to meet people where they are, but walk with them and accompany them. In any case, it must not shrink from recognizing even in this activity outside its doors the "servant-form" of its Lord and be prepared, in this respect too, to say, "Here I will stand with you. . . ."

As I have said, my intent in these brief outlines has not been to write what is called a "theological treatise." All of us are still struggling just to keep our heads above water in the surging sea of problems into which we have been cast by the upheaval of our times. I have tried to do only two things:

First, I could not refrain from speaking out about one of the great needs of preaching today and at least indicating something of its background, a need that must concern anyone who is conscious that he is called to the twofold task of teaching theology and preaching in the church and is constantly being distressed by the necessity of concluding that most of the subjects which are generally being discussed in theology and the church today are simply irrelevant. In any case, I believe that in this essay I have touched upon a theme, which (with all respect for the persons who have responsibilities of this kind in theology and the church and for their assuredly respectable concerns) ought to concern us more poignantly than the interminable discussion of union and confession, the question whether the EKD[7] is a church or a federation of churches, whether the head of a territorial church should be called bishop, presiding officer, president, or brother-bishop, etc., whether the Barmen Declaration is a confession or a doctrinal opinion, whether demons exist or not, and so on. I know that many older ministers can no longer think of

---

[7] The Evangelical Church in Germany. (Trans.)

it as their task, and perhaps they should not, to ponder the many questions raised in this essay; but I plead with students and younger ministers to reflect upon them in their studies as in their ministerial meetings (naturally after reading in full the mimeographed official statements handed out at their district and synodical meetings), and for the purpose of clarification to get in touch with very simple lay-preachers, the Christian people who do the work of proclamation in our cities and suburbs and especially among young people. I venture even to beg a man like Wilhelm Busch [a popular preacher] of Essen to give us a practical paper on the preceding theological reflections and questions. If the meetings of ministers are to be regenerated, it will not be sufficient simply to have some pastor who has learned to do good theological work present a paper (though, naturally, this is of the highest value); at the same time themes and questions should be discussed which crop up in services held in the poorest tenements and lead us to the ultimate problems of Christology.

Second, my purpose has been to help those who engage in practical action, such as we see in certain evangelistic movements directed toward man in the mass, to some self-reflection, in order that their endeavors may not degenerate into religious strategy and the utilization of propagandistic methods of suggestion for spiritual ends. As long as the church itself does not see the problem which has called into being these movements (Salvation Army, Moral Rearmament, etc.), or better, as long as it is not profoundly concerned with this problem and merely goes on ministering to the ninety-nine righteous (which has meanwhile dwindled to one percent), it has no right to criticize or even to laugh at these movements. (I am really too much of a theologian not to be able, if I wished to do so, to pour out a whole sackful of misgivings and objections; but I keep the sack closed, for nothing might fall from it but indictments against *us,* and my purpose is not to discourage, but rather to appeal for a new kind of theological thinking.) But it will be the fault of the church if these movements do degenerate, as they actually threaten to do. That degeneration would be a handwriting on the wall that tells us that again we have not been watchful in the sanctuary and have left the vanguard in the lurch without reinforcements. Here too the blood of our brother, whose keeper we have failed to be, may cry out to heaven.

Since these questions are not even remotely seen in the Second Section of Amsterdam, the report remains under the spell of merely technical proposals and ignores all the theological aspects of the problem.

In conclusion I would exhort us all to remember Jesus' parable of the two sons (Matt. 21:28 ff.); I recommend it as a preaching text in order to approach our question from the Scriptures. We theologians may perhaps say, "Yes"—we say a loud, "legitimate," properly theological "Yes"—and then often do not go. The people who rush out into the world as fervent missionaries, often enough turning some grotesque capers, say, "No," theologically speaking; they are not interested in theology and think that what we do in our lecture halls is dogmatic humbug (does the fault lie *only* with them?)—but they go. "Which of the two did the will of his father?" And if it was the second, must we always keep on saying this false "No" and remain in the disobedience of "not going"?

X

THE FREEDOM OF MAN
AND THE AUTONOMY
OF HISTORICAL PROCESS

SURELY IN THESE DAYS EVERYBODY MUST FEEL NOW AND THEN IN HIS heart the leaping flicker of sentimental longing for the good old days when things were "better" and people were a little more "human," when there were loyal neighbors who assisted us and brought us a cup of soup when we were sick in bed, neighbors who helped us and did not denounce us. Those were the days when people were not regimented and "planned" and constantly driven to higher productivity. Those were the days when life was patriarch- ally peaceful, when there was no such thing as good or bad "business atmosphere" (since artificial "air-conditioning" through "human re- lations" had not yet been invented), but only the natural tempera- ture of warm humanity prevailed. Which of us does not occasionally permit himself a jigger of this sentimentality when some of the as- pects of modern life get us down?

And yet it is a good and a sobering thing to take a swallow of water on top of this wine of yearning. That idyl never existed in the first place. Earlier generations too had the Fall behind them and in the warmer atmosphere of the good old days the dragon's teeth sown by the Adversary sprang up quite as lushly as they do today in a plural- istic or socialistic society. If in those days adultery and injustice, intrigue and hardheartedness had not flourished, if the sun had not

194

shone upon both the good and the evil, there never would have been so many exciting tales that came from those times. And when we think of the toothaches people suffered then, of what the village barber and Dr. Quack inflicted upon them, of how their children died in droves, and how gifted people were prevented by social status from ever rising above their own predetermined social class, then the idyllic dreams soon evaporate. Instead of crying like reactionaries over the good old days, we ought rather—more obediently and more disciplinedly—to remember the fact that it is God the Lord who has set us down in this *present-day* society, whether it be democratic or totalitarian, even if there be much in it that goes against the grain. And if it is our heavenly Father who has put us in this place, then it cannot be too bad; for the waves that would sometimes threaten to swallow us up and carry us where we would not go are but the breath of his mouth, and besides they are subject to his governing hand. And he who sleeps beside us in the ship is none other than Jesus Christ himself.

So why are we so lacking in faith, so fainthearted? Sometimes, it is true, we seem hardly to have a chance to live and also to speak out as we would like and as our conscience demands. But have we forgotten that no one, no man, and no regime can contest God's chances, above all the one great chance that he will make all things work out for our good, if we love him above all things (Rom. 8:28)?

It is necessary to state this at the very beginning. For this fixes the place where our thinking must begin. We can pursue all the sociological analyses we please to discover some few places where we still have room to move freely in our society today with all its autonomisms, but this will be of no help to us at all if we forget that God reigns and that he not only consoles us in our little ship as it hurtles on its ineluctable course, but that he is also in command of the swirling flood that threatens to swallow us up. If we forget this, then our analyses and studies, all our intellectual endeavors take on the character of worry and anxiousness; then, despite their acuteness and sagacity, they become products of spiritual decay, which eat away our joy and our courage, and cripple us, becoming partisans of the spirit of care, when all the time the Lord "gives to his beloved in sleep" (Ps. 27:2).

The most important thing therefore is not that we do some careful and sober thinking; the most important is the *place* where we do our thinking. We can do our thinking either in the abyss of dread, and this may be very acute thinking; but we may end up as existentialists with a philosophy of dread. Or we can do our thinking as men who know they are called to security and peace, we can begin our thinking at the heart of God, knowing that the Father's arms are around us. There we will think more calmly and therefore perhaps more objectively.

All of us have heard what Luther said: "A Christian man is a perfectly free lord of all, subject to none." Sometimes this statement seems to be almost too strong: think of all the things we are subject to, bound to, even chained to—especially laws and regulations, but also to what people around us expect of us, to our date and appointment books, the daily grind, not to speak of our floundering about in the net of worry, fear that the door will be closed and we will miss out on life, and concern for our children. The statement, as cited and torn from its context, is in fact too strong; in any case, it is too one-sided. And Luther did mean it (as the continuation of the quotation shows) in a very definite sense. The freedom he is talking about is not the freedom I gain by breaking my shackles in Promethean defiance and rather madly and arrogantly declaring myself free. Sartre perhaps can do this, but he has little luck with it, for it is a hopeless experiment. A Christian, however, can never talk about freedom in this way. He knows that he is free only as he is bound to God, only as he is God's child and keeps looking to him.

We see this very clearly in Jesus' parable of the prodigal son (Luke 15:11). Here is a rebellious lad who declares his independence and breaks out into the free paths of the far country where there are no masters and no prohibitions, where he need pay no heed to anybody and nobody pays any attention to him, where he can be free to his heart's content and do what he pleases. We know how this little song ended: it began in C-major and ended in B-minor. In the place of the fatherly lord came other lords, who made him a slave, whereas before he was the child in the house. These lords were hunger, which assailed his belly, for no one gave him a crust of bread, no one cared any more; the far country was no longer wonderful; it was terrible; then ambition that consumed him, homesickness that devoured his soul, and finally an overwhelming feeling of lostness.

How strange and wonderful—God's people never feel really free and superior to all the hostile powers unless they are bound to their Lord and thus allied with him. "We cannot but speak of what we have seen and heard," they say when men would forbid them to preach and stifle their witness (Acts 4:20; 5:29). This is to say, they are equal to the compulsion of the enemy because they are under the compulsion of God, and his compulsion is stronger. The enemies say, "You must stop speaking; we are stronger than you." And they answer, "We cannot but speak, for God is stronger than we are; and he is also stronger than your terror." So always we are free only if we are bound and we are never free if we are libertines. We are free when we are mature children of God, but never when we are rebels. True, we are not free over against God; but God makes us free over against men and their power. When we put ourselves under Jesus we rise above things; when we put ourselves above Jesus things rise above us.

Again and again Christians have put it to the test: they know that no one is able to snatch them out of the hand of God and therefore that no one can take away from them their fundamental, cardinal freedom, the freedom to be his children. They have tested this freedom even in prisons, concentration camps, and penitentiaries, and it was precisely in these places of extreme constraint that it proved itself.

Why were they free though chained? There are three reasons.

First, their world may have been enclosed by narrow prison walls and their radius of action reduced to a minimum, but yet access to the above remained open. They could pray, even though they were surrounded with silence. They could even praise God in the very midst of oppression (Acts 2:27), and thus were transported from the narrowness of their fetters to the breadth of eternity.

Second, they knew what Paul Gerhardt knew: "Nothing can befall me, save what thou has foreseen and what is good for me." They knew more, therefore, than just the fact that God was with them, giving their souls room to breathe. They also knew that he can pass through doors and walls; that he holds judges, hangmen, spies, and informers in his hand like marionettes; that he not only gave them strength in their lot, but that he also ordained this lot and kept it in his power. For even the forces of oppression are in his hand, and

Nebuchadnezzar and Herod only imagine that they can merrily ride roughshod over the children of God according to *their* plan; but they themselves are in a plan, the higher plan of that Lord who at one moment "forsakes" them (Isa. 54:7) and in the next, "laughs" and "has them in derision" (Ps. 2:4).

And there is still a third thing that makes the chidren of God free and lets them escape "as a bird from the snare of the fowlers" (Ps. 124:7): *They can praise God,* even in the depths. But to praise God really means nothing else but to see history from the perspective of its end, that is, from the throne of God where all the tribulations will be ended and all prayers answered, because then he will be all in all.

This had to be said to begin with, and it must be for us a greater certainty than the powers of oppression themselves as we now proceed to pass these powers in review and observe them in their attempt to take away from us our freedom of conscience.

In any case, no matter how harshly they may deal with us, they are conquered powers. And because these powers are under the control and subject to the triumph of God, there will always be grounds for praise and thanksgiving. There are many who declare, as they look back upon prison camps and times of affliction, that they would not have missed this experience of the depths. For the freedom that God gives us is by no means the freedom to do as we will, but rather, as Paul de Lagarde said, the freedom to become what we ought, namely, children whom he loves and who love him more and more, and thus become free for the essential thing. It is precisely this external pressure that opens our eyes to this, whereas people who can do what they will, because of wealth, power, and privilege, get struck in the mire of temporal things and lose their sense of proportion. The Duke of Windsor has money and leisure enough to do almost anything. But is he really related to the essential thing; is he really happy as he travels from luxury hotel to luxury hotel, from racetrack to racetrack, with his wife carrying her coiffured lapdog? Is he freer than a Christian man in some prison, suffering for the sake of his faith and being lifted up by the praise of God?

Fundamentally, on every page the New Testament is aware that we men are *always* under stress; but it also knows that God wants to turn the very thing that oppresses us into the material of faith and use it to show us the sovereign freedom of the children of God.

The man who lives only in the sunshine, letting the ripe fruit drop into his mouth, never has a chance to learn the "Nevertheless" of faith at all. That is why God *blesses* us with stresses, strains, and trials, and therefore the true children of God have always known what they owed to the hard, oppressive experiences in life, even though it was usually in retrospect that they realized it, as did God's servant Job, for example.

The forms of stress and pressure are infinite in variety. We all get to know them first in our own personal life. How many things we have wished for our life, on the personal level and also for our vocation! But we did not have the freedom to gain them, because the circumstances were against us or because our talents were insufficient. We all have experienced dry and thirsty stretches in our lives, thrown back by illness and misfortune. We have all had things in our own nature with which we could not cope, and still have not mastered: strong passions, neurotic bondages, our temperament, our anxious spirit. We have all had to go through periods when we were thrown back upon the gracious help and forgiveness of our God, and then have found that these were really places of blessing. And always it was the depths from which we cried that were the places where the miracles happened. The depths are the very nurseries where the vital germs of our faith grow and prosper.

It is in this light that we must also see the pressure that certain structures of society exert upon us in the modern world, including both spheres of our divided world.

In the East the pressure comes from that organization of society which we call planned economy in the broadest sense. Here the individual is given no room to make his own decision of conscience. He may be able to criticize details and the practical execution of plans, but there is no doubt that he is debarred from questioning the system *as such*.

Here the thing that is really oppressive is not so much that the individual cannot make a free choice as to whether he wants the socialistic order of society or not. On the contrary it might be argued that it could be demanded of him that he simply face the facts and recognize the givenness of this structure of society.

What is far worse is that he should be required to profess the ideological, philosophical presuppositions of this structure, that he should be obliged to espouse the immanental-messianic meaning that

is given to this system, namely, atheism, and that he and his especially defenseless children should be everywhere exposed to the exu-
dations of this system, in schools, factories, streamers stretched across
the streets, and on every television screen.

Despite everything that can be said in the same vein about the
West, it must be admitted that this represents a decided curtailment
of freedom. Speaking very frankly, I would put it this way:

Whatever autonomies and pressures the Western social order may
contain, no one demands that we espouse them, affirm them, and
even glorify them. In every breed of totalitarian regime, however,
man is compelled to confess in word and deed his faith in the powers
of planned economy. When he is forced to do this his conscience is
being impugned; he is being required to deny what is holy to his
conscience and to applaud what he considers a power of untruth.
He finds himself enclosed in a state structure that lays hands upon
the souls of men, instead of merely ordering external life, which is its
proper function. He therefore finds himself confronted, not by a
"state" in the strict sense of the word, a state as Luther, for example,
understood it, but rather by a pseudo-church, as described in the
old Antichrist plays. And the oppressing thing is that there is not a
moment and not a place in his life at which he is not exposed to this
interference. In fact, there is not even a desert to which he could
flee to find some escape from this claim upon him. To me it always
seemed, even back in the Nazi period, that one of the most dismal
aspects of the totalitarian landscape was the fact that there was
not even a desert on its margin, but that one was always compelled
to live in the center of it.

I do not say this with any sense of Western superiority. For I
know that we are constantly abusing the freedom which is bestowed
upon *us* and which spares *us* this particular form of pressure. I know
that a greedy, selfish pursuit of prosperity is being carried on in the
name of this freedom and that even the purveyors of pornographical
literature and youth-corrupting trash appeal to it and flourish in its
name. Nevertheless, I refuse to deride this formal and dilapidated
freedom just because it is being abused, as do some theologians
among us who are blind to reality. Even though our misuse of this
freedom will one day be a main indictment against us in the Last
Judgment, I still know that it is a grace and a blessing when God, by
giving us this formal freedom, gives us the chance freely to confess

him and the *humanitas* that he wills us to possess, and that the chance is no less a grace for being constantly frittered away.

It is very hard for me to give advice to brethren who are exposed to this pressure. When one is not being subjected to the same trials with them, one naturally hesitates to say anything. However, *we* too once lived under the burden of ideologies and we experienced the temptation they confronted us with. And only in view of this do I dare even to try to find a way through to a helpful answer.

In a totalitarian regime we men, we Christians too, are all too easily captivated by the goal that is set up by such a system. Even though those of us who live in the East still have certain freedoms (the word "still" is the important word here, but it is a damnable word), we know that the strategic goal remains unchanged, namely, a religionless social order in which the alleged poison of superstition has been sweated out of men's brains. We are constantly allowing the opponent to palm off on us his familiar distinction between strategy and tactics, namely, that his ultimate strategic goal is the violent or mild extermination of Christianity, whereas in the mean-time he may repeatedly interpose respites, so-called periods of armis-tice, shifting, and thawing. This leads even Christians to an understandable psychological conclusion: they become panicky, fear-ing that the door will be closed upon them, and allow themselves to be overmastered by fatalism, which is, of course, a false faith. They say, "It's no use. We must let things take their course. There's noth-ing we can do about it."

I need not say that this is disobedience and that it is a betrayal of the faith that knows that the future is entrusted to God and cherishes the triumphant certainty that the Lord will scatter them in a mo-ment. Then we are not even using the opportunities that exist. And how many opportunities God is continually giving to us; how often he causes large holes to appear in the cunningly contrived nets; how marvelously he plays with his dispensations of history, so that moments of thawing are made to supervene, now for economic, now for foreign policy reasons! Thus by the grace of God we live, as Martin Fischer said, "from reprieve to reprieve." But we are con-stantly failing to understand these signs of God's activity, simply because panic is unbelief and therefore makes us blind.

And I believe that we also wrong our opponent through this un-belief: after all, he has in principle proclaimed freedom of conviction and wrought it into his constitution. We also owe to our opponent the service of holding him to his word, perhaps to his hypocritical word—"for a testimony against them" (Matt. 10:18). If we do not do him this service, we drive him deeper into his entanglement, so that finally he feels justified in assuming that his analysis that religion and faith are merely a poisoning of the brain has proved to be correct. For, he could argue, my experiment with these Christians shows that just a little pressure is enough to cause this mental illness of faith and this "imaginary" Lord of the believers to evaporate. If this belief that the Christians say they have is really correct, thinks the opponent, then the eternal foundation, which the Christians say they are founded upon, must actually exist. And if they *really* had this Lord, to whom all power in heaven and on earth is given, then these broad hints about the coming of atheism would not shock them so much, nor make them nervous and confused about the chances of their God. If this faith were really as serious as the Christians make it out to be, they would not believe what we say about atheism at all, for then they would have to say that their God is also the Lord of the atheists, that these atheists were also under his rule, but that the poor dupes had not yet found it out.

So we Christians in the East are by no means as unfree as we sometimes think; we become unfree only to the degree that we underestimate the possibilities of God. A great deal more can be said than is generally said; and often even the external danger, which we expect as long as we keep staring like a rabbit at the snake, does not materialize at all.

I frequently wonder whether this unbelief and this unwillingness to risk something in the name of God does not often arise from the fact that we want to preserve intact a particular kind of Christianity and ecclesiastical institution and that we grow nervous when we see God shattering our accustomed forms. There is such a thing as a pious, an ecclesiastical, egoism. But it is a curious thing that God never wants our attention turned to ourselves, or even to "our church." He always points us to our neighbor. A faith that is lived without this service to one's neighbor, that is, without love, passes over into corruption (I John 3:7; 4:8; Jas. 2:14 ff.).

I believe we should accustom ourselves to an altogether different way of putting the question as we face trial and temptation. Instead of asking: How can we as Christians survive this time of oppression and jeopardy? we ought rather to ask: What service do I as a Christian owe to my neighbor? And this neighbor may perhaps be, of all people, the Communist functionary who, by the very way in which he puts pressure on me, is questioning my faith. You may be sure he is watching me like a hawk to see which of two things I may do. I may react with panic and duck into resignation (which will mean that I have denied my faith) or I may assume a "Christian" attitude and remain adamant and unmoved, but do so by defending my "Christian world" against the Bolshevistic world (which will mean that I have denied my love). Then the other person thinks, "For this man Christianity is only a Christian ideology which he opposes to my Bolshevistic ideology. This Christian is not concerned about me and my soul, for which his God is supposed to grieve and which he therefore should be seeking in love and self-sacrifice. O no! I'm not a challenge, an object of love and care to him at all; he's only interested in asserting himself as a Christian."

Both denials—the denial of faith and the denial of love—are noted very clearly by the other person. Then they may perhaps be a painful disappointment to him, because in the furthermost corner of his heart he may still be troubled by the question whether the Christians may not have the truth on their side after all. On the other hand, these denials may be a triumph for him, because now he feels that his opinion that religion is nothing but the opiate of the people has been confirmed.

In either case, however, I as a Christian have failed my atheistic brother. And yet Christ died for him. But I have failed to bear witness to him in a credible way that the honor of his visitation was being set before him. I have betrayed this hour and let it slip uselessly away. I have not touched the bonds that chain him to his idols.

When I say this I am fully aware of how inadequate we are as *individuals* to cope with these tasks; but God did not design us to be merely individuals. He put us into the fellowship that watches with us, the church whose admonition helps us to gain clarity and also speaks for us publicly when the individual is too weak to do so. And as the watcher on the walls of Jerusalem it *must* speak out, it *must* open its mouth against the authorities and enunciate clearly and representatively how a Christian thinks of his mission and the limits beyond which he will not go when, for example, he joins the "Agricultural Production Associations"[1] in order to serve his country through his labor. The church must open its mouth, not only to comfort its members, who are sent out "as sheep in the midst of wolves," and certainly not only to preserve "its interests," but also in order to proclaim the faith and represent it credibly to our neighbors, the functionaries and authorities on the *other* side. Then the church's "interests"—and, naturally, it has interests—will also be taken care of incidentally. Only if we seek first the kingdom of God will all these other things be added unto us—but they will really come only "incidentally." He who advocates Christian interests as an end in itself betrays Christ. There are things which God desires should come to us only as by-products, which he gives to us only "in sleep," and which he withholds from us when we purposely and consciously seek them.

I have already said that it is not the ideological society that exposes us to inevitable pressures. The so-called "free world" of the West also evidences in its social order certain trends that rob us of individual decision or considerably limit its scope. If we take a sharp look, we find innumerable points at which we are by no means so free as we think we are. We can mention only a few examples:

Think of industry. To begin with, there are the many little people, or at least not big people, laborers and salaried employes, who can hardly say whose wagon they are hitched to, whether the ethics of the businesses they serve are just or unjust, whether the goods they produce will promote war or peace. But even the so-called "big shots" and leaders are not anything like so free as we imagine. They certainly are not free in the kind of life they are obliged to lead. We know how they are harried by appointments, how their date books not only rob them of time to enjoy life and reflect upon the essentials, but also give them a "coronary" into the bargain.

But even in the process of business operations itself they are very unfree. Free competitive business is based on the law of moves and

---

[1] *Landwirtschaftlichen Produktionsgenossenschaften* (LPG). (Trans.)

countermoves. I cannot act independently of what the competition does, merely on the basis of my own insight and my own conscience; I must constantly "react," and the scope of this reaction is exceedingly limited. Say I am in the heavy industry in the Ruhr, and I very seriously face the question whether I am not compelled to abolish Sunday and introduce the sliding work week, even though I personally want to abide by the Third Commandment. If I hold on to Sunday as a day of rest, I may, for technical reasons connected with the economical operation of blast furnaces, be faced with a considerable shrinkage of the volume of production. But, considering foreign competition which is not handicapped in this respect, this may be dangerous to the national economy. Thus we see how the autonomy of moves and countermoves, action and reaction, and also supply and demand considerably reduces the scope of my power of decision and also my freedom of conscience.

This is true not only in industry but everywhere in life, even in the realm of science and technology, where we still expect to find more freedom of thought and action. Arnold Gehlen has said with a certain justification that the scientist as well as the technologist appears to have been disqualified and as it were declared incompetent to pursue his own initiative insofar as he has no control over the progress of his research and its application. Strictly speaking, it is not the scientist who pushes ahead his research; it is rather research that pushes itself ahead. And, what is more, it moves in accordance with a chain reaction which impels research to move by automatic processes from definite questions to answers and from there to new questions. For the scientist neither "sets" the problems nor does he "decide" what technological application shall be made of what is discovered. "What must become the problem follows from what is already known, and it is inherent in the very logic of experimentation that exact knowledge already includes control of the (technological) effect. The 'decision' to apply is superfluous." The decision is taken off our hands by the object; one might also say that it is taken away from us. Robert Oppenheimer, one of the builders of the atom bomb, once went further and described this logical inevitability as an irresistible psychic tendency when he said, with reference to his particular task, that what is "technologically sweet" proves to be irresistible, even when it means making the computations for constructing the atom bomb.

The first form in which technological autonomy works itself out is therefore the inseverable connection between question and answer, between theoretical knowledge and technological effect. One inevitably follows the other. The scientist appears to be only the medium through which the sequence occurs. His own intellectual contribution enters in merely in the form of the ability (sometimes the ability amounting to genius) to recognize the "waiting" chain reaction of question and answer and to set it off. But is he the responsible steersman? Does not the ship of scientific and technological progress sail on with no one at all on the bridge?

The second form in which autonomy works itself out is to be found in the process which I described earlier as moves and countermoves. This process can be traced in technology as well as in politics and industry. I mention a few examples. When some important advance, say automation, is introduced in one sector of industry, then companies in the same industry must "follow suit" in order to be able to compete. Here we see the relationship of move and countermove operating almost as a natural law. Or think of the same law as it operates in the question of armaments. If a potential enemy secures atomic weapons, then I am delivered over to the necessity of doing the same thing for my own self-defense, which means at least building up an equivalent force. If I consider this armament madness—and who doesn't?—I cannot fulfill my responsibility for combatting this madness simply by abstaining from making my countermove. This would only stimulate the megalomania of my potential enemy. Confronted by this madness, I can exercise my responsibility of conscience only by considering political measures in order to achieve a controlled disarmament. But this disarmament is itself subject to the law of moves and countermoves; it is a process the individual phases of which are likewise bound to the law of reciprocity.

Once we look at world affairs from this point of view, we discover that this law of moves and countermoves, of *do ut des* (I give in order that you may give) pervades all areas of life, even the personal relationship between my neighbor and myself. Only when we see this clearly can we estimate what a radically new thing came into the picture with the coming of the gospel. For the gospel abrogates the law of retaliation in the I-thou relationship. It breaks this vicious circle and in the Golden Rule imposes upon me the obligation to make a new start, taking a free, venturesome initiative. But this new thing, which can come like a fresh, creative breath into my relationship to my neighbor, making all things new, can be carried over only in a very limited way to the supra-personal areas of life, such as technology, industry, and politics. The endeavor to put this distinction between these two realms of life into intellectual terms, not simply to separate them and allow them to fall apart, but rather to distinguish them, constitutes one of the most difficult and challenging chapters in both Protestant and Catholic theological ethics. Lutheranism deals with this question in its doctrine of the two kingdoms, Catholicism in its doctrine of natural law. However, we need not go into that question here. I merely wanted to indicate that here broad horizons of centuries-long intellectual effort are opened up.

There are two questions, however, which we cannot avoid here, because they touch directly upon the problem of responsibility.

1. I mention first the fundamental question of how from the standpoint of Christian ethics we are to understand these autonomies which appear to mislead men in this way. If I am not mistaken, there are two possibilities here.

The first possibility is to think of these autonomies as an inescapable fate, which, because it is inescapable, relieves me of all responsibility. This was how Machiavelli, for example, interpreted the autonomism of politics. He thought of politics as an arena of *sacro egoismo* and accordingly viewed political action as an ethically neutral play of forces in which the forces of virtue and fortune unfold and develop. Politics and economics thus become a purely physical complex of processes in which energies and matter move and are moved.

If one accepts this fatalistic concept of autonomy, this means, applied to technology, that the sole imperative emerging from this autonomy is that one must play along with these processes without scruple or inhibition in order to be able on this level to meet all competitors with dynamic superiority. Applied to military technology, this would mean unlimited race to build up armaments, at least when one may concede oneself the chance of being the stronger.

The second possibility is that I may interpret these autonomies,

not as an ethically neutral, fatalistic necessity, nor as a law of crea‑
tion incorporated into the structure of the world, but rather as
fateful decree evoked by the guilt of man. I hesitate to say this in
this abrupt form, for one really cannot make this statement with‑
out developing it further in order to avoid the painful impression
that one is sounding off with a dogmatic term like sin. If we had
the time to develop the theological background of this idea further,
I would show that, underlying the Christian concept of sin, es‑
pecially the Fall and original sin, are certain processes which are
astonishingly similar to those unleashed by the autonomisms. For
here too the sequence begins with an initial act, in this case the
eating of the forbidden fruit, and in the next moment this initial
act moves beyond the personal sphere and a decision made *by* man
becomes a decision *concerning* man. From then on this man pro‑
ceeds with the Fall behind him and must finish his course in
accordance with the law with which he began. He has this Fall
behind him and now he is "thrown" into his fate. Unlike the hero
of classical tragedy, however, he cannot disassociate himself from
this guilt by simply calling it fate, but must accept it as "his" act,
that is, as his guilt. The Adam-process keeps repeating itself in
him. He must say, "I am Adam."

Now it seems to me that the same thing is true of the auton‑
omisms about which we have been speaking: I dare not simply
shuffle them off as fate and say, "I can't do anything about it; they
are not my responsibility." Do they not ultimately go back to an
initial act of man? Is not the law of move and countermove, the
law of retaliation, merely a macrocosmic reflection of my own
heart? And hence must I not say, "All this is *I*—this is *my world?*"

I believe that this insight—this theological and Christian in‑
sight—into the guilt-character of the autonomisms is exceedingly
helpful in itself and that it can challenge us to exercise our free‑
dom in the midst of this world, which seems to be so rigidly
established and doomed to run its course on fixed, unbending
rails. For this preserves me from making a virtue of this necessity
of our fallen world. Then I cannot feel that I am justified if I
simply follow the trend of autonomism, if I simply jump to con‑
clusions and say, *because* the law of profit and loss demands the
introduction of the sliding work week, I shall abolish Sunday;
because my competitor secures business advantages by nasty tax

manipulations, I must do the same so that I won't be run over. Rather I now put the question this way (choosing the example of the sliding work week): What did God intend his creation to be? Did he plan his creation to be a perfect economic apparatus and man merely a functioning instrument in it? Or did he intend that man should be in his image, that the main and cardinal question should be the question of his salvation, of the fulfillment of his created life? That therefore the purpose of industry is merely to provide the means of physical existence in order that man may live and fulfill the real purpose and meaning of his life? Or, to put it even more simply, does man exist for industry or does industry exist for man?

Once a person has grasped the Sermon on the Mount and discovered how greatly the orders of this aeon and its laws are called into question, he can no longer think of the autonomisms of this world as ends in themselves; no longer can he make a virtue of the necessity of this world. And therefore he also dare not allow all this to overmaster him.

True, we cannot simply treat these autonomisms as nonexistent. This would be visionary and even in a spiritual sense unrealistic. We Christians too must pay our tribute to these laws; we cannot escape the form of this passing world, otherwise we "would need to go out of the world" (I Cor. 5:10; John 17:14 f.). And we have neither the promise nor the command for this. The concrete structure of our action will always have to be that of *compromise;* we can never simply withdraw and contract out of the situation! This is one of the decisive reasons why we can live only by forgiveness, why we are *peccatores in re* (sinners in fact) and *justi in spe* (just men in hope). And yet the very fact that we may know that this is so keeps us sound and whole. This knowledge is like the gauze placed in a wound which is not supposed to heal. Woe to us if it heals and we indulge the illusion that this world is quite in order and we can accept its order as the standard of our action! But he who has discovered that this is a temporary, provisional world, a ruptured world, in which one goes on living beneath the rainbow of reconciliation with God, that person is always alive and sensitive to the question of where he must take his stand and by no means fall and give in, where he can go along and where he must go on strike, where he can yield and where he must resist in the

name of what God has in mind for his world and his people and
not allow the law of opportunism to become his master.

So when we deal with what I have called the autonomisms in
the organization of society we are dealing with forces that are to
be taken with utter seriousness, even though they are conquered
powers. We have the freedom to see through them and to show
them up for what they are—provisional orders of this passing aeon,
to which, it is true, we must pay a certain tribute, but to which
we need no longer submit, to which we subject ourselves as if we
had not subjected ourselves (I Cor. 7:29). We know that God holds
the real goal before the eyes of his children, that he "has ways
through all the ways," even in the maze of seemingly fixed and
inflexible tracks of this world, and that he takes the liberty to
make everything work for good with those who love him, bringing it to the goals "which he has purposed and desired to have,"
in the words of Paul Gerhardt.

Though, on the one hand, we take these forces and autonomisms
seriously, and on the other hand, do not take them altogether
seriously because in the certainty of our calling they are no longer
to be taken with utter seriousness, there is this to be said in any
case: They do not pervade our *whole* life. That is to say, there
are still some elemental areas of our existence which are beyond
them. I mean those areas in which we are dealing with sin, suffering, and death, in other words, with that which is the most
human and personal of all. In these areas we have to come to
terms with our pains, our sorrows, and our despair. Here is where
we have to justify ourselves before our conscience, and yet cannot
do so. Here we realize that our time is limited and that what lies
behind us we can never bring back, for our time runs out in death.

In these areas we cannot appeal to the commands of men, nor
to the laws that inhere in the structure of our society. Here nobody
can take another's place, but each must freely decide whether he
shall flee or stand fast, whether he shall let himself fall or allow
himself to be upheld, also deciding who or what it is that will
uphold him.

Having said this, I am aware of an objection and I am willing
to take this objection seriously. It probably runs something like
this:

You are retreating into the realm of private life, and what we want to hear from you is whether we as Christians can change anything in *public* life, the life of society, or whether we must simply be passive and let things run their course. True, a well-meaning reader may say, you have said some comforting and encouraging things about our still having some chances and that not everything is so fixed and established as it appears. But here in the second part of your presentation you go steering us back into private life, into the personal areas of sin, suffering, and death, because it is obviously easier to prove that there is still a little leeway for the conscience in this area. And some of my theological colleagues may add, somewhat pensively: After all, it was precisely the failure of nineteenth-century Christianity and theology that it moralized and made a private matter of our relation to God, that it talked of nothing but "the soul and its God"; whereas today we have been given a fresh realization that Christians must also live, serve, influence, and keep watch in the public concerns of life. Not only our "individual souls" belong to God; the state, society, indeed, this whole aeon belongs to God. Therefore we dare not be content to build a wall and a roof over our individual salvation and let the wicked world go on playing its evil games until it topples into the abyss. The salvation which God bestowed through the death and resurrection of his Son is not something with which I dare to feather my own personal nest! This salvation is also for those who bear a political mandate, the representation of the government, the managers, and the functionaries. It is in this world outside that we must prove our faith, not privately at home, after working hours, in a quiet, isolated chamber!

Well, I am quite aware of all this and I thoroughly agree with the statement that we are called to the outside world, that we are the salt of the earth and dare not withdraw to the seclusion of the salt cellar in order to conserve ourselves instead of salting the world.

And yet there is one important point in this objection, which I myself have just raised, that is wrong. And the explanation of this brings us to our second basic question.

It is a mistake to think that whenever I have to come to grips with my guilt, my suffering, and my death I am dealing only with the intimate sphere of my own private, personal life. Why is this so?

Every system, no matter whether it be a social program or a philosophical, ideological concept, possesses a definite view of man, an anthropology.

We may illustrate this in the case of National Socialism, in which man was merely the bearer of functions and biological values. Here, as in the other ideologies that afflict us today, there was no such thing as the infinite value of the human soul. Man was judged rather by what he could be utilized for. If he could no longer be evaluated in terms of his functions in the community, in the collective, he was accounted to be a "life unfit to live" and was thrown on the scrap heap. Not man himself, but a man's function was the sole important thing. Correspondingly, the importance of the individual person was depreciated. The individual lost his significance as a unique being upon whom God has placed the accent of eternity. The individual became a mere leaf on the tree of the nation. The leaf might wither, be torn off, and die, but this did not matter, if only the tree of the nation, the tree of the system and society remained standing. For leaves go on growing, they are replaceable and interchangeable.

In those days I was constantly having to deal as a pastor with people who found their stay in this view of the world and of man. And I saw how this view proved to be simply inadequate when these people faced personal, private crises in their lives, when a marriage broke down, when a son fell ill of leukemia, when a father died—not necessarily on the battlefield—leaving his little children behind. These are cases from my own experience.

Take the case of the young father of a family whom I remember from the days of the war. He was a member of the Party, suddenly snatched away by a malignant disease. I had to bury him. The Nazi formations of storm troopers, the other administrators, district leaders, and party propaganda functionaries stood about the grave, obviously waiting indignantly to hear what the "parson" would have to say to them. I mention a few sentences of what I said then.

You say that man is only a leaf on the tree of the nation. Which of you dares to say at this open grave of a promising young man, beloved by his family, which of you dares to say before this widow and these children, weeping for their father, that this man is only a leaf who can be replaced by another? True, his work, his function, can be taken over by another. But he himself is irreplaceable, as God created him and made him live, as God made him a husband and father. That is to say, before God every man is infinitely precious, for Jesus Christ died for every man. And now you can judge for yourselves who is right: God, who considers his people precious and for whom none is too insignificant; or those men, who see in another man only the bearer of a function and accordingly consider him replaceable, who think of him as being only a blighted leaf.

I believe that group of mourners was really affected. In any case, they were very silent when they parted.

The fact is that this view of man that sees in him only a molecule in the collective, only a potential in the production process, only a function of material relationships, whether they be economic or biological, is simply *false*. For it will not do when man's innermost being becomes the theme. And when we face guilt, suffering, and death this innermost being of man *does* become the theme. Each one of us always bears his own guilt. And this is not at all a matter merely of political guilt over against the socialistic society or some other social order to which I cannot fully accommodate myself and therefore disturb because I am a nonconformist. Rather it is always my own personal guilt, the guilt which I know only in part and God alone knows fully. It is that realm in which I dissipate and bury the talent entrusted to me instead of investing it, the realm in which I fail to give love to my neighbor and those closest to me, where I am consumed by envy and care, where I deny and am proud. And my suffering too is always my own, something which I endure in utter loneliness. Though millions of mothers lost their sons in the war, this certainly was not a collective suffering visited upon them. Rather each mother bore her pain alone, because she had a unique and unexchangeable relationship of personal love with her boy, which she shared with no one else. Therefore she could not share her grief either and simply allow it to be absorbed in the general mourning of the whole nation.

All this was borne in upon me in a very trivial experience I once had. During the time of the Third Reich I saw a company of soldiers marching smartly down the street. The sun was shining and they were blaring out a song. There was certainly nothing unusual about this at all; it was a commonplace, everyday experience. And yet on this occasion I was suddenly struck by this thought, that this company of men was really one single sounding and rhythmically moving body, that the individual was, so to speak, submerged in this supra-personal formation; he no longer had even his own gait or his own voice, but had been swallowed up in this overarching whole.

For a moment the thought flashed through my mind: What a fascinating symbol of the collective! And here you stand on the sidelines as a Christian, believing that everyone is an individual before God and that every human being is personally unique, irreplaceable, and infinitely valuable to God. Is not this unit, singing and tramping with measured tread, a contradiction of this Christian doctrine of the individual and his God? But as the company marched around the next corner and the sound of their singing gradually died away it suddenly became clear to me that afterward this unit breaks up again and each man goes back to his family. Then each one leads his own life, each sins in his own way, each has his own peculiar joys and sorrows. And finally each will also die his own death—alone and with none to accompany him. His last hour will be like a turnstile, which lets him alone pass through—without his luggage. There the noisy, rhythmically moving collective body will break up; before God's throne none will have a "next man" to march beside him. And yet, he will have a "next man," standing close beside him, never leaving him; but this "next man" will be different, altogether different from his earthly comrades. It will be He to whom we pray: "When I depart, depart thou not from me."

This is the true image of man. And in these all-important dimensions the philosophies and world views leave man in the lurch. Here they cannot give him order, support, and comfort; here they abandon him. And because we as Christians address the real, the true man, because we speak of the *forgiveness* of his sin, the *overcoming* of suffering, and the *Victor* over death, this abandoned man knows that he is being addressed. When we do this we also strike at the secret doubts of the functionary. And then something extraordinary happens. When we do this, when we simply deliver the message of forgiveness and the overcoming of the world, then we *drive a breach* into the world view. All the arguments and debates, all the brilliant duels with representatives of the other world view are as nothing compared with what God does here with his

Word: he breaks through the bastions of a hostile, entrenched world because he comes down in mercy to the man who sits in the cold prison of his ideological systems.

What we are saying is that the gospel also has the true image of man. We gain the victory and break the compulsion of the system by addressing ourselves to the true man, whom God purchased at great price. And in order to perform this service and proclaim the victory that has overcome the world, and therefore also overcomes the systems that rule the world, we do not need to control the columns of the newspapers or the microphones of the radio. It is enough if a grandmother teaches her grandchild the Lord's Prayer and the Catechism. For then she not only gives him a remedy that makes him immune to all ideologies, but is at the same time driving a breach into the system. The grandmother (here used as a symbol, of course), indeed, any woman who watches over the souls of children, who teaches them to pray and brings them up to be true men—true men because they stand before God—that woman is not only the guardian of the sphere of private life and the home; she is also one of the secret powers and means of the kingdom of God that influence the public and thaw the ice of the godless systems with the simple, insignificant-seeming grains of salt which are the eternal Word.

Hence it is also false to think that woman finds her real fulfillment in being incorporated in the industrial production process, whereas if she remains in the home she is merely a slave to the cookpot and the beds of her children. It is not merely a matter of the cookpot, but also of the table prayer, not merely the children's beds, but also the prayer, "Now I lay me down to sleep, I pray thee, Lord, my soul to keep," which she teaches her children at these beds. It is when she relinquishes this sphere, in which is planted the seed of the gospel that is meant to become a great, overshadowing tree (Mark 4:31 f.)—I say that when she gives up this sphere she really does become enslaved. Then she betrays her calling; then she lets slip from her hand the key position entrusted to her by God.

This applies both to the East and to the West. In the East woman threatens to be estranged from her calling by being taken away from the family to work on the production line. The same thing happens in the West when, without being forced by need, she becomes addicted to the craze for prosperity, when she brings in a second income to buy hi-fi and television sets and other gadgets of modern culture, deserting her home and leaving homeless "key kids"[2] behind. Without realizing what she is doing, she is committing an act that is worse than a betrayal of her personal sphere of life. Unknowingly she is helping to level the roads on which the ideological powers, nihilism, and the enemies of God march in, roads on which they make good progress and encounter no resistance. For she has torn down the barriers of the family, which would have stood in their way. She has thrown away her chance to change things and call a halt to these processes which are only seemingly inevitable.

It is not only the leaders of history, the "world-historical individuals," who determine the destiny of the world, but rather the quiet guardians of the home, the "meek" of the New Testament, the people to whom a child, a grandchild, or marriage partner is entrusted, whose soul God will one day require of them. These are the realms where the real "switch towers" of the world are located. These above all are the concern of God's higher thoughts. The "ruler of this world" (John 14:30; 16:11) is powerless when faithfulness is practiced *here*. But every little devil, however junior and subaltern, celebrates a triumph when we abandon these seemingly insignificant bastions. God is making his policies in places completely different from those imagined by the editors of the world press.

There is still one last place where freedom is promised to us that must be mentioned. It is the freedom of those who love. In the world there prevails a compulsive law that can be characterized by the words "tit for tat," "give and take," "blow for blow," in a word, the law of retaliation. What it means is that I always treat the other person as he treats me. If he comes to meet me with friendliness, I willingly take his hand. If he approaches me with hostility, I become defensive and hate him. This is the world's law of retaliation that Jesus Christ spoke of and about which he says to us: You, however, are not to act in this way (Luke 9:55). For when I react in this way, I am not free at all; then I am merely a function of my opponent; then I am being ruled by the compulsion of the law of

---

[2] *Schlüsselkinder*, children of working mothers who are given a key to get into the house or apartment after school. (Trans.)

retaliation. But he who has grasped what Jesus meant by the words, "Love your enemies!" (Matt. 5:44) makes a new start. He does not simply "react"; he seizes a creative initiative, and thus becomes free.

Certainly this imperative, "Love your enemies!" is a hard saying. And quite naturally I must ask myself how it is possible at all. Wouldn't it be simply forced and hypocritical for me, confronted by an ideological opponent, a representative of the Terror, to seek to suppress all my defensive instincts, all my contempt and defiance, and try to pump up within myself something like a feeling of love? This, of course, would be purely artificial and my face, instead of being relaxed and loving, would present only a wry grimace. Love of one's enemies cannot be practiced by means of morality and resolutions of the will. This can be done only in a completely different way, which means the way in which Jesus Christ himself did it. He saw in the prostitutes and publicans, the high priests and wine-pullers among his people and even in the hired executioners beneath his cross (Luke 23:34) something altogether different from the representatives of the enemy that was out to destroy him. He saw in them the misguided, unhappy children of his Father in heaven, and he grieved over them. And because he thus separated them in his mind from the enemy front and saw them in a completely different dimension—that is, as misguided and unhappy children—he grieved over these lost souls, and therefore he loved them and his heart was filled with compassion. And because this was his attitude toward them, the law of retaliation could no longer dominate him; he was lifted above into the free spontaneity of love.

I believe that this is the message that is helpful and important precisely for our brethren who are living under the pressure of a rigid, harsh system. We must remember that none of the advocates of this system can believe and accept your message about the love that overcomes the world if you confront them in the form of political self-assertion and therefore in hostile reaction to the Antichrist, negatively and defensively putting forth the claims of the Christian Church.

Externally, this kind of militant self-assertion of Christianity looks very brave and strong in faith. And yet this is precisely what blocks the message and kills the willingness of others to listen. For this kind of Christianity lives only by reaction, by retaliation; it is ruled by the law of earthly power struggles and therefore no one will believe it when it preaches the freedom of the children of God.

Therefore everything depends not upon our merely "reacting," but rather upon our learning to undergo that transformation of vision that took place in the eyes of Jesus when he looked at his enemies, upon our seeing in the functionaries and fanatical ideologists the hidden brothers of our Lord, for whom he died and whom he bought with a great price. If we allow him to give us that vision, we shall experience a miracle: We will become inwardly free from the other's oppression and our witness will gain in authority. For the very thing that will disconcert him will be to see that we are not concerned merely with preserving Christendom, but with him, that we grieve for him and the error of his way. For nothing like this ever happens anywhere else in this world with its law of retaliation. It happens only where Jesus Christ rules and calls us to the freedom of those who love.

Our love, far more than our feeble words, is able to thaw the icy armor of hearts that are closed. *Jesus Christ reigns through those who love in the world.* When they love he also gives them the word of testimony and the authority of witnesses, but *only* when they love. We may be ever so clever theologians, reducing our opponents to silence in discussion, but without this love we are noisy gongs and clanging cymbals (I Cor. 13:1). Only the one who loves has the power to thaw the ice.

So everywhere we see the signs of the freedom promised to us. Yes, we can change things, for we are no longer pawns and objects of inevitable laws; we are the children of our Father. He who learns to praise God, like the apostle in prison, is free despite the bars and walls. For he who praises God sees the world from the vantage of its end, where God has won his victory, where believers and foes, those who pray and those who mock, are gathered about his throne. It is by this sight of the end that our freedom lives; here our fear is assuaged and here we are given the perseverance of those who know that one day the world's battlefields will be empty and God will be all in all. He who laughs last laughs best; and he who is crowned last is king. But this last one will be Jesus Christ our Lord. And he to whom the last hour belongs need not fear the next minute.

INDEX

A

abortion, 79 f., 104
accident, contingency, 168 f.
actus purus, 10
Adenauer, Konrad, 109
Aleksandrov, G., 95, 98
amor fati, 20, 72
anthropology, man, 18, 20, 35, 36, 128,
138, 159, 215
art, 16, 49
atheism, 83 ff., 202
Augustine, 157, 161
autonomy, 13, 207 ff.

B

Barth, Karl, 86
Bengel, Albrecht, 42
Benjamin, Hilde, 108
Bismarck, Otto von, 40, 168, 169
Blumhardt, Johann Christoph, 172
Bochenski, I. M., 100
Bolshevism, 54, 71 f., 93, 111 f., 121,
125 f., 136 f., 180, 203
Bonhoeffer, Dietrich, 58, 62 ff., 86, 164
Borchert, Wolfgang, 58
Brecht, Berthold, 173
Bultmann, Rudolf, 181
Burckhardt, Jacob, 49, 72
Busch, Wilhelm, 31
Busch, Wilhelm (Essen), 192
Buschendorf, G., 105

C

casuistry, 148 ff.
causality, 15, 16, 20, 174

children of God, sonship, 14 f., 19,
27 f., 36 f., 81, 132, 137, 164 f.
Christ-event, the, 27
Churchill, Winston, 70, 71
Clytemnestra, 19, 20
collective, collectivism, 12, 54, 69, 72,
74, 121, 139, 212, 214
Communism, 21, 22, 84 ff., 109 ff.
community, 11, 27, 74, 144, 212
conscience, 26, 46, 74, 181, 198, 200,
205, 210
cosmology, 92, 155, 181
creatio ex nihilo, 20

D

decision, 12, 21, 60, 74, 159 ff., 205, 208
democracy, 31, 53, 68, 78, 195
demonic, 125
demythologizing, 50, 54, 57, 181
dialectical materialism, 22, 72, 86, 117
Dibelius, Otto, 91
dignity, human, 26, 124, 129
Dirnecker, Bert, 107
divorce, 152
Dostoievski, Feodor, 119
Duke of Windsor, 198
duty, 16, 31

E

education, pedagogy, 56, 116, 143
Einstein, Albert, 11, 102, 104
Engels, Friedrich, 22
entelechy, 14, 17, 26, 32
environment, 26, 66, 103, 126
eschaton, 29, 41, 57
ethos, 12, 17

Format by Anne Hallowell
Set in Linotype Baskerville
Composed, printed and bound by The Haddon Craftsmen, Inc.
HARPER & ROW, PUBLISHERS, INCORPORATED